Samuel Johnson

Voltaire's Candide

Or, the optimist. Rasselas, Prince of Abyssinia. Third Edition

Samuel Johnson

Voltaire's Candide
Or, the optimist. Rasselas, Prince of Abyssinia. Third Edition

ISBN/EAN: 9783337164805

Printed in Europe, USA, Canada, Australia, Japan

Cover: Foto ©Thomas Meinert / pixelio.de

More available books at **www.hansebooks.com**

VOLTAIRE'S

CANDIDE OR THE OPTIMIST

AND

RASSELAS PRINCE OF ABYSSINIA

BY

SAMUEL JOHNSON

WITH AN INTRODUCTION BY HENRY MORLEY

LL.D., PROFESSOR OF ENGLISH LITERATURE AT
UNIVERSITY COLLEGE, LONDON

THIRD EDITION

LONDON
GEORGE ROUTLEDGE AND SONS
BROADWAY, LUDGATE HILL
GLASGOW AND NEW YORK
1888

INTRODUCTION.

WHEN Thomas Carlyle spoke of the eighteenth century as an age of "shams and windy sentimentalities," he might have added that the great feature of the century was a reaction against shams, and that the windy sentimentalities represented only some part of the reaction as it touched weak minds. Rousseau's notion that men were overcivilized—whereas the most advanced nation upon earth is, at this day, barely half civilized—and that we should go backwards instead of forwards, returning nearer to the state of primitive man, was expressed in England, before Rousseau was born, by Bernard Mandeville in his " Fable of the Bees." Impatience of dead form in a corrupt civilization led to the question, Whether such a world as men were living in could have been shaped by a just God or directed by wise Providence? Man and Nature seemed to many faithful and earnest searchers through the darkness to answer to that question, No. Such honest scepticism, born of aspiration for the right and good, has been referred to in the Introduction to another volume of this Library, Butler's " Analogy of Religion, Natural and Revealed, to the Constitution and Course of Nature." We pass along one line of thought from Leibnitz's "Théodicée" to Pope's "Essay on Man" and Butler's "Analogy"—all books that sought to arm our reason against doubt. And we may pass also by another line of thought, attacking the wide-spread evil in life ; in Church and State and in society, and even in the home; everywhere dead forms of dead authority, dead worship of conventions that had no more in them of live civilization than the tattoo of the savage; we may pass by that line through books like Swift's "Gulliver's Travels," Gay's "Beggars' Opera," and more especially its sequel, " Polly," expressing the full strength of the conviction of wrong that must precede the struggle for a remedy. And so we come to "Candide" and " Rasselas," both published in the same year, 1759.

Voltaire in "Candide," as Johnson in "Rasselas," expressed the despair of the time over the problem of man's life on earth. Voltaire mocked and Johnson mourned over the notion that this is the best possible world. Each taught the vanity of human wishes. Voltaire, with no glance beyond, ended the first part of " Candide" with a shrug of light-hearted despair ; every man has his bit work to do, his garden to dig, "he must take care of his garden." Johnson took good care of his garden, but in "Rasselas" his glance is ever across the waves of this life to the life beyond. He finds in time the schoolhouse for eternity.

It must not be forgotten that these utterances in 1759 preceded by only thirty years the struggle of the French Revolution. That came upon many a young heart as endeavour prompted by an ardent hope to raise men by one great effort to the higher ground that we seek now to reach only by slow and patient climbing. There is no reason why, as men rise in civilization, they should not come to build their happiness on sure foundations, paying less heed to the "Lo here" and "Lo there," as they learn more surely that the kingdom of God is within them.

Voltaire was about fifteen years older than Johnson ; for he was born in February 1694, and Johnson in September 1709. Voltaire was sixty-five years old when he published " Candide ;" Johnson fifty when, at the same time, he published "Rasselas." Voltaire died in May 1778, Johnson in December 1784; both were dead, therefore, at the time of the outburst of the French Revolution.

Voltaire was the third child of François Arouet, a rich notary. His mother died when he was five years old. His brother Armand, ten years older than himself, was drawn towards the Jansenists ; but he was himself placed in a school of the Jesuits —the Collége Louis le Grand—that was favoured by the nobility, among whose sons he could make friends for the future. He was a lively student, and when but eleven years old earned credit for his verse. He won the favour of Ninon l'Enclos, who left him at her death, in 1705, two thousand livres to buy books with. Voltaire left the Jesuit school in 1711, with the credit of brilliant success as a student, and much literary skill. He passed into a law school that disgusted him, then turned to literature and wrote odes in 1712 and 1713; that of 1713 was "Sur les Malheurs du Temps." Then he began a tragedy on Œdipus. His father, to send him away from the temptation to rhyme and live idly, attached him as secretary to an ambassador to the Hague.

But at the Hague he consoled himself by an increase of dissipation, and was sent back to Paris, where he had at first to hide from the wrath of his father. Then he allowed himself to be placed as clerk with a lawyer, but picked up friends among young poets, who became companions in his dissipation. In 1715 his father placed François-Marie Arouet under the care of M. de Caumartin, who had a father loud often in praise of Henri IV. Here he conceived the plan of his "Henriade," and of a history of the age of Louis XIV. He worked on at his "Œdipus," and resolved to give all energies to literature that were not occupied with dissipation.

Louis XIV. died on the 1st of September 1715, and soon afterwards young Arouet was made answerable for verses on the Regent. He was banished to Sully-sur-Loire, and found there so much idle pleasure that nothing, he said, was wanting to his enjoyment of the place except the liberty to leave it. As verses had caused his banishment, verses obtained his recall to Paris; but a spy having fixed on him the writing of another satire on the Regency, he was arrested in May 1717, and sent to the Bastille. There he remained prisoner for a year, wrote the two first books of the "Henriade," and finished "Œdipus." It was when he left the Bastille that he changed his name to Voltaire. "I have been very unhappy," he said, "with the old name; let me see whether I shall do better with the new." The first sign of improvement was the success of his "Œdipus," first acted in November 1718. He was now sought as a poet by the world of fashion. There was another banishment to Sully, much dissipation, much work with the pen. The "Henriade" was finished; more plays were written and acted. In 1722, his father's death left Voltaire a fortune, and he received also a pension of two thousand livres from the King. Insulted by the Chevalier de Rohan, who caused him to be fallen upon and beaten, Voltaire challenged him, and was again locked up in the Bastille. The indignity and wrong thus suffered caused Voltaire, when set free, to ask for his passport to England. He came to England in August 1726. In England, in 1728, he published the "Henriade." In the spring of 1729 he returned to Paris. The mocking spirit in which he dealt with the religion of England in his "Lettres sur les Anglais" caused that book to be burned and his own liberty to be again in danger. He withdrew to Cirey, and wrote for Madame du Châtelet a "Traité de Metaphysique." His literary energy remained unbroken; his works multiplied. In 1740 he first met Frederick II. of Prussia. In 1750, after many changes of life in France, he accepted the invitation of Frederick to live with him at his Court, with a large pension. But after three years at Potsdam, he escaped from his Majesty, and settled in France with a niece, Madame Denis. He had bought an estate at Tourney and another at Ferney. It was not until 1760 that he settled wholly upon his property at Ferney, and became the patriarch of the place. Ferney was the garden in which he worked, and he helped to transform the place from a poor hamlet into a town of thriving watchmakers. Wherever Voltaire went he spent energies freely for evil and for good. He could share in the false pleasures of life, well knowing their emptiness, and mock at vanity without finding in it vexation of spirit. Witty, not wise, he made just war upon all hypocrisies of life, but could not separate them from its truths.'

Samuel Johnson, born with a taint of scrofula that throughout life unfitted the physical frame for the uses of the mind within, born also to long struggle against poverty, achieved within himself that conquest over difficulty which is the problem of the race of man.

Johnson's father was a bookseller in Lichfield, who died, little prosperous, when his son, aged 22, had struggled through a liberal education that had been hard to secure, and had included work at Pembroke College, Oxford, under conditions of almost absolute penury, and with depression of mind that sometimes made insanity seem very near. He struggled on, married, attempted in vain to earn his bread as a schoolmaster, was forced to live by his pen, and with a stout heart and humble trust in God bore toil and poverty, and infirmity of a body that had to be daily conquered to the uses of the soul. He lifted no voice of complaint ; said, " I hate a complainer." But he fought steadily in the battle that brings out those energies through use of which alone man can draw nearer to the life that is in God.

As we toil on towards a higher civilization, the difficulties caused by our own yet imperfect sense of right will slowly pass away, and there will remain only the healthy battle against surrounding nature, with the contests of opinion through which God bids us use our energies for the securing of new power from new truth, contests of which the issues will be no longer obscured by anger and evil-speaking. Who would forego the use of energies by which alone man feels that he is made in the likeness of God, to become one of many creatures all born to attain one definite perfection ; to be as one cabbage in a cabbage garden, or one peach in the ripe crop upon a sunny wall? All evils of life, wittily heaped together in "Candide," when they arise from man's fraud and wrong-doing are conquerable in long course of time ; and conquest of them means that advance of civilization towards which we have begun to labour in this century with more definite aims than heretofore. The struggle of the French Revolution to lift men at once above those grosser ills of life which pressed upon them in the eighteenth century, and wrung from them such books as "Candide" and "Rasselas," failed only in its immediate aim. Its highest hope is with us still, quickened though sobered by the failure of immediate attainment. A State can be no better than the citizens of which it is composed. Our labour now is not to mould States but make citizens.

Voltaire, when in witty mockery he wrote "Candide," was a rich man owning two estates. Johnson, when he wrote "Rasselas" in humble faith, was very poor. His old mother had just died, and that he might have money to pay the little debts she left, and bury her, he wrote "Rasselas" in the evenings and nights of a single week.

H. M.

November 1884.

CANDIDE;

OR,

THE OPTIMIST.

CANDIDE.

―――+―

PART I.

CHAPTER I.

How Candide was brought up in a magnificent castle ; and how he was driven from thence.

IN the country of Westphalia, in the castle of the most noble baron of Thunder-ten-tronckh, lived a youth, whom nature had endowed with a most sweet disposition. His face was the true index of his mind. He had a solid judgment joined to the most unaffected simplicity ; and hence, I presume, he had his name of Candide. The old servants of the house suspected him to have been the son of the baron's sister by a mighty good sort of a gentleman of the neighbourhood, whom that young lady refused to marry, because he could produce no more than threescore and eleven quarterings in his arms, the rest of the genealogical tree belonging to the family having been lost through the injuries of time.

The baron was one of the most powerful lords in Westphalia, for his castle had not only a gate, but even windows, and his great hall was hung with tapestry. He used to hunt with his mastiffs and spaniels instead of greyhounds ; his groom served him for huntsman, and the parson of the parish officiated as his grand almoner. He was called " My

Lord " by all his people, and he never told a story but every one laughed at it.

My Lady Baroness weighed three hundred and fifty pounds, consequently was a person of no small consideration ; and then she did the honours of the house with a dignity that commanded universal respect. Her daughter was about seventeen years of age, fresh-coloured, comely, plump, and amiable. The baron's son seemed to be a youth in every respect worthy of the father he sprung from. Pangloss, the preceptor, was the oracle of the family, and little Candide listened to his instructions with all the simplicity natural to his age and disposition.

Master Pangloss taught the metaphysico-theologo-cosmolo-nigology. He could prove to admiration that there is no effect without a cause, and in this best of all possible worlds the baron's castle was the most magnificent of all castles, and my lady the best of all possible baronesses.

"It is demonstrable," said he, "that things cannot be otherwise than they are ; for as all things have been created for some end, they must necessarily be created for the best end. Observe, for instance, the nose is formed for spectacles ; therefore we wear spectacles. The legs are visibly designed for stockings; accordingly we wear stockings. Stones were made to be hewn and to construct castles; therefore my lord has a magnificent castle ; for the geatest baron in the province ought to be the best lodged. Swine were intended to be eaten ; therefore we eat pork all the year round. And they who assert that everything is *right*, do not express themselves correctly ; they should say that everything is *best*."

Candide listened attentively, and believed implicitly; for he thought Miss Cunegund excessively handsome, though he never had the courage to tell her so. He concluded that next to the happiness of being Baron of Thunder-ten-tronckh, the next was that of being Miss Cunegund, the next that of seeing her every day, and the last that of hearing the doctrine of Master Pangloss, the greatest philosopher of the whole province, and consequently of the whole world.

One day, when Miss Cunegund went to take a walk in a little neighbouring wood, which was called a park, she saw, through the bushes, the sage Doctor Pangloss giving a lecture in experimental philosophy to her mother's chambermaid, a little brown wench, very pretty and very tractable.

In her way back she happened to meet Candide. She blushed; he blushed also. She wished him a good morning in a flattering tone; he returned the salute without knowing what he said. The next day, as they were rising from dinner, Cunegund and Candide slipped behind the screen; Miss dropped her handkerchief; the young man picked it up. She innocently took hold of his hand, and he as innocently kissed hers with a warmth, a sensibility, a grace—all very particular: their lips met; their eyes sparkled; their knees trembled; their hands strayed. The baron chanced to come by; he beheld the cause and effect, and without hesitation salutes Candide with some notable kicks on the rear, and drove him out of doors. Miss Cunegund, the tender, the lovely Miss Cunegund, fainted away, and, as soon she came to herself, the baroness boxed her ears. Thus a general consternation was spread over this most magnificent and most agreeable of all possible castles.

CHAPTER II.

What befell Candide among the Bulgarians.

CANDIDE, thus driven out of this terrestrial paradise, rambled a long time without knowing where he went; sometimes he raised his eyes, all bedewed with tears, towards heaven, and sometimes he cast a melancholy look towards the mag-

nificent castle, where dwelt the fairest of young baronesses.
He laid himself down to sleep in a furrow, heart-broken and
supperless.   The snow fell in great flakes, and in the morning when he awoke, he was almost frozen to death; however, he made shift to crawl to the next town, which was
called Walds-berghoff-trarbk-dikdorff, without a penny in his
pocket, and half-dead with hunger and fatigue.   He took up
his stand at the door of an inn.   He had not been long
there, before two men dressed in blue fixed their eyes stedfastly upon him.   "Faith, comrade," said one of them to
the other, "yonder is a well-made young fellow, and of the
right size;" upon which they made up to Candide, and with
the greatest civility and politeness invited him to dine with
them.   "Gentlemen," replied Candide, with a most engaging
modesty, "you do me much honour; but upon my word I
have no money."   "Money, sir," said one of the blues to
him, "young persons of your appearance and merit never
pay anything; why, are not you five feet five inches high?"
"Yes, gentlemen, that is really my size," replied he, with a
low bow.   "Come then, sir, sit down along with us; we will
not only pay your reckoning, but will never suffer such a
clever young fellow as you to want money.   Mankind were
born to assist one another."   "You are perfectly right,
gentlemen," said Candide, "this is precisely the doctrine of
Master Pangloss; and I am convinced that everything is
for the best."   His generous companions next entreat him
to accept of a few crowns, which he readily complies with,
at the same time offering them his note for the payment,
which they refuse, and sit down to table.   "Have you not
a great affection for ―― " "O yes; I have a great affection
for the lovely Miss Cunegund."   "Maybe so," replied one
of the blues; "but that is not the question.   We ask you
whether you have not a great affection for the King of the
Bulgarians?"   "For the King of the Bulgarians?" said Candide. "Oh, Lord! not at all; why, I never saw him in my life."

"Is it possible ! Oh, he is a most charming king. Come, we must drink his health." " With all my heart, gentlemen," says Candide, and off he tosses his glass. " Bravo ! " cry the blues ; " you are now the support, the defender, the hero of the Bulgarians ; your fortune is made ; you are in the high road to glory." So saying, they handcuff him, and carry him away to the regiment. There he is made to wheel about to the right, to the left, to draw his rammer, to return his rammer, to present, to fire, to march ; and they give him thirty blows with a cane. The next day he performs his exercise a little better, and they give him but twenty. The day following he comes off with ten, and is looked upon as a young fellow of surprising genius by all his comrades.

Candide was struck with amazement, and could not, for the soul of him, conceive how he came to be a hero. One fine spring morning he took it into his head to take a walk, and he marched straight forward, conceiving it to be a privilege of the human species, as well as of the brute creation, to make use of their legs how and when they pleased. He had not gone above two leagues when he was overtaken by four other heroes, six feet high, who bound him neck and heels, and carried him to a dungeon. A court-martial sat upon him, and he was asked which he liked best, either to run the gauntlet six-and-thirty times through the whole regiment, or to have his brains blown out with a dozen of musket-balls. In vain did he remonstrate with them, that the human will is free, and that he chose neither. They obliged him to make a choice, and he determined, in virtue of that divine gift called free-will, to run the gauntlet six-and-thirty times. He had gone through his discipline twice, and the regiment being composed of 2,000 men, they composed for him exactly 4,000 strokes, which laid bare all his muscles and nerves from the nape of his neck to his rump. As they were preparing to make him set out the third time, our young hero, unable to support it any longer, begged as a favour they would be so obliging as to shoot him through the head. The favour being granted, a bandage was tied over his eyes, and he was made to kneel down. At that very instant his Bulgarian Majesty happening to pass by, made a stop, and inquired into the delinquent's crime, and being a prince of great penetration, he found, from what he heard of Candide, that he was a young metaphysician, entirely ignorant of the world; and therefore, out of his great clemency, he condescended to pardon him, for which his name will be celebrated in every journal and in every age. A skilful surgeon made a cure of the flagellated Candide in three weeks, by means of emollient unguents prescribed by Dioscorides. His sores were now skinned over, and he was able to march, when the King of the Bulgarians gave battle to the King of the Abares.

CHAPTER III.

How Candide escaped from the Bulgarians, and what befell him afterwards.

NEVER was anything so gallant, so well accoutred, so brilliant, and so finely disposed as the two armies. The trumpets, fifes, hautboys, drums, and cannon made such harmony as never was heard in hell itself. The entertainment began by a discharge of cannon, which in the twinkling of an eye laid flat about 6,000 men on each side. The musket bullets swept away, out of the best of all possible worlds, nine or ten thousand scoundrels that infected its surface. The bayonet was next the *sufficient reason* of the deaths of several thousands. The whole might amount to 30,000 souls. Candide trembled like a philosopher, and concealed himself as well as he could during this heroic butchery.

At length, while the two kings were causing " Te Deum "

to be sung in each of their camps, Candide took a resolution to go and reason somewhere else upon causes and effects. After passing over heaps of dead or dying men, the first place he came to was a neighbouring village in the Abarian territories, which had been burnt to the ground by the Bulgarians, agreeably to the laws of war. Here lay a number of old men covered with wounds, who beheld their wives dying with their throats cut, and hugging their children to their breasts, all stained with blood. There several young virgins, whose bodies had been ripped open, after they had satisfied the natural necessities of the Bulgarian heroes, breathed their last; while others, half-burnt in the flames, begged to be despatched out of the world. The ground about them was covered with the brains, arms, and legs of dead men.

Candide made all the haste he could to another village, which belonged to the Bulgarians, and there he found that the heroic Abares had acted the same tragedy. From thence, continuing to walk over palpitating limbs or through ruined buildings, at length he arrived beyond the theatre of war, with a little provision in his budget and Miss Cunegund's image in his heart. When he arrived in Holland, his provisions failed him; but having heard that the inhabitants of that country were all rich and Christians, he made himself sure of being treated by them in the same manner as at the baron's castle, before he had been driven from thence through the power of Miss Cunegund's bright eyes.

He asked charity of several grave-looking people, who one and all answered him, that if he continued to follow this trade, they would have him sent to the house of correction, where he should be taught to get his bread.

He next addressed himself to a person who was just come from haranguing a numerous assembly for a whole hour on the subject of charity. The orator, squinting at him under his broad-brimmed hat, asked him sternly what brought

him thither, and whether he was for the good old cause?
"Sir," said Candide in a submissive manner, "I conceive
there can be no effect without a cause; everything is necessarily concatenated and arranged for the best. It was
necessary that I should be banished the presence of Miss
Cunegund; that I should afterwards run the gauntlet; and
it is necessary I should beg my. bread, till I am able to
get it: all this could not have been otherwise." "Hark
ye, friend," said the orator, "do you hold the Pope to be
Antichrist?" "Truly, I never heard anything about it,"
said Candide; "but whether he is or not, I am in want of
something to eat." "Thou deservest not to eat or to drink,"
replied the orator, "wretch, monster that thou art! Hence !
avoid my sight, nor ever come near me again while thou
livest." The orator's wife happened to put her head out
of the window at that instant, when, seeing a man who
doubted whether the Pope was Antichrist, she discharged
upon his head a chamber-pot full of ——. Good heavens !
to what excess does religious zeal transport the female
kind !

A man who had never been christened, an honest Anabaptist named James, was witness to the cruel and igno-
minious treatment showed to one of his brethren, to a
rational, two-footed, unfledged being. Moved with pity, he
carried him to his own house, caused him to be cleaned,
gave him meat and drink, and made him a present of two
florins, at the same time proposing to instruct him in his
own trade of weaving Persian silks, which are fabricated
in Holland. Candide, penetrated with so much goodness,
threw himself at his feet, crying, "Now I am convinced that
my master Pangloss told me truth when he said that everything was for the best in this world; for I am infinitely
more affected with your extraordinary generosity than with
the inhumanity of that gentleman in the black coat, and his
wife." The next day, as Candide was walking out, he met

a beggar all covered with scabs, his eyes were sunk in his head, the end of his nose eaten off, his mouth drawn on one side, his teeth as black as a cloak, snuffling and coughing most violently, and every time he attempted to spit, out dropped a tooth.

CHAPTER IV.

How Candide found his old Master Pangloss again, and what happened to them.

CANDIDE, divided between compassion and horror, but giving way to the former, bestowed on this shocking figure the two florins which the honest Anabaptist James had just before given to him. The spectre looked at him very earnestly, shed tears, and threw his arms about his neck. Candide started back aghast. "Alas!" said the one wretch to the other, "don't you know your dear Pangloss?" "What do I hear? Is it you, my dear master—you I behold in this piteous plight? What dreadful misfortune has befallen you? What has made you leave the most magnificent and delightful of all castles? What has become of Miss Cunegund, the mirror of young ladies, and Nature's masterpiece?" "Oh Lord!" cried Pangloss, "I am so weak I cannot stand;" upon which Candide instantly led him to the Anabaptist's stable, and procured him something to eat. As soon as Pangloss had a little refreshed himself, Candide began to repeat his inquiries concerning Miss Cunegund. "She is dead," replied the other. "Dead!" cried Candide, and immediately fainted away. His friend recovered him by the help of a little bad vinegar, which he found by chance in the stable. Candide opened his eyes, and again repeated, "Dead! Is Miss Cunegund dead? Ah, where is the best of worlds now? But of what illness did she die? Was it for grief upon seeing her father

kick me out of his magnificent castle ? "   "No," replied
Pangloss.   " Her body was ripped open by the Bulgarian
soldiers after they had ravished her as much as it was possible for damsel to be ravished.   They knocked the baron
her father on the head for attempting to defend her ; my
lady her mother was cut in pieces ; my poor pupil was
served just in the same manner as his sister ; and as for the
castle, they have not left one stone upon another.   They
have destroyed all the ducks and the sheep, the barns and
the trees ; but we have had our revenge, for the Abares
have done the very same thing in a neighbouring barony,
which belonged to a Bulgarian lord."

At hearing this, Candide fainted away a second time,
but having come to himself again, he said all that it became
him to say.   He inquired into the cause and effect, as well
as into the *sufficing reason,* that had reduced Pangloss to so
miserable a condition.   "Alas," replied the preceptor, " it
was love ; love, the comfort of the human species ; love, the
preserver of the universe the soul of all sensible beings ;
love, tender love ! "   "Alas," replied Candide, " I have had
some knowledge of love myself, this sovereign of hearts, this
soul of souls ; yet it never cost me more than a kiss and
twenty kicks in the rear.   But how could this beautiful
cause produce in you so hideous an effect ? "

Pangloss made answer in these terms : " Oh, my dear
Candide, you must remember Pacquette, that pretty wench
who waited on our noble baroness ; in her arms I tasted the
pleasures of paradise, which produced these hell torments
with which you see me devoured.   She was infected with
disease, and perhaps is since dead of it.   She received this
present of a learned cordelier, who derived it from the
fountain-head.   He was indebted for it to an old countess,
who had it of a captain of horse, who had it of a marchioness, who had it of a page, the page had it of a Jesuit,
who during his noviciate had it in a direct line from one of

the fellow-adventurers of Christopher Columbus. For my part, I shall give it to nobody. I am a dying man."

"O sage Pangloss," cried Candide, "what a strange genealogy is this. Is not the devil the root of it?" "Not at all," replied the great man; "it was a thing unavoidable, a necessary ingredient in the best of worlds; for if Columbus had not caught in an island in America this disease, which is evidently opposite to the great end of nature, we should have had neither chocolate nor cochineal. It is also to be observed that, even to the present time, in this continent of ours, this malady, like our religious controversies, is peculiar to ourselves. The Turks, the Indians, the Persians, the Chinese, the Siamese, and the Japanese are entirely unacquainted with it; but there is a *sufficing reason* for them to know it in a few centuries. In the meantime, it is making prodigious havoc among us, especially in those armies composed of well-disciplined hirelings, who determine the fate of nations; for we may safely affirm that, when an army of 30,000 men fights another equal in number, there are about 20,000 of them so diseased on each side."

"Very surprising indeed," said Candide, "but you must get cured." "Lord help me! how can I?" said Pangloss. "My dear friend, I have not a penny in the world; and you know one cannot be bled or have a glister without a fee."

This last speech had its effect on Candide. He flew to the charitable Anabaptist James. He flung himself at his feet, and gave him so striking a picture of the miserable situation of his friend, that the good man, without any further hesitation, agreed to take Dr. Pangloss into his house and to pay for his cure. The cure was effected with only the loss of one eye and an ear. As he wrote a good hand and understood accounts tolerably well, the Anabaptist made him his bookkeeper. At the expiration of two months, being obliged to go to Lisbon about some mercantile affairs, he took the two philosophers with him in the same ship.

Pangloss during the course of the voyage explained to him how everything was so constituted that it could not be better. James did not quite agree with him on this point. "Mankind," said he, "must in some things have deviated from their original innocence; for they were not born wolves, and yet they worry one another like those beasts of prey. God never gave them twenty-four pounders nor bayonets, and yet they have made cannon and bayonets to destroy one another. To this account I might add not only bankruptcies, but the law which seizes on the effects of bankrupts, only to cheat the creditors." "All this was indispensably necessary," replied the one-eyed doctor; "for private misfortunes are public benefits; so that the more private misfortunes there are the greater is the general good." While he was arguing in this manner the sky was overcast, the winds blew from the four quarters of the compass, and the ship was assailed by a most terrible tempest within sight of the port of Lisbon.

CHAPTER V.

A Tempest, a Shipwreck, an Earthquake, and what else befell
Dr. Pangloss, Candide, and James the Anabaptist.

ONE-HALF of the passengers, weakened and half-dead with the inconceivable anxiety and sickness which the rolling of a vessel at sea occasions through the whole human frame, were lost to all sense of the danger that surrounded them. The other made loud outcries, or betook themselves to their prayers. The sails were blown into shivers, and the masts were brought by the board. The vessel was a perfect wreck. Every one was busily employed, but nobody could be either heard or obeyed. The Anabaptist, being upon deck, lent a helping hand as well as the rest, when a brutish sailor gave him a blow and laid him speechless; but with the violence of the blow the tar himself tumbled head-foremost overboard, and fell upon a piece of the broken mast, which he immediately grasped. Honest James, forgetting the injury he had so lately received from him, flew to his assistance, and with great difficulty hauled him in again, but in the attempt was, by a sudden jerk of the ship, thrown overboard himself, in sight of the very fellow whom he had risked his life to save, and who took not the least notice of him in this distress. Candide, who beheld all that passed, and saw his benefactor one moment rising above water and the next swallowed up by the merciless waves, was preparing to jump after him; but was prevented by the philosopher Pangloss, who demonstrated to him that the coast of Lisbon had been made on purpose for the Anabaptist to be drowned there. While he was proving his argument *à priori*, the ship foundered, and the whole crew perished, except Pangloss, Candide, and the sailor who had been the means of drowning the good Anabaptist. The villain swam ashore, but Pangloss and Candide got to land upon a plank.

As soon as they had recovered themselves from their surprise and fatigue, they walked towards Lisbon. With what little money they had left they thought to save themselves from starving after having escaped drowning.

Scarce had they done lamenting the loss of their benefactor and set foot in the city, when they perceived the earth to tremble under their feet, and the sea, swelling and foaming in the harbour, dash in pieces the vessels that were riding at an anchor. Large sheets of flame and cinders covered the streets and public places. The houses tottered, and were tumbled topsy-turvy, even to their foundations, which were themselves destroyed; and thirty thousand inhabitants of both sexes, young and old, were buried beneath the ruins. The sailor, whistling and swearing, cried, " Damn it, there's something to be got here ! " " What can be the 'sufficient reason' of this phenomenon ? " said Pangloss. " It is

certainly the Day of Judgment," said Candide.   The sailor,
defying death in the pursuit of plunder, rushed into the
midst of the ruin, where he found some money, with which
he got drunk, and after he had slept himself sober, he purchased the favours of the first good-natured wench that came
in his way, amidst the ruins of demolished houses and the
groans of half-buried and expiring persons.   Pangloss pulled
him by the sleeve : " Friend," said he, " this ¦is not right ;
you trespass against the *universal reason*, and have mistaken
your time."   " Death and 'ounds ! " answered the other, " I
am a sailor and born at Batavia, and have trampled four
times upon the crucifix in as many voyages to Japan ; you
are come to a good hand with your *universal reason.*"

In the meantime, Candide, who had been wounded by
some pieces of stone that fell from the houses, lay stretched
in the street, almost covered with rubbish.   " For God's
sake," said he to Pangloss, " get me a little wine and oil ; I
am dying."   " This concussion of the earth is no new thing,"
replied Pangloss ; " the city of Lima in America experienced
the same last year : the same cause, the same effect ; there
is certainly a train of sulphur all the way underground from
Lima to Lisbon."   " Nothing more probable," said Candide ;
" but for the love of God a little oil and wine."   " Probable ! "
replied the philosopher.   " I maintain that the thing is
demonstrable."   Candide fainted away, and Pangloss fetched
him some water from a neighbouring spring.

The next day, in searching among the ruins, they found
some eatables, with which they repaired their exhausted
strength.   After this they assisted the inhabitants in relieving
the distressed and wounded. Some whom they had humanely
assisted, gave them as good a dinner as could be expected
under such terrible circumstances.   The repast, indeed, was
mournful, and the company moistened their bread with their
tears ; but Pangloss endeavoured to comfort them under
this affliction by affirming that things could not be otherwise

than they were : " for," said he, " all this is for the very best end, for if there is a volcano at Lisbon, it could be in no other spot ; for it is impossible but things should be as they are, for everything is for the best."

By the side of the preceptor sat a little man dressed in black, who was one of the *familiars* of the Inquisition. This person, taking him up with great complaisance, said, " Possibly, my good sir, you do not believe in original sin ; for if everything is best, there could have been no such thing as the fall or punishment of men."

" I humbly ask your excellency's pardon," answered Pangloss, still more politely ; " for the fall of man, and the curse consequent thereupon, necessarily entered into the system of the best of worlds." " That is as much as to say, sir," rejoined the *familiar*, " you do not believe in free-will." " Your excellency will be so good as to excuse me," said Pangloss ; " free-will is consistent with absolute necessity ; for it was necessary we should be free, for in that the will——"

Pangloss was in the midst of his proposition when the Inquisitor beckoned to his attendant to help him to a glass of port wine.

CHAPTER VI.

How the Portuguese made a superb Auto da-fé to prevent any future Earthquakes, and how Candide underwent public flagellation.

AFTER the earthquake, which had destroyed three-fourths of the city of Lisbon, the sages of that country could think of no means more effectual to preserve the kingdom from utter ruin than to entertain the people with an *auto-da-fé*, it having been decided by the University of Coimbra that the burning a few people alive by a slow fire, and with great ceremony, is an infallible secret to prevent earthquakes.

In consequence thereof, they had seized on a Biscayner for marrying his godmother, and on two Portuguese for taking out the bacon of a larder pullet they were eating; after dinner, they came and secured Doctor Pangloss and his pupil Candide, the one for speaking his mind, and the other for seeming to approve what he had said. They were conducted to separate apartments, extremely cool, where they were never incommoded with the sun. Eight days afterwards they were each dressed in a *san-benito*, and their heads were adorned with paper mitres. The mitre and *san-benito* worn by Candide were painted with flames reversed, and with devils that had neither tails nor claws; but Doctor Pangloss's devils had both tails and claws, and his flames were upright. In these habits they marched in procession, and heard a very pathetic sermon, which was followed by an anthem accompanied by bagpipes. Candide was flogged to some tune while the anthem was singing; the Biscayner and the two men who would not eat bacon were burnt; and Pangloss was hanged, which is not a common custom at these solemnities. The same day there was another earthquake, which made most dreadful havoc.

Candide, amazed, terrified, confounded, astonished, all bloody and trembling from head to foot, said to himself, "If this is the best of all possible worlds, what are the others? If I had only been whipped, I could have put up with it, as I did among the Bulgarians; but, oh my dear Pangloss! my beloved master! thou greatest of philosophers! that ever I should live to see thee hanged, without knowing for what! O my dear Anabaptist, thou best of men, that it should be thy fate to be drowned in the very harbour! O Miss Cunegund, you mirror of young ladies! that it should be your fate to be ripped open!"

He was making the best of his way from the place where he had been preached to, whipped, absolved, and received benediction, when he was accosted by an old woman, who said to him, "Take courage, child, and follow me."

CHAPTER VII.

How the Old Woman took care of Candide, and how he found the Object
of his Love.

CANDIDE followed the old woman, though without taking courage, to a decayed house, where she gave him a pot of pomatum to anoint his sores, showed him a very neat bed with a suit of clothes hanging up by it, and set victuals and drink before him. "There," said she, "eat, drink, and sleep; and may our Blessed Lady of Atocha, and the great St. Anthony of Padua, and the illustrious St. James of Compostella, take you under their protection. I shall be back to-morrow." Candide, struck with amazement at what he had seen, at what he had suffered, and still more with the charity of the old woman, would have shown his acknowledgment by kissing her hand. "It is not my hand you ought to kiss," said the old woman; "I shall be back to-morrow. Anoint your back, eat, and take your rest."

Candide, notwithstanding so many disasters, ate and slept. The next morning the old woman brought him his breakfast, examined his back, and rubbed it herself with another ointment. She returned at the proper time and brought him his dinner, and at night she visited him again with his supper. The next day she observed the same ceremonies. "Who are you?" said Candide to her. "What God has inspired you with so much goodness? What return can I make you for this charitable assistance?" The good old beldame kept a profound silence. In the evening she returned, but without his supper. "Come along with me," said she, "but do not speak a word." She took him under her arm, and walked with him about a quarter of a mile into the country, till they came to a lonely house surrounded with moats and gardens. The old conductress knocked at

a little door, which was immediately opened, and she
showed him up a pair of back-stairs into a small but richly-
furnished apartment. There she made him sit down on a
brocaded sofa, shut the door upon him, and left him.
Candide thought himself in a trance; he looked upon his
whole life hitherto as a frightful dream, and the present
moment a very agreeable one.

The old woman soon returned, supporting, with great
difficulty, a young lady, who appeared scarce able to stand.
She was of a majestic mien and stature, her dress was rich
and glittering with diamonds, and her face was covered
with a veil. "Take off that veil," said the old woman to
Candide. The young man approaches, and with a trembling hand takes off her veil. What a happy moment!
What surprise! He thought he beheld Miss Cunegund.
He did behold her: it was she herself! His strength fails
him, he cannot utter a word, he falls at her feet. Cunegund
faints upon the sofa. The old woman bedews them with
spirits; they recover; they begin to speak. At first they
could express themselves only in broken accents; their
questions and answers were alternately interrupted with
sighs, tears, and exclamations. The old woman desired
them to make less noise, and after this prudent admonition,
left them together. "Good heavens!" cried Candide, "is
it you? Is it Miss Cunegund I behold, and alive? Do I
find you again in Portugal? Then you have not been
ravished? They did not rip you open, as the philosopher Pangloss informed me?" "Indeed, but they did,"
replied Miss Cunegund; "but these two accidents do not
always prove mortal." "But were your father and mother
killed?" "Alas!" answered she, "it is but too true!"
and she wept. "And your brother?" "And my brother
also." "And how came you into Portugal? And how did
you know of my being here? And by what strange adventure did you contrive to have me brought into this house?

And how——" "I will tell you all," replied the lady; "but first you must acquaint me with all that has befallen you since the innocent kiss you gave me, and the rude kicking you received in consequence of it."

Candide, with the greatest submission, prepared to obey the commands of his fair mistress, and though he was still wrapt in amazement, though his voice was low and tremulous, though his back pained him, yet he gave her a most ingenious account of everything that had befallen him since the moment of their separation. Cunegund, with her eyes uplifted to heaven, shed tears when he related the death of the good Anabaptist James, and of Pangloss; after which she thus related her adventures to Candide, who lost not one syllable she uttered, and seemed to devour her with his eyes all the time she was speaking.

CHAPTER VIII.

The History of Cunegund.

"I was in bed and fast asleep when it pleased heaven to send the Bulgarians to our delightful castle of Thunder-ten-tronckh, where they murdered my father and brother, and cut my mother in pieces. A tall Bulgarian soldier, six feet high, perceiving that I had fainted away at this sight, attempted to ravish me. The operation brought me to my senses. I cried, I struggled, I bit, I scratched, I would have torn the tall Bulgarian's eyes out, not knowing that what had happened at my father's castle was a customary thing. The brutal soldier, enraged at my resistance, gave me a cut in the left groin with his hanger, the mark of which I still carry." "Methinks I long to see it," said Candide, with all imaginable simplicity. "You shall," said Cunegund; "but let me proceed." "Pray do," replied Candide.

She continued: "A Bulgarian captain came in, and saw

me weltering in my blood, and the soldier still as busy as if no one had been present. The officer, enraged at the fellow's want of respect to him, killed him with one stroke of his sabre. This captain took care of me, had me cured, and carried me prisoner of war to his quarters. I washed what little linen he was master of, and dressed his victuals. He was very fond of me, that was certain ; neither can I deny that he was well-made, and had a white soft skin ; but he was very stupid, and knew nothing of philosophy. It might plainly be perceived that he had not been educated under Doctor Pangloss. In three months' time, having gamed away all his money, and being grown tired of me, he sold me to a Jew named Don Issachar, who traded to Holland and Portugal, and was passionately fond of women. This Jew showed me great kindness, in hopes to gain my favours ; but he never could prevail on me. A modest woman may be once outraged, but her virtue is greatly strengthened thereby. In order to make sure of me, he brought me to this country-house you now see. I had hitherto believed that nothing could equal the beauty of the castle of Thunder-ten-tronckh, but I found I was mistaken.

" The Grand Inquisitor saw me one day at mass, ogled me all the time of service, and when it was over sent to let me know he wanted to speak with me about some private business. I was conducted to his palace, where I told him all my story. He represented to me how much it was beneath a person of my birth to belong to a circumcised Israelite. He caused a proposal to be made to Don Issachar, that he should resign me to his lordship. Don Issachar, being the court banker and a man of credit, was not easy to be prevailed upon. His lordship threatened him with an *auto-da-fé* ; in short, my Jew was frightened into a composition, and it was agreed between them that the house and myself should belong to both in common ; that the Jew should

have Monday, Wednesday, and the Sabbath to himself, and
the Inquisitor the other four days of the week. This agreement has subsisted almost six months, but not without several
contests whether the space from Saturday night to Sunday
morning belonged to the old or the new law. For my part,
I have hitherto withstood them both, and truly I believe that
this is the very reason why they are both so fond of me.

"At length, to turn aside the scourge of earthquakes, and
to intimidate Don Issachar, my Lord Inquisitor was pleased
to celebrate an *auto-da-fé*. He did me the honour to
invite me to the ceremony. I had a very good seat; and
refreshments of all kinds were offered the ladies between
mass and the execution. I was dreadfully shocked at the
burning the two Jews and the honest Biscayner who
married his godmother; but how great was my surprise, my
consternation, and concern, when I beheld a figure so like
Pangloss, dressed in a *san-benito* and mitre! I rubbed my
eyes, I looked at him attentively. I saw him hanged, and
I fainted away. Scarce had I recovered my senses when I
beheld you, stark naked: this was the height of horror,
grief, and despair. I must confess to you for a truth, that
your skin is far whiter and more blooming than that of the
Bulgarian captain. This spectacle worked me up to a pitch
of distraction. I screamed out, and would have said, 'Hold,
barbarians!' but my voice failed me; and indeed my cries
would have signified nothing. After you had been severely
whipped, 'How is it possible,' said I to myself, 'that the
lovely Candide and the sage Pangloss should be at Lisbon,
the one to receive an hundred lashes, and the other to be
hanged, by order of my Lord Inquisitor, of whom I am so
great a favourite?' Pangloss deceived me most cruelly in
saying that everything is fittest and best.

"Thus agitated and perplexed, now distracted and lost,
now half-dead with grief, I revolved in my mind the murder
of my father, mother, and brother, committed before my

eyes ; the insolence of the rascally Bulgarian soldier ; the
wound he gave me in the groin ; my servitude ; my being a
cook wench to my Bulgarian captain ; my subjection to the
dirty Jew and my cruel Inquisitor ; the hanging of Doctor
Pangloss ; the *Miserere* sung while you were whipping ; and
particularly the kiss I gave you behind the screen the last
day I ever beheld you.   I returned thanks to God for
having brought you to the place where I was after so many
trials.   I charged the old woman who attends me to bring
you hither as soon as was convenient.   She has punctually
executed my orders, and I now enjoy the inexpressible
satisfaction of seeing you, hearing you, and speaking to you.
But you must certainly be half-dead with hunger ; I myself
have a great inclination to eat ; and so let us sit down to
supper."

Upon this the two lovers immediately placed themselves
at table, and after having supped, they returned to seat
themselves again on the magnificent sofa already mentioned,
where they were in amorous dalliance when Signor Don
Issachar, one of the masters of the house, entered unexpectedly.   It was the Sabbath-day, and he came to enjoy
his privilege, and sigh forth his passion at the feet of the
fair Cunegund.

CHAPTER IX.

*What happened to Cunegund, Candide, the Grand Inquisitor,
and the Jew.*

THIS same Issachar was the most choleric little Hebrew
that had ever been in Israel since the captivity of Babylon.
"What, then," said he, "thou Galilean wretch?   The
Inquisitor was not enough for thee, but this rascal must
come in for a share with me !"   In uttering these words he
drew out a long poignard which he always carried about with
him, and never dreaming that his adversary had any arms,

he attacked him most furiously ; but our honest Westphalian had received a handsome sword of the old woman with the suit of clothes. Candide draws his rapier, and though he was the most gentle, sweet-tempered young man breathing, he whips it into the Israelite, and lays him sprawling on the floor at the fair Cunegund's feet.

"Holy Virgin !" cried she, "what will become of us? A man killed in my apartment! If the peace officers come we are undone." " Had not Pangloss been hanged," replied Candide, "he would have given us most excellent advice in this emergency, for he was a profound philosopher. But since he is not here, let us consult the old woman." She was very understanding, and was beginning to give her advice, when another door opened on a sudden. It was now one o'clock in the morning, and of course the beginning of Sunday, which, by agreement, fell to the lot of my Lord Inquisitor. Entering, he discovers the flagellated Candide, with his drawn sword in his hand, a dead body stretched on the floor, Cunegund frightened out of her wits, and the old woman giving advice.

At that very moment a sudden thought came into Candide's head. "If this holy man," thought he, "should call assistance, I shall most undoubtedly be consigned to the flames, and Miss Cunegund may perhaps meet with no better treatment. Besides, he was the cause of my being so cruelly whipped ; he is my rival ; and as I have now begun to dip my hands in blood, I will kill away, for there is no time to hesitate." This whole train of reasoning was clear and in-stantaneous ; so that, without giving time to the Inquisitor to recover from his surprise, he ran him through the body, and laid him by the side of the Jew. "Good God !" cries Cunegund, "here's another fine piece of work! Now there can be no mercy for us ; we are excommunicated to all the devils in hell ; our last hour has come ! But how in the name of wonder could you, who are of so mild a temper, despatch

B

a Jew and Inquisitor in two minutes' time?" "Beautiful miss," answered Candide, "when a man is in love, is jealous, and has been flogged by the Inquisition, he becomes lost to all reflection."

The old woman then put in her word. "There are three Andalusian horses in the stable," said she, "with as many bridles and saddles. Let the brave Candide get them ready; madame has a parcel of moidores and jewels. Let us mount immediately, though I have only one side to sit upon. Let us set out for Cadiz; it is the finest weather in the world, and there is great pleasure in travelling in the cool of the night."

Candide, without any further hesitation, saddles the three horses; and Miss Cunegund, the old woman, and he set out, and travelled thirty miles without once baiting. While they were making the best of their way, the Holy Brotherhood entered the house. My lord the Inquisitor was interred in a magnificent manner; and Master Issachar's body was thrown upon a dunghill.

Candide, Cunegunde, and the old woman had by this time reached the little town of Avecina, in the midst of the mountains of Sierra Morena, and were engaged in the following conversation in an inn where they had taken up their quarters.

CHAPTER X.

*In what distress Candide, Cunegund, and the Old Woman arrive at
Cadiz; and of their Embarkation.*

"Who could it be that has robbed me of my moidores and jewels?" exclaimed Miss Cunegund, all bathed in tears. "How shall we live? what shall we do? where shall I find Inquisitors and Jews who can give me more?" "Alas!" said the old woman, "I have a shrewd suspicion of a reverend Father Cordelier, who lay last night in the same inn with us at Badajoz. God forbid I should condemn any one wrongfully, but he came into our room twice, and he set off in the morning long before us." "Alas!" said Candide, "Pangloss has often demonstrated to me that the goods of this world are common to all men, and that every one has an equal right to the enjoyment of them; but according to these principles, the Cordelier ought to have left us enough to carry us to the end of our journey. Have you nothing at all left, my dear Miss Cunegund?" "Not a sous," replied she. "What is to be done, then?" said Candide. "Sell one of the horses," replied the old woman. "I will get behind Miss Cunegund, though I have only one side to ride on; and we shall reach Cadiz, never fear."

In the same inn there was a Benedictine friar, who bought the horse very cheap. Candide, Cunegund, and the old woman, after passing through Lucina, Chellas, and Letrixa, arrived at length at Cadiz. A fleet was then getting ready, and troops were assembling, in order to reduce the reverend father Jesuits of Paraguay, who were accused of having excited one of the Indian tribes in the neighbourhood of the town of the Holy Sacrament to revolt against the kings of Spain and Portugal. Candide, having been in the Bulgarian service, performed the military exercise of that nation before the general of this little army with so intrepid an air, and with such agility and expedition, that he gave him the command of a company of foot. Being now made a captain, he embarks with Miss Cunegund, the old woman, two valets, and the two Andalusian horses which had belonged to the Grand Inquisitor of Portugal.

During their voyage they amused themselves with many profound reasonings on poor Pangloss's philosophy. "We are now going into another world, and surely it must be there that everything is best; for I must confess that we have had some little reason to complain of what passes in ours, both as to the physical and moral part. Though I have a sincere

love for you," said Miss Cunegund, " yet I still shudder at
the reflection of what I have seen and experienced."   " All
will be well," replied Candide.   " The sea of this new world
is already better than our European seas ; it is smoother, and
the winds blow more regularly."   " God grant it," said
Cunegund.   "But I have met with such terrible treatment
in this that I have almost lost all hopes of a better."
" What murmuring and complaining is here indeed ! " cried
the old woman.   " If you had suffered half what I have done
there might be some reason for it."   Miss Cunegund could
scarce refrain laughing at the good old woman, and thought
it droll enough to pretend to a greater share of misfortunes
than herself.   "Alas ! my good dame," said she, " unless
you had been ravished by two Bulgarians, had received two
deep wounds in your body, had seen two of your own castles
demolished, had lost two fathers and two mothers, and seen
both of them barbarously murdered before your eyes, and,
to sum up all, had two lovers whipped at an *auto-da-fé*,
I cannot see how you could be more unfortunate than I.
Add to this, though born a baroness, and bearing seventy-
two quarterings, I have been reduced to a cook-wench."
" Miss," replied the old woman, "you do not know my
family as yet; but if I were to show you everything, you
would not talk in this manner, but suspend your judgment."
This speech raised a high curiosity in Candide and Cunegund, and the old woman continued as follows.

CHAPTER XI.

The History of the Old Woman.

" I HAVE not always been blear eyed ; my nose did not
always touch my chin; nor was I always a servant.   You
must know that I am the daughter of Pope Urban X. and
of the Princess of Palestrina.   To the age of fourteen I was

brought up in a castle, to which all the castles of the German barons would not have been fit for stabling, and one of my robes would have bought half the province of Westphalia. I grew up, and improved in beauty, wit, and every graceful accomplishment; and in the midst of pleasures, homage, and the highest expectations. I already began to inspire the men with love. My breast began to take its right form; and such a breast—white, firm, and formed like that of Venus of Medicis. My eyebrows were as black as jet; and as for my eyes, they darted flames, and eclipsed the lustre of the stars, as I was told by the poets of our part of the world. My maids, when they dressed and undressed me, used to fall into an ecstasy in viewing me before and behind; and all the men longed to be in their places.

I was contracted to a sovereign prince of Massa Carara. Such a prince! as handsome as myself, sweet-tempered, agreeable, witty, and in love with me over head and ears. I loved him too, as our sex generally do for the first time, with rapture, transport, and idolatry. The nuptials were prepared with surprising pomp and magnificence; the ceremony was attended with feasts, carousals, and burlettas: all Italy composed sonnets in my praise, though not one of them was tolerable. I was on the point of reaching the summit of bliss, when an old marchioness, who had been mistress to the prince my husband, invited him to drink chocolate. In less than two hours after he returned from the visit, he died of most terrible convulsions. But this is a mere trifle. My mother, distracted to the highest degree, and yet less afflicted than I, determined to absent herself for some time from so fatal a place. As she had a very fine estate in the neighbourhood of Gaieta, we embarked on board a galley, which was gilded like the high altar of St. Peter's at Rome. In our passage we were boarded by a Sallee rover. Our men defended themselves like true pope's soldiers; they flung themselves upon their knees, laid down their arms, and begged the corsair to give them absolution *in articulo mortis.*

The Moors presently stripped us as bare as ever we were born. My mother, my maids of honour, and myself, were served all in the same manner. It is amazing how quick these gentry are at undressing people. But what surprised me most was, that they thrust their fingers into every part of our bodies that their fingers could in any way reach. I thought it a very strange kind of ceremony; for thus we are generally apt to judge of things when we have not seen the world. I afterwards learnt that it was to discover if we had no diamonds concealed. This practice has been established time immemorial among those civilized nations that scour the seas. I was informed that the religious Knights of Malta never fail to make this search whenever any Moors of either sex fall into their hands. It is a part of the law of nations, from which they never deviate.

I need not tell you how great a hardship it was for a young princess and her mother to be made slaves and carried to Morocco. You may easily imagine what we must have suffered on board a corsair. My mother was still extremely handsome, our maids of honour, and even our common waiting-women, had more charms than were to be found in all Africa. As to myself, I was enchanting; I was beauty itself, and then I had my innocence. But, alas! I did not retain it long; this precious flower, which was reserved for the lovely prince of Massa Carara, was cropt by the captain of the Moorish vessel, who was a hideous negro, and thought he did me infinite honour. Indeed, both the Princess of Palestrina and myself must have had very strong constitutions to undergo all the hardships and violences we suffered till our arrival at Morocco. But I will not detain you any longer with such common things; they are hardly worth mentioning.

Upon our arrival at Morocco we found that kingdom bathed in blood. Fifty sons of the Emperor Muley Ishmael were each at the head of a party. This produced fifty civil wars of blacks against blacks, of tawnies against tawnies, and of mulattoes against mulattoes. In short, the whole empire was one continued scene of carcases.

No sooner were we landed than a party of blacks, of a contrary faction to that of my captain, came to rob him of his booty. Next to the money and jewels we were the most valuable things he had. I was witness on this occasion to such a battle as you never beheld in your cold European climates. The northern nations have not that fermentation in their blood, nor that raging lust for women that is so common in Africa. The natives of Europe seem to have their veins filled with milk only ; but fire and vitrol circulate in those of the inhabitants of Mount Atlas and the neighbouring provinces. They fought with the fury of the lions, tigers, and serpents of their country, to know who should have us. A Moor seized my mother by the right arm, while my captain's lieutenant held her by the left ; another Moor laid hold of her by the right leg, and one of our corsairs held her by the other. In this manner were almost every one of our women dragged between four soldiers. My captain kept me concealed behind him, and with his drawn scymetar cut down every one who opposed him ; at length I saw all our Italian women and my mother mangled and torn in pieces by the monsters who contended for them. The captives, my companions, the Moors who took us, the soldiers, the sailors, the blacks, the whites, the mulattoes, and lastly my captain himself, were all slain, and I remained alone, expiring upon a heap of dead bodies. The like barbarous scenes were transacted every day over the whole country, which is an extent of three hundred leagues, and yet they never missed the five stated times of prayer enjoined by their prophet Mahomet.

I disengaged myself with great difficulty from such a heap of slaughtered bodies, and made a shift to crawl to a large orange tree that stood on the bank of a neighbouring rivulet, where I fell down exhausted with fatigue, and overwhelmed with horror, despair, and hunger. My senses being over-powered, I fell asleep, or rather seemed to be in a trance. Thus I lay in a state of weakness and insensibility, between life and death, when I felt myself pressed by something that moved up and down upon my body. This brought me to myself; I opened my eyes, and saw a pretty fair-faced man, who sighed, and muttered these words between his teeth: " O che sciagura d'essere senza coglioni ! "

CHAPTER XII.

The Adventures of the Old Woman (continued).

ASTONISHED and delighted to hear my native language, and no less surprised at the young man's words, I told him that there were far greater misfortunes in the world than what he complained of. And to convince him of it, I gave him a short history of the horrible disasters that had befallen me ; and as soon as I had finished, fell into a swoon again. He carried me in his arms to a neighbouring cottage, where he had me put to bed, procured me something to eat, waited on me with the greatest attention, comforted me, caressed me, told me that he had never seen anything so perfectly beautiful as myself, and that he had never so much regretted the loss of what no one could restore to him. " I was born at Naples," said he, " where they caponize two or three thousand children every year ; several die of the operation ; some acquire voices far beyond the most tuneful of your ladies ; and others are sent to govern states and empires. I underwent this operation very happily, and was one of the singers in the Princess of Palestrina's chapel." "How," cried I, "in my mother's chapel!" "The Princess of

Palestrina, your mother!" cried he, bursting into a flood of tears. "Is it possible you should be the beautiful young princess whom I had the care of bringing up till she was six years old, and who at that tender age promised to be as fair as I now behold you?" "I am the same," replied I. "My mother lies about a hundred yards from hence, cut in pieces, and buried under a heap of dead bodies."

I then related to him all that had befallen me, and he, in return, acquainted me with all his adventures, and how he had been sent to the court of the King of Morocco by a Christian prince, to conclude a treaty with that monarch; in consequence of which he was to be furnished with military stcres and ships to enable him to destroy the commerce of other Christian governments. "I have executed my commission," said the eunuch; "I am going to take shipping at Ceuta, and I'll take you along with me to Italy. 'Ma che sciagura d'essere senza coglioni!'"

I thanked him with tears of joy; and instead of taking me with him into Italy, he carried me to Algiers, and sold me to the Dey of that province. I had not been long a slave, when the plague, which had made the tour of Africa, Asia, and Europe, broke out at Algiers with redoubled fury. You have seen an earthquake; but tell me, miss, had you ever the plague? "Never," answered the young baroness.

If you ever had (continued the old woman) you would own an earthquake was a trifle to it. It is very common in Africa; I was seized with it. Figure to yourself the distressed situation of the daughter of a pope, only fifteen years old, and who in less than three months had felt the miseries of poverty and slavery; had been ravished almost every day; had beheld her mother cut into four quarters; had experienced the scourges of famine and war, and was now dying of the plague at Algiers. I did not, however, die of it; but my eunuch and the Dey, and almost the whole seraglio of Algiers, were swept off,

As soon as the first fury of this dreadful pestilence was over, a sale was made of the Dey's slaves. I was purchased by a merchant, who carried me to Tunis. This man sold me to another merchant, who sold me again to another at Tripoli; from Tripoli I was sold to Alexandria, from Alexandria to Smyrna, and from Smyrna to Constantinople. After many changes, I at length became the property of an aga of the janissaries, who, soon after I came into his possession, was ordered away to the defence of Asoph, then besieged by the Russians.

The aga, being very fond of women, took his whole seraglio with him, and lodged us in a small fort, with two black eunuchs and twenty soldiers for our guard. Our army made a great slaughter among the Russians; but they soon returned us the compliment. Asoph was taken by storm, and the enemy spared neither age, sex, nor condition, but put all to the sword, and laid the city in ashes. Our little fort alone held out; they resolved to reduce us by famine. The twenty janissaries, who were left to defend it, had bound themselves by an oath never to surrender the place. Being reduced to the extremity of famine, they found themselves obliged to kill our two eunuchs, and eat them, rather than violate their oath. But this horrible repast soon failing them, they next determined to support the remains of life by devouring the women.

We had a very pious and humane iman, who made them a most excellent sermon on this occasion, exhorting them not to kill us all at once; " Only cut off one of the buttocks of each of those ladies," said he, " and you will fare extremely well; if ye are still under the necessity of having recourse to the same expedient again, ye will find the like supply a few days hence. Heaven will approve of so charitable an action, and work your deliverance."

By the force of this eloquence he easily persuaded them, and all underwent the operation. The imam applied the same balsam as they do to children after circumcision. We were all ready to give up the ghost.

The janissaries had scarcely time to finish the repast with which we had supplied them, when the Russians attacked the place by means of flat-bottomed boats, and not a single janissary escaped. The Russians paid no regard to the condition we were in; but as there are French surgeons in all parts of the world, a skilful operator took us under his care, and made a cure of us; and I shall never forget while I live, that as soon as my wounds were perfectly healed he made me certain proposals. In general, he desired us all to have a good heart, assuring us that the like had happened in many sieges and that it was perfectly agreeable to the laws of war.

As soon as my companions were in a condition to walk, they were sent to Moscow. As for me, I fell to the lot of a boyard, who put me to work in his garden, and gave me twenty lashes a day. But this nobleman having in about two years afterwards been broke alive upon the wheel, with about thirty others, for some court intrigues, I took advantage of the event, and made my escape. I travelled over great part of Russia. I was a long time an innkeeper's servant at Riga, then at Rostock, Wismar, Leipsick, Cassel, Utrecht, Leyden, the Hague, and Rotterdam : I have grown old in misery and disgrace, living with only one buttock, and in the perpetual remembrance that I was a pope's daughter. I have been an hundred times upon the point of killing myself, but still was fond of life. This ridiculous weakness is perhaps one of the dangerous principles implanted in our nature. For what can be more absurd than to persist in carrying a burden of which we wish to be eased? to detest, and yet to strive to preserve our existence? In a word, to caress the serpent that devours us, and hug him close to our bosoms till he has gnawed into our hearts?

In the different countries which it has been my fate to traverse, and the many inns where I have been a servant, I have observed a prodigious number of people who held their existence in abhorrence, and yet I never knew more than twelve who voluntarily put an end to their misery; namely, three negroes, four Englishmen, as many Genoese, and a German professor named Robek. My last place was with the Jew, Don Issachar, who placed me near your person, my fair lady; to whose fortunes I have attached myself, and have been more affected to your misfortunes than my own. I should never have even mentioned the latter to you, had you not a little piqued me on the head of sufferings; and if it was not customary to tell stories on board a ship in order to pass away the time. In short, my dear miss, I have a great deal of knowledge and experience in the world; therefore take my advice—divert yourself, and prevail upon each passenger to tell his story, and if there is one of them all that has not cursed his existence many times, and said to himself over and over again that he was the most wretched of mortals, I give you leave to throw me head-foremost into the sea.

CHAPTER XIII.

How Candide was obliged to leave the fair Cunegund and the Old Woman.

THE fair Cunegund, being thus made acquainted with the history of the old woman's life and adventures, paid her all the respect and civility due to a person of her rank and merit. She very readily came into her proposal of engaging every one of the passengers to relate their adventures in their turns, and was at length, as well as Candide, compelled to acknowledge that the old woman was in the right. "It is a thousand pities," said Candide, "that the sage Pangloss should have been hanged, contrary to the custom of an *auto-da-fé*, for he would have read us a most admirable lecture on the moral and physical evil which overspread the earth and sea ; and I think I should have courage enough to presume to offer, with all due respect, some few objections."

While every one was reciting his adventures, the ship continued on her way, and at length arrived at Buenos Ayres, where Cunegund, Captain Candide, and the old woman landed, and went to wait upon the Governor, Don Fernando d'Ibaraa y Figueora y Mascarenes y Lampourdos y Souza. This nobleman carried himself with a haughtiness suitable to a person who bore so many names. He spoke with the most noble disdain to every one, carried his nose so high, strained his voice to such a pitch, assumed so imperious an air, and stalked with so much loftiness and pride, that every one who had the honour of conversing with him was violently tempted to bastinade his excellency. He was immoderately fond of women, and Miss Cunegund appeared in his eyes a paragon of beauty. The first thing he did was to ask her if she was not the captain's wife. The air with which he made this demand alarmed Candide, who did not dare to say he was married to her, because indeed he was not ; neither durst he say she was his sister, because she was not ; and though a lie of this nature proved of great service to one of the ancients, and might possibly be useful to some of the moderns, yet the purity of his heart would not permit him to violate the truth. "Miss Cunegund," replied he, "is to do me the honour to marry me, and we humbly beseech your excellency to condescend to grace the ceremony with your presence."

Don Fernando d'Ibaraa y Figueora y Mascarenes y Lampourdos y Souza, twirling his mustachio, and putting on a sarcastic smile, ordered Captain Candide to go and review his company. The gentle Candide obeyed, and the Governor was left with Miss Cunegund. He made her a strong declaration of love, protesting that he was ready to give her his hand in the face of the Church, or otherwise, as should appear most agreeable to a young lady of her prodigious beauty. Cunegund desired leave to retire a quarter of an hour to consult the old woman, and determine how she should proceed.

The old woman gave her the following counsel: " Miss, you have seventy-two quarterings in your arms, it is true, but you have not a penny to bless yourself with. It is your own fault if you are not wife to one of the greatest noblemen in South America, with an exceeding fine mustachio. What business have you to pride yourself upon an unshaken constancy? You have been ravished by a Bulgarian soldier; a Jew and an Inquisitor have both tasted of your favours. People take advantage of misfortunes. I must confess, were I in your place I should without the least scruple give my hand to the Governor, and thereby make the fortune of the brave Captain Candide." While the old woman was thus haranguing, with all the prudence that old age and experience furnish, a small bark entered the harbour, in which was an alcayde and his alguazils. Matters had fallen out as follows :—

The old woman rightly guessed that the Cordelier with the long sleeves was the person who had taken Miss Cunegund's money and jewels, while they and Candide were at Badajoz, in their flight from Lisbon. This same friar attempted to sell some of the diamonds to a jeweller, who presently knew them to have belonged to the Grand Inquisitor, and stopped them. The Cordelier, before he was hanged, acknowledged that he had stolen them, and described the persons and the road they had taken. The flight of Cunegund and Candide was already the town talk. They sent in pursuit of them to Cadiz; and the vessel which had been sent to make the greater despatch had now reached the port of Buenos Ayres. A report was spread that an alcayde was going to land, and that he was in pursuit of the murderers of my lord the Inquisitor. The sage old woman immediately saw what was to be done. " You cannot run away," said she to Cunegund ; " but you have nothing to fear. It was not you who killed my Lord Inquisitor. Besides, as the Governor is in love with you, he will not suffer you to be ill-treated. Therefore stand your ground." Then hurrying away to Candide, " Begone," said she, " from hence this instant, or you will be burnt alive ! " Candide found there was no time to be lost. But how could he part from Cunegund, and whither must he fly for shelter ?

CHAPTER XIV.

The reception Candide and Cacambo met with among the Jesuits in Paraguay.

CANDIDE had brought with him from Cadiz such a footman as one often meets with on the coasts of Spain and in the colonies. He was the fourth part of a Spaniard, of a mongrel breed, and born in Tucuman. He had successfully gone through the profession of a singing boy, sexton, sailor, monk, pedlar, soldier, and lacquey. His name was Cacambo. He had a great affection for his master, because his master was a mighty good man. He immediately saddled the two Andalusian horses. " Come, my good master, let us follow the old woman's advice, and make all the haste we can from this place without staying to look behind us." Candide burst into a flood of tears : " Oh, my dear Cunegund, must I then be compelled to quit you just as the governor was going to honour us with his presence at our wedding ? Cunegund, so long lost and found again, what will now become of you ? " " Lord," said Cacambo, " she must do as well as she can: women are never at a loss. God takes care of them, and so let us make the best of our way." " But whither wilt thou carry me? Where can we go? What can we do without Cunegund?" cried the disconsolate Candide. " By St. James of Compostella," said Cacambo, " you were going to fight against the Jesuits of Paraguay ; now let us e'en go and fight for them. I know the road perfectly well ; I'll conduct you to their kingdom ; they will be delighted with a captain that under-stands the Bulgarian exercise ; you will certainly make a prodigious fortune. If we cannot find our account in this world we may in another. It is a great pleasure to see new objects and perform new exploits."

" Then you have been to Paraguay," said Candide. " Ay, marry, have I," replied Cacambo. " I was a scout in the College of the Assumption, and am as well acquainted with the new government of Los Padres as I am with the streets of Cadiz. Oh, it is an admirable government, that is most certain ! The kingdom is at present upwards of three hundred leagues in diameter, and divided into thirty provinces ; the fathers are there masters of everything, and the people have no money at all. This you must allow is the masterpiece of justice and reason. For my part, I see nothing so divine as the good fathers, who wage war in this part of the world against the troops of Spain and Portugal, at the same time that they hear the confessions of those very princes in Europe ; who kill Spaniards in America, and send them to heaven at Madrid. This pleases me exceedingly ; but let us push forward ; you are going to see the happiest and most fortunate of all mortals. How charmed will those fathers be to hear that a captain who understands the Bulgarian exercise is coming among them."

As soon as they reached the first barrier, Cacambo called to the advance-guard, and told them that a captain wanted to speak to my lord the general. Notice was given to the main-guard, and immediately a Paraguayan officer ran to throw himself at the feet of the commandant, to impart this news to him. Candide and Cacambo were immediately disarmed, and their two Andalusian horses were seized. The two strangers are now conducted between two files of musketeers. The commandant was at the farther end with a three-cornered cap on his head, his gown tucked up, a sword by his side, and a half-pike in his hand. He made a sign, and instantly four-and-twenty soldiers drew up round the new-comers. A sergeant told them that they must wait, the commandant could not speak to them ; and that the reverend father provincial did not suffer any Spaniard to open his mouth but in his presence, or to stay above three hours in the province. "And where is the reverend father provincial ? " said Cacambo. " He is just come from mass, and is at the parade," replied the sergeant, "and in about three hours time you may possibly have the honour to kiss his spurs." " But," said Cacambo, " the captain, who as well as myself is perishing with hunger, is no Spaniard, but a German ; therefore, pray, might we not be permitted to break our fast till we can be introduced to his reverence ? "

The serjeant immediately went and acquainted the commandant with what he heard. " God be praised," said the reverend commandant ; "since he is a German, I will hear what he has to say; let him be brought to my arbour. Immediately they conducted Candide to a beautiful pavilion adorned with a colonnade of green marble spotted with yellow, and with an intertexture of vines, which served as a kind of cage for parrots, humming-birds, fly-birds, Guinea hens, and all other curious kinds of birds. An excellent breakfast was provided in vessels of gold, and while the Paraguayans were eating coarse Indian corn out of wooden dishes in the open air, and exposed to the burning heat of the sun, the reverend father commandant retired to his cool arbour.

He was a very handsome young man, round-faced, fair,

and fresh-coloured, his eyebrows were finely arched, he had a piercing eye, the tips of his ears were red, his lips vermilion, and he had a bold and commanding air; but such a boldness as neither resembled that of a Spaniard nor of a Jesuit. He ordered Candide and Cacambo to have their arms restored to them, together with their two Andalusian horses. Cacambo gave the poor beasts some oats to eat close by the arbour, keeping a strict eye upon them all the while for fear of surprise.

Candide having kissed the hem of the commandant's robe, they sat down to table. " It seems you are a German," says the Jesuit to him in that language. " Yes, reverend father," answered Candide. As they pronounced these words they looked at each other with great amazement, and with an emotion that neither could conceal. " From what part of Germany do you come ? " said the Jesuit. " From the dirty province of Westphalia," answered Candide. " I was born in the castle of Thunder-ten-tronckh." " Oh heavens ! is it possible ? " said the commandant. " What a miracle !" cried Candide. " Can it be you ? " said the commandant. On this they both retired a few steps backwards, then running into each other's arms, embraced, and let fall a shower of tears. " Is it you, then, reverend father ? You are the brother of the fair Miss Cunegund ? you that were slain by the Bulgarians ! you the baron's son ! you a Jesuit in Paraguay ! I must confess this is a strange world we live in. O Pangloss ! Pangloss ! what joy would this have given you if you had not been hanged."

The commandant dismissed the negro slaves and the Paraguayans, who presented them with liquor in crystal goblets. He returned thanks to God and St. Ignatius a thousand times; he clasped Candide in his arms, and both their faces were bathed in tears. " You will be more surprised, more affected, more transported," said Candide, " when I tell you that Miss Cunegund, your sister, whose body was supposed to have been ripped open, is in perfect health." " Where ? " " In your neighbourhood, with the governor of Buenos Ayres ; and I myself was going to fight against you." Every word they uttered during this long conversation was productive of some new matter of astonishment. Their souls fluttered on their tongues, listened in their ears, and sparkled in their eyes. Like true Germans, they continued a long while at table, waiting for the reverend father, and the commandant spoke to his dear Candide as follows.

CHAPTER XV.

How Candide killed the Brother of his dear Cunegund.

" NEVER while I live shall I lose the remembrance of that horrible day on which I saw my father and brother barbarously butchered before my eyes, and my sister ravished. When the Bulgarians retired, we searched in vain for my dear sister. She was nowhere to be found ; but the bodies of my father, mother, and myself, with two servant-maids and three little boys, all of whom had been murdered by the remorseless enemy, were thrown into a cart to be buried in a chapel belonging to the Jesuits, within two leagues of our family seat. A Jesuit sprinkled us with some holy water, which was confoundedly salt, and a few drops of it went into my eyes. The father perceived that my eyelids stirred a little ; he put his hand upon my breast, and felt my heart beat, upon which he gave me proper assistance, and at the end of three weeks I was perfectly recovered. You know, my dear Candide, I was very handsome. I became still more so, and the reverend father Croust, superior of that house, took a great fancy to me. He gave me the habit of the order, and some years afterwards I was sent to Rome. Our general stood in need of new levies of young German

Jesuits. The sovereigns of Paraguay admit of as few Spanish Jesuits as possible; they prefer those of other nations, as being more obedient to command. The reverend father-general looked upon me as a proper person to work in that vineyard. I set out in company with a Polander and a Tyrolese. Upon my arrival I was honoured with a sub-deaconship and a lieutenancy. Now I am colonel and priest. We shall give a warm reception to the King of Spain's troops; I can assure you they will be well excommunicated and beaten. Providence has sent you hither to assist us. But is it true that my dear sister Cunegund is in the neighbourhood with the governor of Buenos Ayres?" Candide swore that nothing could be more true; and the tears began again to trickle down their cheeks.

The baron knew no end of embracing Candide; he called him his brother, his deliverer. "Perhaps," said he, "my dear Candide, we shall be fortunate enough to enter the town sword in hand, and recover my sister Cunegund." "Ah! that would crown my wishes," replied Candide, "for I intended to marry her; and I hope I shall still be able to effect it." "Insolent fellow!" replied the baron. "You! you have the impudence to marry my sister, who bears seventy-two quarterings! Really I think you have an insufferable degree of assurance to dare so much as to mention such an audacious design to me." Candide, thunderstruck at the oddness of this speech, answered: "Reverend father, all the quarterings in the world are of no signification. I have delivered your sister from a Jew and an Inquisitor; she is under many obligations to me, and she is resolved to give me her hand. My master Pangloss always told me that mankind are by nature equal. Therefore, you may depend upon it that I will marry your sister." "We shall see that, villain!" said the Jesuit baron of Thunder-ten-Tronckh, and struck him across the face with the flat side of his sword. Candide in an instant draws his rapier, and plunges it up to the hilt in the Jesuit's body; but in pulling it out, reeking hot, he burst into tears. "Good God!" cried he, "I have killed my old master, my friend, my brother-in-law. I am the best man in the world, and yet I have already killed three men; and of these three two were priests."

Cacambo, who was standing sentry near the door of the arbour, instantly ran up. "Nothing remains," said his master, "but to sell our lives as dearly as possible. They will undoubtedly look into the arbour; we must die sword in hand." Cacambo, who had seen many of these kind of adventures, was not discouraged. He stripped the baron of his Jesuit's habit and put it upon Candide, then gave him the dead man's three-cornered cap, and made him mount on horseback. All this was done as quick as thought. "Gallop, master," cried Cacambo; "everybody will take you for a Jesuit going to give orders, and we shall have passed the frontiers before they will be able to overtake us." He flew as he spoke these words, crying out aloud in Spanish, "Make way! make way for the reverend father-colonel!"

CHAPTER XVI.

What happened to our two Travellers with two Girls, two Monkeys, and the Savages called Oreillons.

CANDIDE and his valet had already passed the frontiers before it was known that the German Jesuit was dead. The wary Cacambo had taken care to fill his wallet with bread, chocolate, some ham, some fruit, and a few bottles of wine. They penetrated with their Andalusian horses into a strange country, where they could discover no beaten path. At length, a beautiful meadow, intersected with purling rills, opened to their view. Cacambo proposed to his master to take some nourishment, and he set him an example. "How can you desire me to feast upon ham when I have killed the baron's son, and am doomed never more to see the beautiful Cunegund? What will it avail me to prolong a wretched life that might be spent far from her in remorse and despair? And then what will the journal of Trevoux say?"

While he was making these reflections he still continued eating. The sun was now on the point of setting when the ears of our two wanderers were assailed with cries which seemed to be uttered by a female voice. They could not tell whether these were cries of grief or joy; however, they instantly started up, full of that inquietude and apprehension which a strange place naturally inspires. The cries proceeded from two young women who were tripping stark naked along the mead, while two monkeys followed close at their heels, biting their backs. Candide was touched with compassion; he had learned to shoot while he was among the Bulgarians, and he could hit a filbert in a hedge without touching a leaf. Accordingly he takes up his double-barrel Spanish fusil, pulls the trigger, and lays the two monkeys lifeless on the ground. "God be praised, my dear Cacambo, I have rescued two poor girls from a most perilous situation. If I have committed a sin in killing an Inquisitor and a Jesuit, I made ample amends by saving the lives of these two distressed damsels. Who knows but they may be young ladies of a good family, and that this assistance I have been so happy to give them may procure us great advantage in this country."

He was about to continue when he felt himself struck speechless at seeing the two girls embracing the dead bodies of the monkeys in the tenderest manner, bathing their wounds with their tears, and rending the air with the most doleful lamentations. "Really," said he to Cacambo, I should not have expected to see such a prodigious share of good-nature." "Master," replied the knowing valet, "you have made a precious piece of work of it: do you know that you have killed the lovers of these two ladies."

"Their lovers, Cacambo! You are jesting; it cannot be; I can never believe it." "Dear sir," replied Cacambo, "you are surprised at everything; why should you think it so strange that there should be a country where monkeys insinuate themselves into the good graces of the ladies? They are the fourth part of a man, as I am the fourth part of a Spaniard." "Alas!" replied Candide, "I remember to have heard my master Pangloss say that such accidents as these frequently came to pass in former times; and that these commixtures are productive of centaurs, fauns, and satyrs; and that many of the ancients had seen such monsters; but I looked upon the whole as fabulous." "Now you are convinced," said Cacambo, "that it is very true; and you see what use is made of those creatures by persons who have not had a proper education. All I am afraid of is, that these same ladies will play us some ugly trick."

These judicious reflections operated so far on Candide as to make him quit the meadow and strike into a thicket. There he and Cacambo supped; and after heartily cursing the Grand Inquisitor, the Governor of Buenos Ayres, and the baron, they fell asleep on the ground. When they awoke, they were surprised to find that they could not move. The reason was, that the Oreillons, who inhabit that country, and to whom the ladies had given information of these two strangers, had bound them with cords made of the bark of trees. They saw themselves surrounded by fifty naked Oreillons, armed with bows and arrows, clubs, and hatchets of flint; some were making a fire under a large cauldron; and others were preparing spits, crying out one and all: "A Jesuit! a Jesuit! We shall be revenged; we shall have excellent cheer; let us eat this Jesuit; let us eat him up."

"I told you, master," cried Cacambo mournfully, "that these two wenches would play us some scurvy trick.' Candide, seeing the cauldron and the spits, cried out, "I suppose they are going either to boil or roast us. Ah! what would Pangloss say if he was to see how pure nature is formed? Everything is right. It may be so; but I must confess it is something hard to be bereft of dear Miss Cunegund, and to be spitted like a rabbit by these barbarous Oreillons." Cacambo, who never lost his presence of mind in distress, said to the disconsolate Candide: "Do not despair. I understand a little of the jargon of these people; I will speak to them." "Ay, pray do," said Candide; "and be sure you make them sensible of the horrid barbarity of boiling and roasting of human creatures, and how little of Christianity there is in such practices."

"Gentlemen," said Cacambo, "you think perhaps you are going to feast upon a Jesuit; if so, it is mighty well; nothing can be more agreeable to justice than thus to treat your enemies. Indeed, the law of nature teaches us to kill our neighbour; and accordingly we find this practised all over the world; and if we do not indulge ourselves in eating human flesh, it is because we have much better fare; but for your parts, who have not such resources as we, it is certainly much better judged to feast upon your enemies than to throw their bodies to the fowls of the air, and thus lose all the fruits of your victory. But surely, gentlemen, you would not choose to eat your friends. You imagine you are going to roast a Jesuit, whereas my master is your friend, your defender; and you are going to spit the very man who has been destroying your enemies. As to myself, I am your countryman; this gentleman is my master; and so far from being a Jesuit, give me leave to tell you he has very lately killed one of that order, whose spoils he now wears, and which have probably occasioned your mistake. To convince you of the truth of what I say, take the habit he has now on, and carry it to the first barrier of the Jesuits' kingdom, and inquire whether my master did not kill one of their officers. There will be little or no time lost by this, and you may still reserve our bodies in your power to feast on, if you should find what we have told you to be false; but, on the contrary, if you find it to be true, I am persuaded you are too well acquainted with the principles of the laws of society, humanity, and justice, not to use us courteously, and suffer us to depart unhurt."

This speech appeared very reasonable to the Oreillons. They deputed two of their people with all expedition to inquire into the truth of this affair, who acquitted themselves of their commission like men of sense, and soon returned with good tidings for our distressed adventurers. Upon this they were both loosed, and those who were so lately going to roast and boil them, now showed them all sorts of civilities, offered them friends, gave them refreshments, and reconducted them to the confines of their country, crying before them all the way, in token of joy, " He is no Jesuit, he is no Jesuit."

Candide could not help admiring the cause of his deliverance. " What men ! what manners ! " cried he ; " if I had not fortunately run my sword up to the hilt in the body of Miss Cunegund's brother, I should have infallibly been eaten alive. But, after all, pure nature is an excellent thing ; since these people, instead of eating me, showed me a thousand civilities as soon as they knew I was not a Jesuit."

CHAPTER XVII.

Candide and his Valet arrive in the Country of El Dorado. What they saw there.

WHEN they got to the frontiers of the Oreillons, "You see," said Cacambo to Candide, " this hemisphere is not better than the other ; e'en take my advice, and let us return to Europe by the shortest way possible." " But how can we get back," said Candide, " and whither shall we go ? To my own country? The Bulgarians and the Abares are laying that waste with fire and sword; or shall we go to Portugal? There I shall be burnt; and if we abide here, we are every moment in danger of being spitted. But how can I bring myself to quit that part of the world where my dear Miss Cunegund has her residence?"

"Let us turn towards Cayenne," said Cacambo; "there we shall meet with some Frenchmen; for you know those gentry ramble all over the world; perhaps they will assist us, and God will look with pity on our distress."

It was not so easy to get to Cayenne. They knew pretty nearly whereabouts it lay; but the mountains, rivers, precipices, robbers, savages, were dreadful obstacles in the way. Their horses died with fatigue, and their provisions were at an end. They subsisted a whole month upon wild fruit, till at length they came to a little river bordered with cocoa trees, the sight of which at once revived their drooping spirits, and furnished nourishment for their enfeebled bodies.

Cacambo, who was always giving as good advice as the old woman herself, said to Candide: "You see there is no holding out any longer; we have travelled enough on foot. I spy an empty canoe near the river-side; let us fill it with cocoa-nuts, get into it, and go down with the stream: a river always leads to some inhabited place. If we do not meet with agreeable things, we shall at least meet with something new." "Agreed," replied Candide; "let us recommend ourselves to Providence."

They rowed a few leagues down the river, the banks of which were in some places covered with flowers, in others barren; in some parts smooth and level, and in others steep and rugged. The stream widened as they went farther on, till at length it passed under one of the frightful rocks whose summits seemed to reach the clouds. Here our two travellers had the courage to commit themselves to the stream, which, contracting in this part, hurried them along with a dreadful noise and rapidity. At the end of four-and-twenty hours they saw daylight again; but their canoe was dashed to pieces against the rocks. They were obliged to creep along from rock to rock for the space of a league, till at length a spacious plain presented itself to their sight. This place was bounded by a chain of inaccessible mountains. The country appeared cultivated equally for pleasure and to produce the necessaries of life. The useful and agreeable were here equally blended. The roads were covered, or rather adorned, with carriages formed of glittering materials, in which were men and women of a surprising beauty, drawn with great rapidity by red sheep of a very large size, which far surpassed the finest coursers of Andalusia, Tetuan, or Mecquinez.

" Here is a country, however," said Candide, " preferable to Westphalia." He and Cacambo landed near the first village they saw, at the entrance of which they perceived some children, covered with tattered garments of the richest brocade, playing at quoits. Our two inhabitants of the other hemisphere amused themselves greatly with what they saw. The quoits were large round pieces, yellow, red, and green, which cast a most glorious lustre. Our travellers picked some of them up, and they proved to be gold, emeralds, rubies, and diamonds, the least of which would have been the greatest ornament to the superb throne of the Great Mogul. "Without doubt," said Cacambo, "those children must be the king's sons that are playing at quoits." As he was uttering these words the schoolmaster of the village appeared, who came to call them to school. "There," said Candide, " is the preceptor of the royal family."

The little ragamuffins immediately quitted their diversion, leaving the quoits on the ground with all their other playthings. Candide gathers them up, runs to the schoolmaster, and, with a most respectful bow, presents them to him, giving him to understand by signs, that their royal highnesses had forgot their gold and precious stones. The schoolmaster, with a smile, flung them upon the ground; then examining Candide from head to foot with an air of admiration, he turned his back and went on his way.

Our travellers took care, however, to gather up the gold, the rubies, and the emeralds. "Where are we?" cried Candide: "The king's children in this country must have an excellent education, since they are taught to show such a contempt for gold and precious stones." Cacambo was as much surprised as his master. They then drew near the first house in the village, which was built after the manner of an European palace. There was a crowd of people about the door, and a still greater number in the house. The sound of the most delightful instruments of music was heard, and the most agreeable smell came from the kitchen. Cacambo went up to the door, and heard those within talking in the Peruvian language, which was his mother tongue; for every one knows that Cacambo was born in a village of Tucuman, where no other language is spoken. "I will be your interpreter here," said he to Candide, "let us go in; this is an eating-house."

Immediately two waiters and two servant-girls, dressed in cloth of gold, and their hair braided with ribbands of tissue, accost the strangers, and invite them to sit down to the ordinary. Their dinner consisted of four dishes of different soups, each garnished with two young paroquets, a large dish of bouillé that weighed two hundredweight, two roasted monkeys of a delicious flavour, three hundred humming-birds in one dish, and six hundred fly-birds in another; some excellent ragouts, delicate tarts, and the whole served up in dishes of rock-crystal. Several sorts of liquors, extracted from the sugar-cane, were handed about by the servants who attended.

Most of the company were chapmen and waggoners, all

extremely polite ; they asked Cacambo a few questions with the utmost discretion and circumspection ; and replied to his in a most obliging and satisfactory manner.

As soon as dinner was over, both Candide and Cacambo thought they should pay very handsomely for their entertainment by laying down two of those large gold pieces which they had picked off the ground ; but the landlord and landlady burst into a fit of laughing, and held their sides for some time. When the fit was over : " Gentlemen," said the landlord, " I plainly perceive you are strangers, and such we are not accustomed to see ; pardon us therefore for laughing when you offered us the common pebbles of our highways for payment of your reckoning. To be sure, you have none of the coin of this kingdom ; but there is no necessity for having any money at all to dine in this house. All the inns, which are established for the convenience of those who carry on the trade of this nation, are maintained by the government. You have found but very indifferent entertainment here, because this is only a poor village ; but in almost every other of these public-houses you will meet with a reception worthy of persons of your merit." Cacambo explained the whole of this speech of the landlord to Candide, who listened to it with the same astonishment with which his friend communicated it. "What sort of a country is this," said the one to the other, " that is unknown to all the world, and in which Nature has everywhere so different an appearance to what she has in ours? Possibly this is that part of the globe where everything is right, for there must certainly be some such place. And for all that Master Pangloss could say, I often perceived that things went very ill in Westphalia."

CHAPTER XVIII.

What they saw in the Country of El Dorado.

CACAMBO vented all his curiosity upon his landlord by a thousand different questions: the honest man answered him thus: "I am very ignorant, sir, but I am contented with my ignorance; however, we have in this neighbourhood an old man retired from Court, who is the most learned and communicative person in the kingdom." He then carried Cacambo to the old man; Candide acted now only a second character, and attended his valet. They entered a very plain house, for the door was nothing but silver, and the ceiling was only of beaten gold, but wrought in so elegant a taste as to vie with the richest. The antechamber, indeed, was only incrusted with rubies and emeralds; but the order in which everything was disposed made amends for this great simplicity.

The old man received the strangers on his sofa, which was stuffed with humming-birds, feathers, and ordered his servants to present them with liquors in golden goblets; after which he satisfied their curiosity in the following terms:—

"I am now one hundred and seventy-two years old; and I learnt of my late father, who was equerry to the king, the amazing revolutions of Peru to which he had been an eyewitness. This kingdom is the ancient patrimony of the Incas, who very imprudently quitted it to conquer another part of the world, and were at length conquered and destroyed themselves by the Spaniards.

"Those princes of their family who remained in their native country acted more wisely. They ordained, with the consent of their whole nation, that none of the inhabitants of our little kingdom should ever quit it; and to this wise ordinance we owe the preservation of our innocence and happiness. The Spaniards had some confused notion of this country, to which they gave the name of *El Dorado;* and Sir Walter Raleigh, an Englishman, actually came very near it about three hundred years ago; but the inaccessible rocks and precipices with which our country is surrounded on all sides, has hitherto secured us from the rapacious fury of the people of Europe, who have an unaccountable fondness for the pebbles and dirt of our land, for the sake of which they would murder us all to the very last man."

The conversation lasted some time, and turned chiefly on the form of government, their manners, their women, their public diversions, and the arts. At length, Candide, who had always had a taste for metaphysics, asked whether the people of that country had any religion.

The old man reddened a little at this question. "Can you doubt it?" said he. "Do you take us for wretches lost to all sense of gratitude?" Cacambo asked in a respectful manner what was the established religion of El Dorado. The old man blushed again, and said: "Can there be two religions then? Ours, I apprehend, is the religion of the whole world. We worship God from morning till night." "Do you worship but one God?" said Cacambo, who still acted as the interpreter of Candide's doubts. "Certainly," said the old man; "there are not two nor three nor four Gods. I must confess the people of your world ask very extraordinary questions." However, Candide could not refrain from making many more inquiries of the old man. He wanted to know in what manner they prayed to God in El Dorado. "We do not pray to him at all," said the reverend sage. "We have nothing to ask of him. He has given us all we want, and we give him thanks incessantly." Candide had a curiosity to see some of their priests, and desired Cacambo to ask the old man where they were; at which he, smiling, said: "My friends, we are all of us priests. The king and all the heads of families sing solemn hymns of thanksgiving every morning, accompanied by five or six thousand musicians." "What!" says Cacambo, "have you no monks among you to dispute, to govern, to intrigue, and to burn people who are not of the same opinion with themselves?" "Do you take us for fools?" said the old man; "here we are all of one opinion, and know not what you mean by your monks." During the whole of this discourse Candide was in raptures, and he said to himself: "What a prodigious difference is there between this place and Westphalia, and this house and the baron's castle! Ah, Master Pangloss! had you ever seen El Dorado you would no longer have maintained that the castle of Thunder-ten-tronckh was the finest of all possible edifices. There is nothing like seeing the world, that's certain."

This long conversation being ended, the old man ordered six sheep to be harnessed and put to the coach, and sent twelve of his servants to escort the travellers to Court. "Excuse me," said he, "for not waiting on you in person; my age deprives me of that honour. The king will receive you in such a manner that you will have no reason to complain; and doubtless you will make a proper allowance for the customs of the country if they should not happen altogether to please you."

Candide and Cacambo got into the coach, the six sheep flew, and in less than a quarter of an hour they arrived at the king's palace, which was situated at the further end of the capital. At the entrance was a portal two hundred and twenty feet high, and one hundred wide; but it is impossible for words to express the materials of which it was built. The reader, however, will readily conceive they must have a prodigious superiority over the pebbles and sand which we call gold and precious stones.

Twenty beautiful young virgins in waiting received Candide and Cacambo at their alighting from the coach, conducted them to the bath, and clad them in robes wove of the down of humming-birds; after which they were introduced by the great officers of the Crown, of both sexes, to the king's apartment, between two files of musicians, each file consisting of a thousand, agreeably to the custom of the country. When they drew near to the presence-chamber, Cacambo asked one of the officers in what manner they were to pay their obeisance to his majesty; whether it was the custom to fall upon their knees, or to prostrate themselves upon the ground? whether they were to put their hands upon their heads or behind their backs? whether they were to lick the dust off the floor? in short, what was the ceremony usual on such occasions? "The custom," said the great officer, "is to embrace the king, and kiss him on each cheek." Candide and Cacambo accordingly threw their arms around his majesty's neck, who received them in the most gracious manner imaginable, and very politely asked them to sup with him.

While supper was preparing, orders were given to show them the city, where they saw public structures that reared their lofty heads to the clouds; the market-places decorated with a thousand columns; fountains of spring-water, besides others of rose-water, and of liquors drawn from the sugar-cane, incessantly flowing in the great squares, which were paved with a kind of precious stones that emitted an odour like that of cloves and cinnamon. Candide asked to see the High Court of Justice, the Parliament; but was answered that they have none in that country, being utter strangers to lawsuits. He then inquired if they had any prisons; they replied, none. But what gave him at once the greatest surprise and pleasure was the Palace of Sciences, where he saw a gallery, two thousand feet long, filled with the various apparatus in mathematics and natural philosophy. ·

After having spent the whole afternoon in seeing only about the thousandth part of the city, they were brought back

C

to the king's palace.   Candide sat down at the table with his majesty, his valet Cacambo, and several ladies of the Court.   Never was entertainment more elegant, nor could any one possible show more wit than his majesty displayed while they were at supper.   Cacambo explained all the king's *bon mots* to Candide, and although they were translated, they still appeared to be *bon mots*.   Of all the things that surprised Candide, this was not the least.   They spent a whole month in this hospitable place, during which time Candide was continually saying to Cacambo, " I own, my friend, once more that the castle where I was born is a mere nothing in comparison with the place where we now are ; but still Miss Cunegund is not here, and you yourself have doubtless some fair one for whom you sigh in Europe.   If we remain here, we shall only be as others are ; whereas, if we return to our own world with only a dozen of El Dorado sheep loaded with the pebbles of this country, we shall be richer than all the kings in Europe ; we shall no longer need to stand in awe of the inquisitors ; and we may easily recover Miss Cunegund."

This speech was perfectly agreeable to Cacambo.   A fondness for roving, for making a figure in their own country, and for boasting of what they had seen in their travels, was so prevalent in our two wanderers, that they resolved to be no longer happy ; and demanded permission of the king to quit the country.

"You are about to do a rash and silly action." said the king.   " I am sensible my kingdom is an inconsiderable spot; but when people are tolerably at their ease in any place, I should think it would be to their interest to remain there. Most assuredly I have no right to detain you or any strangers against your wills : this is an act of tyranny to which our manners and our laws are equally repugnant : all men are by nature free; you have therefore an undoubted liberty to depart whenever you please, but you will have many and great difficulties to encounter in passing the frontiers. It is impossible to ascend that rapid river which runs under high and vaulted rocks, and by which you were conveyed hither by a kind of miracle. The mountains by which my kingdom are hemmed in on all sides, are ten thousand feet high, and perfectly perpendicular; they are above ten leagues over each, and the descent from them is one continued precipice. However, since you are determined to leave us, I will immediately give orders to the superintendent of my carriages to cause one to be made that will convey you very safe. When they have conducted you to the back of the mountains, nobody can attend you farther; for my subjects have made a vow never to quit the kingdom, and they are too prudent to break it. Ask me whatever else you please." "All we shall ask of your majesty," said Cacambo, is only a few sheep laden with provisions, pebbles, and the clay of your country." The king smiled at the request, and said, "I cannot imagine what pleasure you Europeans find in our yellow clay; but take away as much of it as you will, and much good may it do you."

He immediately gave orders to his engineers to make a machine to hoist these two extraordinary men out of the kingdom. Three thousand good mathematicians went to work and finished it in about fifteen days; and it did not cost more than twenty millions sterling of that country's money. Candide and Cacambo were placed on this machine, and they took with them two large red sheep, bridled and saddled, to ride upon when they got on the other side of the mountains; twenty others to serve as sumpters for carrying provisions; thirty laden with presents of whatever was most curious in the country; and fifty with gold, diamonds, and other precious stones. The king, at parting with our two adventurers, embraced them with the greatest cordiality.

It was a curious sight to behold the manner of their

setting off, and the ingenious method by which they and their sheep were hoisted to the top of the mountains. The mathematicians and engineers took leave of them as soon as they had conveyed them to a place of safety; and Candide was wholly occupied with the thoughts of presenting his sheep to Miss Cunégund. "Now," says he, "thanks to Heaven, we have more than sufficient to pay the Governor of Buenos Ayres for Miss Cunegund, if she is redeemable. Let us make the best of our way to Cayenne, where we will take shipping, and then we may at leisure think of what kingdom we shall purchase with our riches."

CHAPTER XIX.

What happened to them at Surinam, and how Candide came acquainted with Martin.

OUR travellers' first day's journey was very pleasant; they were elated with the prospect of possessing more riches than were to be found in Europe, Asia, and Africa together. Candide, in amorous transports, cut the name of Miss Cunegund on almost every tree he came to. The second day, two of their sheep sunk in a morass, and were swallowed up, with their lading; two more died of fatigue; some few days afterwards, seven or eight perished with hunger in a desert; and others, at different times, tumbled down precipices, or were otherwise lost; so that, after travelling about a hundred days, they had only two sheep left of the hundred and two they brought with them from El Dorado. Said Candide to Cacambo: "You see, my dear friend, how perishable the riches of this world are; there is nothing solid but virtue." "Very true," said Cacambo; "but we have still two sheep remaining, with more treasure than ever the King of Spain will be possessed of; and I espy a town at a distance, which I take to be Surinam, a town belonging to the Dutch. We are now at the end of our troubles, and at the beginning of happiness."

As they drew near the town, they saw a negro stretched on the ground with only one-half of his habit, which was a kind of linen frock, for the poor man had lost his left leg and his right hand. "Good God," said Candide in Dutch; "what dost thou here, friend, in this deplorable condition?" "I am waiting for my master, Mynheer Vanderdendur, the famous trader," answered the negro. "Was it Mynheer Vanderdendur that used you in this cruel manner?" "Yes, sir," said the negro; "it is the custom here. They give a linen garment twice a year, and that is all our covering. When we labour in the sugar-works, and the mill happens to snatch off a finger, they instantly chop off our hand; and when we attempt to run away, they cut off a leg. Both these cases have happened to me; and it is at this expense that you eat sugar in Europe; and yet when my mother sold me for ten patacoons on the coast of Guinea, she said to me: 'My dear child, bless our fetishes; adore them for ever; they will make thee live happy; thou hast the honour to be a slave to our lords the whites, by which thou wilt make the fortune of us thy parents.' Alas! I know not whether I have made their fortunes; but they have not made mine. Dogs, monkeys, and parrots are a thousand times less wretched than I. The Dutch fetishes who converted me tell me every Sunday that the blacks and whites are all children of one father, whom they call Adam. As for me, I do not understand anything of genealogies; but if what these preachers say is true, we are all second cousins; and you must allow that it is impossible to be worse treated by our relations than we are."

"O Pangloss!" cried out Candide, "such horrid doings never entered thy imagination. Here is an end of the matter; I find myself, after all, obliged to renounce thy optimism." "Optimism," said Cacambo, "what is that?"

" Alas ! " replied Candide, " it is the obstinacy of maintaining that everything is best when it is worst ; " and so saying, he turned his eyes towards the poor negro, and shed a flood of tears ; and in this weeping mood he entered the town of Surinam.

Immediately upon their arrival our travellers inquired if there was any vessel in the harbour which they might send to Buenos Ayres. The person they addressed themselves to happened to be the master of a Spanish bark, who offered to agree with them on moderate terms, and appointed them a meeting at a public-house. Thither Candide and his faithful Cacambo went to wait for him, taking with them their two sheep.

Candide, who was all frankness and sincerity, made an ingenuous recital of his adventures to the Spaniard, declaring to him at the same time his resolution of carrying off Miss Cunegund from the Governor of Buenos Ayres. " Oh, oh ! " said the shipmaster, " if that is the case, get whom you please to carry you to Buenos Ayres ; for my part, I wash my hands of the affair. It would prove a hanging matter to us all. The fair Cunegund is the Governor's favourite mistress." These words were like a clap of thunder to Candide ; he wept bitterly for a long time, and, taking Cacambo aside, he says to him : " I'll tell you, my dear friend, what you must do. We have each of us in our pockets to the value of five or six millions in diamonds ; you are cleverer at these matters than I ; you must go to Buenos Ayres and bring off Miss Cunegund. If the Governor makes any difficulty, give him a million ; if he holds out, give him two ; as you have not killed an Inquisitor, they will have no suspicion of you : I'll fit out another ship, and go to Venice, where I will wait for you. Venice is a free country, where we shall have nothing to fear from Bulgarians, Abares, Jews, or Inquisitors. Cacambo greatly applauded this wise resolution. He was inconsolable at the thoughts of parting with so good a master, who treated him more like an intimate friend than a servant; but the pleasure of being able to do him a service soon got the better of his sorrow. They embraced each other with a flood of tears. Candide charged him not to forget the old woman. Cacambo set out the same day. This Cacambo was a very honest fellow.

Candide continued some days longer at Surinam, waiting for any captain to carry him and his two remaining sheep to Italy. He hired domestics, and purchased many things necessary for a long voyage; at length, Mynheer Vanderdendur, skipper of a large Dutch vessel, came and offered his service. "What will you have," said Candide, to carry me, my servants, my baggage, and these two sheep you see here, directly to Venice?" The skipper asked ten thousand piastres; and Candide agreed to his demand without hesitation.

"Ho, ho!" said the cunning Vanderdendur to himself, "this stranger must be very rich; he agrees to give me ten thousand piastres without hesitation." Returning a little while after, he tells Candide that, upon second consideration he could not undertake the voyage for less than twenty thousand. "Very well; you shall have them," said Candide.

"Zounds!" said the skipper to himself, "this man agrees to pay twenty thousand piastres with as much ease as ten." Accordingly he goes back again, and tells him roundly that he will not carry him to Venice for less than thirty thousand piastres. "Then you shall have thirty thousand," said Candide.

"Odso!" said the Dutchman once more to himself, "thirty thousand piasters seem a trifle to this man. Those sheep must certainly be laden with an immense treasure. I'll e'en stop here and ask no more; but make him pay down the thirty thousand piastres, and then we may see what is to be done farther." Candide sold two small diamonds, the least

of which was worth more than all the skipper asked. He
paid him beforehand; the two sheep were put on board, and
Candide followed in a small boat to join the vessel in the
roads. The skipper takes his opportunity, hoists sail, and
puts out to sea with a favourable wind. Candide, confounded and amazed, soon lost sight of the ship. "Alas!"
said he, "this is a trick like those in our old world!" He
returns back to the shore overwhelmed with grief; and
indeed he had lost what would have made the fortune of
twenty monarchs.

Immediately upon his landing he applied to the Dutch
magistrate. Being transported with passion, he thunders at
the door, which being opened, he goes in, tells his case,
and talks a little louder than was necessary. The magistrate began with fining him ten thousand piastres for his
petulance, and then listened very patiently to what he had
to say; promised to examine into the affair on the skipper's
return; and ordered him to pay ten thousand piastres more
for the fees of the court.

This treatment put Candide out of all patience. It is
true he had suffered misfortunes a thousand times more
grievous; but the cool insolence of the judge and the villainy
of the skipper raised his choler and threw him into a deep
melancholy. The villainy of mankind presented itself to
his mind in all its deformity, and his soul was a prey to the
most gloomy ideas. After some time, hearing that the captain of a French ship was ready to set sail for Bordeaux, as
he had no more sheep loaded with diamonds to put on board,
he hired the cabin at the usual price; and made it known in
the town that he would pay the passage and board of any
honest man who would give him his company during the
voyage, besides making him a present of ten thousand piastres,
on condition that such person was the most dissatisfied
with his condition, and the most unfortunate in the whole
province.

Upon this there appeared such a crowd of candidates, that a large fleet could not have contained them. Candide, willing to choose among those who appeared most likely to answer his intention, selected twenty, who seemed to him the most sociable, and who all pretended to merit the preference. He invited them to his inn, and promised to treat them with a supper, on condition that every man should bind himself by an oath to relate his own history; declaring at the same time that he would make choice of that person who should appear to him the most deserving of compassion and the most justly dissatisfied with his condition of life, and that he would make a present to the rest.

This extraordinary assembly continued sitting till four in the morning. Candide, while he was listening to their adventures, called to mind what the old woman had said to him in their voyage to Buenos Ayres, and the wager she had laid that there was not a person on board the ship but had met with some great misfortunes. Every story he heard put him in mind of Pangloss. " My old master," said he, " would be confoundedly put to it to demonstrate his favourite system. Would he were here ! Certainly, if everything is for the best, it is in El Dorado, and not in the other parts of the world." At length he determined in favour of a poor scholar, who had laboured ten years for the booksellers at Amsterdam, being of opinion that no employment could be more detestable.

This scholar, who was in fact a very honest man, had been robbed by his wife, beaten by his son, and forsaken by his daughter, who had run away with a Portuguese. He had been likewise deprived of a small employment on which he subsisted, and he was persecuted by the clergy of Surinam, who took him for a Socinian. It must be acknowledged that the other competitors were at least as wretched as he. But Candide was in hopes that the company of a man of letters would relieve the tediousness of the voyage. All the other candidates complained that Candide had done them great injustice, but he stopped their mouths by a present of a hundred piastres to each.

CHAPTER XX.

What befell Candide and Martin on their Passage.

THE old philosopher, whose name was Martin, took shipping with Candide for Bordeaux. They both had seen and suffered a great deal; and had the ship been to go from Surinam to Japan round the Cape of Good Hope, they could have found sufficient entertainment for each other during the whole voyage in discoursing upon moral and natural evil.

Candide, however, had one advantage over Martin; he lived in the pleasing hopes of seeing Miss Cunegund once more whereas the poor philosopher had nothing to hope for; besides, Candide had money and jewels, and notwithstanding he had lost an hundred red sheep laden with the greatest treasure on the earth, and though he still smarted from the reflection of the Dutch skipper's knavery, yet when he considered what he had still left, and repeated the name of Cunegund, especially after meal times, he inclined to Pangloss's doctrine.

"And pray," said he to Martin, "what is your opinion of the whole of this system? What notion have you of moral and natural evil?" "Sir," replied Martin, "our priest accused me of being a Socinian; but the real truth is, I am a Manichæan." "Nay, you are jesting," said Candide, "there are no Manichæans existing at present in the world." "And yet I am one," said Martin; "but I cannot help it; I cannot for the soul of me think otherwise." "Surely the devil must be in you," said Candide. "He concerns himself so much," replied Martin, "in the affairs of this world, that it is very probable he may be in me as

well as everywhere else ; but I must confess, when I cast
my eye on this globe, or rather globule, I cannot help thinking that God has abandoned it to some malignant being. I
always except El Dorado. I scarce ever knew a city that did
not wish the destruction of its neighbouring city, nor a
family that did not desire to exterminate some other family.
The poor in all parts of the world bear an inveterate hatred
to the rich, even while they creep and cringe to them ; and
the rich treat the poor like sheep, whose wool and flesh they
barter for money : a million of regimental assassins traverse
Europe from one end to the other, to get their bread by
regular depredation and murder, because it is the most
gentleman-like profession. Even in those cities which seem
to enjoy the blessings of peace, and where the arts flourish,
the inhabitants are devoured with envy, care, and in-
quietudes, which are greater plagues than any experienced
in a town besieged. Private chagrins are still more dreadful than public calamities. In a word," concluded the
philosopher, "I have seen and suffered so much that I am
a Manichæan."

"And yet there is some good in the world," replied
Candide. "Maybe so," said Martin ; "but it has escaped
my knowledge."

While they were deeply engaged in this dispute they heard
the report of cannon, which redoubled every moment. Each
takes out his glass, and they espy two ships warmly engaged
at the distance of about three miles. The wind brought
them both so near the French ship that those on board her
had the pleasure of seeing the fight with great ease. After
several smart broadsides, the one gave the other a shot
between wind and water, which sunk her outright. Then
could Candide and Martin plainly perceive an hundred men
on the deck of the vessel which was sinking, who, with hands
uplifted to heaven, sent forth piercing cries, and were in a
moment swallowed up by the waves.

" Well," said Martin, you now see in what manner mankind treat each other." " It is certain," said Candide, " that there is something diabolical in this affair." As he was speaking thus, he spied something of a shining red hue, which swam close to the vessel. The boat was hoisted out to see what it might be, when it proved to be one of his sheep. Candide felt more joy at the recovery of this one animal than he did grief when he lost the other hundred, though laden with the large diamonds of El Dorado.

The French captain quickly perceived that the victorious ship belonged to the crown of Spain ; that the other was a Dutch pirate, and the very same captain who had robbed Candide. The immense riches which this villain had amassed were buried with him in the deep, and only this one sheep saved out of the whole. " You see," said Candide to Martin, " that vice is sometimes punished ; this villain the Dutch skipper has met with the fate he deserved." " Very true," said Martin, " but why should the passengers be doomed also to destruction ? God has punished the knave, and the devil has drowned the rest."

The French and Spanish ships continued their cruise, and Candide and Martin their conversation. They disputed fourteen days successively, at the end of which they were just as far advanced as the first moment they began. However, they had the satisfaction of disputing, of communicating their ideas, and of mutually comforting each other. Candide embraced his sheep with transport : " Since I have found thee again," said he," I may possibly find my Cunegund once more,"

CHAPTER XXI.

Candide and Martin, while thus reasoning with each other, draw near to the coast of France.

AT length they descried the coast of France, when Candide said to Martin, " Pray, Mr. Martin, were you ever in France ? " " Yes, sir," said Martin, " I have been in several provinces of that kingdom. In some one-half of the people are fools and madmen ; in some they are too artful ; in others, again, they are in general either very good-natured or very brutal ; while in others they affect to be witty ; and in all, their ruling passion is love, the next is slander, and the last is to talk nonsense." " But pray, Mr. Martin, were you ever in Paris ? " " Yes, sir, I have been in that city, and it is a place that contains the several species just described. It is a chaos, a confused multitude, where every one seeks for pleasure without being able to find it : at least, as far as I have observed during my short stay in that city. At my arrival I was robbed of all I had in the world by pickpockets and sharpers, at the fair of St. Germain. I was taken up myself for a robber, and confined in prison a whole week, after which I hired myself as corrector to a press, in order to get a little money towards defraying my expenses back to Holland on foot. I knew the whole tribe of scribblers, malcontents, and fanatics. It is said the people of that city are very polite : I believe they may be so."

" For my part, I have no curiosity to see France," said Candide. " You may easily conceive, my friend, that after spending a month at El Dorado, I can desire to behold nothing upon earth but Miss Cunegund ; I am going to wait for her at Venice. I intend to pass through France in my way to Italy ; will you not bear me company ? " " With all my heart," said Martin. " They say Venice is agreeable to none but noble Venetians, but that, nevertheless, strangers are well received there when they have plenty of money. Now I have none, but you have ; therefore I will attend you whither you please." " Now we are upon this subject," said Candide, " do you think that the earth was originally sea, as we read in that great book which belongs to the captain of the ship ? " " I believe nothing of it," replied Martin, " any more than I do of the many other chimeras which have been related to us for some time past." " But then to what end," said Candide, " was the world formed ? " " To make us mad," said Martin. " Are you not surprised," continued Candide, "at the love which the two girls in the country of the Oreillons had for those two monkeys ? You know I have told you the story." "Surprised !" replied Martin, " not in the least ; I see nothing strange in this passion. I have seen so many extraordinary things that there is nothing extraordinary to me now." " Do you think," said Candide, "that mankind always massacred each other as they do now ? Were they always guilty of lies, fraud, treachery, ingratitude, inconstancy, envy, ambition, and cruelty ? Were they always thieves, fools, cowards, gluttons, drunkards, misers, calumniators, debauchees, fanatics, and hypocrites ? " " Do you believe," said Martin, " that hawks have always been accustomed to eat pigeons when they came in their way ? " " Doubtless," said Candide. " Well, then," replied Martin, " if hawks have always had the same nature, why should you pretend that mankind change theirs ? " " Oh !" said Candide, "there is a great deal of difference ; for free will——" And reasoning thus, they arrived at Bourdeaux.

CHAPTER XXII.

What happened to Candide and Martin in France.

CANDIDE stayed no longer at Bourdeaux than was necessary to dispose of a few of the pebbles he had brought from El Dorado, and to provide himself with a post-chaise for two persons, for he could no longer stir a step without his philosopher Martin. The only thing that gave him concern was the being obliged to leave his sheep behind him, which he entrusted to the care of the Academy of Sciences at Bourdeaux, who proposed, as a prize subject for the year, to prove why the wool of this sheep was red ; and the prize was adjudged to a northern sage, who demonstrated by A *plus* B *minus* C, divided by Z, why the sheep must necessarily be red, and die of the mange.

In the meantime, all the travellers whom Candide met with in the inns or on the road told him to a man that they were going to Paris. This general eagerness gave him likewise a great desire to see this capital, and it was not much out of his way to Venice.

He entered the city by the suburbs of St. Marceau, and thought himself in one of the vilest hamlets in all Westphalia.

Candide had not been long at his inn before he was seized with a slight disorder, owing to the fatigue he had undergone. As he wore a diamond of an enormous size on his finger, and had among the rest of his equipage a strong box that seemed very weighty, he soon found himself between two physicians whom he had not sent for, a number of intimate friends whom he had never seen and who would not quit his bedside, and two female devotees, who were very careful in providing him hot suppers.

" I remember," said Martin to him, " that the first time I

came to Paris I was likewise taken ill. I was very poor, and accordingly I had neither friends, nurses, nor physicians, and yet I did very well."

However, by dint of purging and bleeding, Candide's disorder became very serious. The priest of the parish came with all imaginable politeness to desire a note of him, payable to the bearer in the other world. Candide refused to comply with his request, but the two devotees assured him that it was a new fashion. Candide replied that he was not one that followed the fashion. Martin was for throwing the priest out of the window. The clerk swore Candide should not have Christian burial. Martin swore in his turn that he would bury the clerk alive if he continued to plague them any longer. The dispute grew warm ; Martin took him by the shoulders and turned him out of the room, which gave great scandal, and occasioned a verbal process.

Candide recovered, and till he was in a condition to go abroad, had a great deal of very good company to pass the evenings with him in his chamber. They played deep. Candide was surprised to find he could never turn a trick, and Martin was not at all surprised at the matter.

Among those who did him the honours of the place was a little spruce Abbé of Perigord—one of those insinuating, busy, fawning, impudent necessary fellows that lay wait for strangers at their arrival, tell them all the scandal of the town, and offer to minister to their pleasures at various prices. This man conducted Candide and Martin to the playhouse : they were acting a new tragedy. Candide found himself placed near a cluster of wits. This, however, did not prevent him from shedding tears at some parts of the piece, which were most affecting and best acted. One of these talkers said to him between the acts : "You are greatly to blame to shed tears. That actress plays horribly, and the man that plays with her still worse, and the piece itself is still more execrable than the representation. The author does not understand a word of Arabic, and yet he has laid his scene in Arabia ; and what is more, he is a fellow who does not believe in innate ideas. To-morrow I will bring you a score of pamphlets that have been written against him." " Pray, sir," said Candide to the Abbé, " how many theatrical pieces have you in France ? " " Five or six thousand," replied the other. " Indeed ! that is a great number," said Candide ; " but how many good ones may there be ? " " About fifteen or sixteen." " Oh ! that is a great number," said Martin.

Candide was greatly taken with an actress who performed the part of Queen Elizabeth in a dull kind of tragedy that is played sometimes. " 'That actress," said he to Martin, " pleases me greatly. She has some sort of resemblance to Miss Cunegund. I should be very glad to pay my respects to her." The Abbé of Perigord offered his service to introduce him to her at her own house. Candide, who was brought up in Germany, desired to know what might be the ceremonial used on those occasions, and how a Queen of England was treated in France. " There is a necessary distinction to be observed in these matters," said the Abbé. " In a country town we take them to a tavern ; here in Paris they are treated with great respect during their lifetime, provided they are handsome, and when they die we throw their bodies upon a dunghill." " How," said Candide, " throw a queen's body upon a dunghill ! " " The gentleman is quite right," said Martin ; " he tells you nothing but the truth. I happened to be at Paris when Miss Monimia made her exit, as one may say, out of this world into another. She was refused what they call here the rites of sepulture ; that is to say, she was denied the privilege of rotting in a churchyard by the side of all the beggars in the parish. They buried her at the corner of Burgundy Street, which must certainly have shocked her extremely, as she had very exalted notions of things." " This is acting very unpolitely," said Candide. " Lord ! " said Martin, "what can be said to it ? It is the way of these people. Figure to yourself all the contradictions, all the inconsistencies possible, and you may meet with them in the government, the courts of justice, the churches, and the public spectacles of this odd nation." " Is it true," said Candide, "that the people of Paris are always laughing ? " " Yes," replied the Abbé ; " but it is with anger in their hearts. They express all their complaints by loud bursts of laughter, and commit the most detestable crimes with a smile on their faces."

" Who was that great overgrown beast," said Candide, " who spoke so ill to me of the piece with which I was so much affected, and of the players who gave me so much pleasure ? " " A very good-for-nothing sort of a man, I assure you," answered the Abbé ; " one who gets his liveli-hood by abusing every new book and play that is written or performed. He abominates to see any one meet with success, like eunuchs who detest every one that possesses those powers they are deprived of. He is one of those vipers in literature who nourish themselves with their own venom ; a pamphlet-monger." " A pamphlet-monger ? " said Candide ; " what is that ? " " Why, a pamphlet-monger," replied the Abbé, " is a writer of pamphlets, a fool."

Candide, Martin, and the Abbé of Perigord argued thus on the staircase while they stood to see the people go out of the playhouse. " Though I am very earnest to see Miss Cunegund again," said Candide, " yet I have a great incli-nation to sup with Miss Clairon, for I am really much taken with her."

The Abbé was not a person to show his face at this lady's house, which was frequented by none but the best company. "She is engaged this evening," said he ; " but I will do my-self the honour to introduce you to a lady of quality of my acquaintance, at whose house you will see as much of tne manners of Paris as if you had lived here for forty years."

Candide, who was naturally curious, suffered himself to be conducted to this lady's house, which was in the suburbs of St. Honoré. The company were engaged at basset; twelve melancholy punters held each in his hand a small pack of cards, the corners of which, doubled down, were so many registers of their ill-fortune. A profound silence reigned through the assembly, a pallid dread had taken possession of the countenances of the punters, and restless inquietude stretched every muscle of the face of him who kept the bank; and the lady of the house, who was seated next to him, observed with lynx's eyes every parole and *sept-le-va* as they were going, as likewise those who tallied, and made them undouble their cards with a severe exactness, though mixed with a politeness, which she thought necessary not to frighten away her customers. This lady assumed the title of Marchioness of Parolignac. Her daughter, a girl of about fifteen years of age, was one of the punters, and took care to give her mamma an item, by signs, when any one of them attempted to repair the rigour of their ill-fortune by a little innocent deception. The company were thus occupied, when Candide, Martin, and the Abbé, made their entrance. Not a creature rose to salute them, or indeed took the least notice of them, being wholly intent upon the business in hand. "Ah!" said Candide, "my Lady Baroness of Thunder-ten-tronckh would have behaved more civilly."

However, the Abbé whispered the Marchioness in the ear, who, half raising herself from her seat, honoured Candide with a gracious smile, and gave Martin a nod of her head with an air of inexpressible dignity. She then ordered a seat for Candide, and desired him to make one at their party of play. He did so, and in a few deals lost near a thousand pieces; after which they supped very elegantly, and every one was surprised at seeing Candide lose so much money, without appearing to be the least disturbed at it. The servants in waiting said to each other, " This is certainly some English lord."

The supper was like most others of this kind at Paris. At first every one was silent ; then followed a few confused murmurs, and afterwards several insipid jokes passed and repassed, with false reports, false reasonings, a little politics, and a great deal of scandal. The conversation then turned upon the new productions in literature. " Pray," said the Abbé, "good folks, have you seen the romance written by the Sieur Gauchat, doctor of divinity ? " " Yes," answered one of the company, " but I had not patience to go through it. The town is pestered with a swarm of imperti- nent productions, but this of Dr. Gauchat's outdoes them all. In short, I was so horribly tired of reading this vile stuff, that I even resolved to come here, and make a party at basset." " But what say you to the Archdeacon T——'s miscellaneous collection," said the Abbé. " Oh, my God !" cried the Marchioness of Parolignac, never mention the tedious creature. Only think what pains he is at to tell one things that all the world knows; and how he labours an argument that is hardly worth the slightest consideration ! How absurdly he makes use of other people's wit ! how miserably he mangles what he has pilfered from them ! The man makes me quite sick. A few pages of the good archdeacon are enough in conscience to satisfy any one."

There was at the table a person of learning and taste, who supported what the Marchioness had advanced. They next began to talk of tragedies, The lady desired to know how it came about that there were several tragedies which still continued to be played, though they would not bear reading ? The man of taste explained very clearly, how a piece may be in some manner interesting without having a grain of merit. He showed, in a few words, that it is not

sufficient to throw together a few incidents that are to be met
with in every romance, and that dazzle the spectator; the
thoughts should be new without being far-fetched; frequently
sublime, but always natural; the author should have a
thorough knowledge of the human heart, and make it speak
properly; he should be a complete poet, without showing an
affectation of it in any of the characters of his piece; he should
be a perfect master of his language, speak it with all its purity
and with the utmost harmony, and yet so as not to make the
sense a slave to the rhyme. "Whoever," added he, "neglects
any one of these rules, though he may write two or three
tragedies with tolerable success, will never be reckoned in the
number of good authors. There are very few good tragedies;
some are idylliums, in well written and harmonious dialogue;
and others a chain of political reasonings that set one asleep;
or else pompous and high-flown amplifications, that disgust
rather than please. Others again are the ravings of a
madman, in an uncouth style, unmeaning flights, or long
apostrophes to the deities, for want of knowing how to
address mankind: in a word, a collection of false maxims
and dull commonplace."

Candide listened to this discourse with great attention,
and conceived a high opinion of the person who delivered
it; and as the Marchioness had taken care to place him near
her side, he took the liberty to whisper her softly in the
ear, and ask who this person was that spoke so well. "He
is a man of letters," replied her ladyship, "who never plays,
and whom the Abbé brings with him to my house sometimes
to spend an evening. He is a great judge of writing,
especially in tragedy: he has composed one himself, which
was damned, and has written a book that was never seen
out of his bookseller's shop, excepting only one copy, which
he sent me with a dedication, to which he had prefixed my
name." "Oh, the great man!" cried Candide: "he is a
second Pangloss."

4

4

Then turning towards him : "Sir," said he, you are doubtless of opinion that everything is for the best in the physical and moral world, and that nothing could be otherwise than it is?" "I, sir!" replied the man of letters ; "I think no such thing, I assure you ; I find that all in this world is set the wrong end uppermost. No one knows what is his rank, his office, nor what he does, nor what he should do ; and that except our evenings, which we generally pass tolerably merrily, the rest of our time is spent in idle disputes and quarrels: Jansenists against Molinists, the Parliament against the Church, and one armed body of men against another ; courtier against courtier, husband against wife, and relations against relations. In short, this world is nothing but one continued scene of civil war."

"Yes," said Candide, "and I have seen worse than all that ; and yet a learned man, who had the misfortune to be hanged, taught me that everything was marvellously well, and that these evils you are speaking of were only so many shades in a beautiful picture." "Your hempen sage," said Martin, "laughed at you. These shades, as you call them, are the most horrible blemishes." "The men make these blemishes," rejoined Candide, "and they cannot do otherwise." "Then it is not their fault," added Martin. The greatest part of the gamesters, who did not understand a syllable of this discourse, amused themselves with drinking, while Martin reasoned with the learned gentleman ; and Candide entertained the lady of the house with a part of his adventures.

After supper the Marchioness conducted Candide into her dressing-room, and made him sit down under a canopy. "Well," said she, "are you still so violently fond of Miss Cunegund of Thunder-ten-tronck ? "Yes, madam," replied Candide. The Marchioness says to him, with a tender smile, "You answer me like a young man born in Westphalia. A Frenchman would have said, 'It is true, madam,

I had a great passion for Miss Cunegund ; but since I have seen you I fear I can no longer love her as I did.' " " Alas ! madam," replied Candide, " I will make you what answer you please." "You fell in love with her, I find, in stooping to pick up her handkerchief, which she had dropped. You shall pick up my garter." " With all my heart, madam," said Candide ; and he picked it up. " But you must tie it on again," said the lady. " Look ye, young man," said the Marchioness, "you are a stranger. I make some of my lovers here in Paris languish for me a whole fortnight ; but I surrender to you the first night, because I am willing to do the honours of my country to a young Westphalian." The fair one having cast her eye on two very large diamonds that were upon the young stranger's finger, praised them in so earnest a manner that they were in an instant transferred from his finger to hers.

As Candide was going home with the Abbé he felt some qualms of conscience for having been guilty of infidelity to Miss Cunegund. The Abbé took part with him in his uneasiness. He had but an inconsiderable share in the thousand pieces Candide had lost at play, and the two diamonds which had been in a manner extorted from him ; and therefore very prudently designed to make the most he could of his new acquaintance which chance had thrown in his way. He talked much of Miss Cunegund ; and Candide assured him that he would heartily ask pardon of that fair one for his infidelity to her when he saw her at Venice.

The Abbé redoubled his civilities, and seemed to interest himself warmly in everything that Candide said, did, or seemed inclined to do.

" And so, sir, you have an engagement at Venice ? " " Yes, Monsieur l'Abbé," answered Candide, " I must absolutely wait upon Miss Cunegund ;" and then the pleasure he took in talking about the object he loved led him insensibly to relate, according to custom, part of his adventures with that illustrious Westphalian beauty.

"I fancy," said the Abbé, "Miss Cunegund has a great deal of wit, and that her letters must be very entertaining." "I never received any from her," said Candide, "for you are to consider that, being expelled from the castle upon her account, I could not write to her, especially as soon after my departure I heard she was dead ; but, thank God, I found afterwards she was living. I left her again after this, and now I have sent a messenger to her near two thousand leagues from hence, and wait here for his return with an answer from her."

The artful Abbé let not a word of all this escape him, though he seemed to be musing upon something else. He soon took his leave of the two adventurers, after having embraced them with the greatest cordiality. The next morning, almost as soon as his eyes were open, Candide received the following billet :—

"My dearest Lover,—I have been ill in this city these eight days. I have heard of your arrival, and should fly to your arms were I able to stir. I was informed of your being on the way hither at Bourdeaux, where I left the faithful Cacambo and the old woman, who will soon follow me. The Governor of Buenos Ayres has taken everything from me but your heart, which I still retain. Come to me immediately on receipt of this. Your presence will either give me new life or kill me with the pleasure."

At the receipt of this charming, this unexpected letter, Candide felt the utmost transports of joy ; though, on the other hand, the indisposition of his beloved Miss Cunegund, overwhelmed him with grief. Distracted between these two passions, he takes his gold and his diamonds, and procured a person to conduct him and Martin to the house where Miss Cunegund lodged. Upon entering the room he felt his limbs tremble, his heart flutter, his tongue falter. He attempted to undraw the curtain, and called for a light to the bedside. "Lord, sir," cried a maid-servant, who was waiting in the room, " take care what you do; Miss cannot bear the least light." And so saying, she pulls the curtain close again. " Cunegund! my dear Cunegund !" cried Candide, bathed in tears, " how do you do ? If you cannot bear the light, speak to me at least." " Alas ! she cannot speak," said the maid. The sick lady then puts a plump hand out of the bed, and Candide first bathes it with his tears, then fills it with diamonds, leaving a purse of gold upon the easy chair.

In the midst of his transports comes an officer into the room, followed by the Abbé and a file of musketeers. " There," said he, " are the two suspected foreigners." At the same time he orders them to be seized and carried to prison. " Travellers are not treated in this manner in the country of El Dorado," said Candide. " I am more of a Manichæan now than ever," said Martin. " But pray, good sir, where are you going to carry us," said Candide. " To a dungeon, my dear sir," replied the officer.

When Martin had a little recovered himself, so as to for a cool judgment of what had passed, he plainly perceived that the person who had acted the part of Miss Cunegund was a cheat, that the Abbé of Perigord was a sharper, who had imposed upon the honest simplicity of Candide, and that the officer was a knave, whom they might easily get rid of.

Candide, following the advice of his friend Martin, and burning with impatience to see the real Miss Cunegund, rather than be obliged to appear at a court of justice, proposes to the officer to make him a present of three small diamonds, each of them worth three thousand pistoles. " Ah, sir," said this understrapper of justice, " had you committed ever so much villainy, this would render you the honestest man living in my eyes. Three diamonds worth three thousand pistoles ! Why, my dear sir, so far from carrying you to jail, I would lose my life to serve you. There are orders for stopping all strangers ; but leave it to me. I have a brother at Dieppe, in Normandy. I myself will conduct you thither, and if you have a diamond left to give him, he will take as much care of you as I myself should."

"But why," said Candide, "do they stop all strangers?" The Abbé of Perigord made answer that it was because a poor devil of the country of Atrebata heard somebody tell foolish stories, and this induced him to commit a parricide; not such a one as that in the month of May 1610, but such as that in the month of December in the year 1594, and such as many that have been perpetrated in other months and years by other poor devils who had heard foolish stories.

The officer then explained to them what the Abbé meant. "Horrid monsters!" exclaimed Candide. "Is it possible that such scenes should pass among a people who are perpetually singing and dancing? Is there no flying this abominable country immediately, this execrable kingdom, where monkeys provoke tigers? I have seen bears in my country, but men I have beheld nowhere but in El Dorado. In the name of God, sir," said he to the officer, "do me the kindness to conduct me to Venice, where I am to wait for Miss Cunegund." "Really, sir," replied the officer, "I cannot possibly wait on you farther than Lower Normandy." So saying, he ordered Candide's irons to be struck off, acknowledged himself mistaken, and sent his followers about their business; after which he conducted Candide and Martin to Dieppe, and left them to the care of his brother. There happened just then to be a small Dutch ship in the roads. The Norman, whom the other three diamonds had converted into the most obliging, serviceable being that ever breathed, took care to see Candide and his attendants safe on board this vessel, that was just ready to sail for Portsmouth in England. This was not the nearest way to Venice indeed; but Candide thought himself escaped out of hell, and did not in the least doubt but he should quickly find an opportunity of resuming his voyage to Venice.

CHAPTER XXIII.

Candide and Martin touch upon the English Coast: what they see there.

"AH, Pangloss! Pangloss! Ah, Martin! Martin! Ah, my dear Miss Cunegund! What sort of a world is this?" Thus exclaimed Candide as soon as he had got on board the Dutch ship. "Why, something very foolish and very abominable," said Martin. "You are acquainted with England," said Candide; "are they as great fools in that country as in France?" "Yes; but in a different manner," answered Martin. "You know that these two nations are at war about a few acres of barren land in the neighbourhood of Canada, and that they have expended much greater sums in the contest than all Canada is worth. To say exactly whether there are a greater number fit to be inhabitants of a madhouse in the one country than the other, exceeds the limits of my imperfect capacity. I know in general that the people we are going to visit are of a very dark and gloomy disposition."

As they were chatting thus together they arrived at Portsmouth. The shore on each side the harbour was lined with a multitude of people, whose eyes were stedfastly fixed on a lusty man who was kneeling down on the deck of one of the men-of-war, with something tied over his eyes. Opposite to this personage stood four soldiers, each of whom shot three bullets into his skull with all the composure imaginable; and when it was done, the whole company went away perfectly well satisfied. "What the devil is all this for?" said Candide; "and what demon or foe to mankind lords it thus tyrannically over the world?" He then asked who was that lusty man who had been sent out of the world with so much ceremony, when he received for answer that it was an admiral. "And pray why do you put your admiral to death?" "Because he did not put a sufficient number of his fellow-creatures to death. You must know, he had an engagement with a French admiral, and it has been proved against him that he was not near enough to his antagonist." "But," replied Candide, "the French admiral must have been as far from him." "There is no doubt of that; but in this country it is found requisite, now and then, to put one admiral to death in order to spirit up the others to fight."

Candide was so shocked at what he saw and heard that he would not set foot on shore, but made a bargain with the Dutch skipper (were he even to rob him like the captain of Surinam) to carry him directly to Venice.

The skipper was ready in two days. They sailed along the coast of France, and passed within sight of Lisbon, at which Candide trembled. From thence they proceeded to the straits, entered the Mediterranean, and at length arrived at Venice. "God be praised," said Candide, embracing Martin, "this is the place where I am to behold my beloved Cunegund once again. I can confide in Cacambo like another self. All is well—all very well; all as well as possible."

CHAPTER XXIV.

Of Pacquette and Friar Giroflée.

Upon their aerival at Venice he went in search of Cacambo at every inn and coffee-house, and among all the ladies of pleasure; but could hear nothing of him. He sent every day to inquire what ships were come in; still no news of Cacambo. "It is strange," said he to Martin, "very strange, that I should have had time to sail from Surinam to Bourdeaux; to travel from thence to Paris, to Dieppe, to Portsmouth; to sail along the coast of Portugal and Spain, and up the Mediterranean to spend some months at Venice; and that my lovely Cunegund should not be arrived. Instead of her, I only met with a Parisian impostor and a rascally Abbé of Perigord. Cunegund is actually dead, and I have nothing to do but to follow her. Alas! how much better would it have been for me to have remained in the paradise of El Dorado, than to have returned to this wicked Europe! You are in the right, my dear Martin; you are certainly in the right : all is misery and deceit."

He fell into a deep melancholy, and neither went to the opera in vogue, nor partook of any of the diversions of the Carnival : nay, he even slighted the fair sex. Martin said to him, "Upon my word, I think you are very simple to imagine that a rascally valet, with five or six millions in his pocket, would go in search of your mistress to the further end of the world, and bring her to Venice to meet you. If he finds her, he will take her for himself; if he does not, he will take another. Let me advise you to forget your valet Cacambo, and your mistress Cunegund." Martin's speech was not the most consolatory to the dejected Candide. His melancholy increased, and Martin never left proving to him, that there is very little virtue or happiness in this world—except, perhaps, in El Dorado, where hardly anybody can gain admittance.

While they were disputing on this important subject, and still expecting Miss Cunegund, Candide perceived a young Theatin friar in St. Mark's Place, with a girl under his arm. The Theatin looked fresh-coloured, plump, and vigorous; his eyes sparkled; his air and gait were bold and lofty. The girl was very pretty, and was singing a song; and every now and then gave her Theatin an amorous ogle, and wantonly pinched his ruddy cheeks. "You will at least allow," said Candide to Martin, " that these two are happy. Hitherto I have met with none but unfortunate people in the whole habitable globe, except in El Dorado ; but as to this couple, I would venture to lay a wager that they are happy." " Done!" said Martin ; "they are not, for what you will." " Well, we have only to ask them to dine with us," said Candide, "and you will see whether I am mistaken or not."

Thereupon he accosts them, and with great politeness invites them to his inn to eat some macaroni, with Lombard partridges and caviare, and to drink a bottle of Montepulciano, Lacryma Christi, Cyprus and Samos wine. The girl blushed; the Theatin accepted the invitation, and she followed him, eyeing Candide every now and then with a mixture of surprise and confusion, while the tears stole down her cheeks. No sooner did she enter his apartment than she cried out : " How, Mr. Candide, have you quite forgot your Pacquette? Do you not know her again?" Candide, who had not regarded her with any degree of attention before, being wholly occupied with the thoughts of his dear Cunegund: "Ah! is it you, child? Was it you that reduced Doctor Pangloss to that fine condition I saw him in?"

" Alas! sir," answered Pacquette, " it was I indeed. I find you are acquainted with everything; and I have been informed of all the misfortunes that happened to the whole family of my lady baroness and the fair Cunegund. But I can safely swear to you that my lot was no less deplorable ; I was innocence itself when you saw me last. A Cordelier, who was my confessor, easily misled me ; the consequences proved terrible. I was obliged to leave the castle some time after the baron kicked you out from thence ; and if a famous surgeon had not taken compassion on me, I had been a dead woman. Gratitude obliged me to live with him some time as a companion. His wife, who was a very devil for jealousy, beat me unmercifully every day. Oh! she was a perfect fury. The doctor himself was the most ugly of all mortals, and I the most wretched creature existing, to be continually beaten for a man whom I did not love. You are sensible, sir, how dangerous it was for an ill-natured

woman to be married to a physician. Incensed at the behaviour of his wife, he one day gave her so affectionate a
remedy for a slight cold she had caught, that she died in less
than two hours in most dreadful convulsions. Her relations
prosecuted the husband, who was obliged to fly, and I was
sent to prison. My innocence would not have saved me,
if I had not been tolerably handsome. The judge gave me
my liberty on condition he should succeed the doctor. However, I was soon supplanted by a rival, turned off without a
farthing, and obliged to continue the abominable trade which
you men think so pleasing, but which to us unhappy creatures
is the most dreadful of all sufferings. At length I came to
follow the business at Venice. Ah, sir ! did you but know
what it is to be companion with every fellow—with old trades-
men, with counsellors, with monks, watermen, and abbés ;
to be exposed to all their insolence and abuse ; to be often
obliged to borrow the gay clothes we wear; to be robbed by
one gallant of what we get from another ; to be subject to
the extortions of civil magistrates ; and to have for ever
before one's eyes the prospect of old age, an hospital, or a
dunghill, you would conclude that I am one of the most
unhappy wretches breathing."

Thus did Pacquette unbosom herself to honest Candide
in his closet, in the presence of Martin, who took occasion
to say to him, " You see I have won the wager already."

Friar Giroflée was all this time in the parlour refreshing
himself with a glass or two of wine till dinner was ready.
" But," said Candide to Pacquette, " you looked so gay and
content when I met you, you sang and caressed the Theatin
with so much fondness, that I absolutely thought you as
happy as you say you are now miserable." " Ah ! dear
sir," said Pacquette, " this is one of the miseries of the trade ;
yesterday I was stripped and beaten by an officer, yet to-
day I must appear good-humoured and gay to please a
friar.

Candide was convinced, and acknowledged that Martin was in the right. They sat down to table with Pacquette and the Theatin; the entertainment was very agreeable, and towards the end they began to converse together with some freedom. "Father," said Candide to the friar, "you seem to me to enjoy a state of happiness that even kings might envy; joy and health are painted in your countenance. You have a beautiful friend to divert you; and you seem to be perfectly well contented with your condition as a Theatin."

"Faith, sir," said Friar Giroflée, "I wish with all my soul the Theatins were every one of them at the bottom of the sea. I have been tempted a thousand times to set fire to the convent and go and turn Turk. My parents obliged me at the age of fifteen to put on this detestable habit, only to increase the fortune of an elder brother of mine, whom God confound! Jealousy, discord, and fury reside in our convent. It is true I have preached often paltry sermons by which I have got a little money, part of which the prior robs me of, and the remainder helps to buy my joys; but at night when I go hence to my convent, I am ready to dash my brains against the walls of the dormitory; and this is the case with all the rest of our fraternity."

Martin, turning towards Candide with his usual indifference, said, "Well, what think you now? Have I won the wager entirely?" Candide gave two thousand piastres to Pacquette and a thousand to Friar Giroflée, saying, "I will answer that this will make them happy." "I am not of your opinion," said Martin; "perhaps this money will only make them wretched." "Be that as it may," said Candide, "one thing comforts me; I see that one often meets with those whom we expected never to see again; so that perhaps, as I have found my red sheep and Pacquette, I may be lucky enough to find Miss Cunegund also." "I wish," said Martin, "she one day may make you happy;

but I doubt it much." " You are very hard of belief," said Candide. " It is because," said Martin, " I have seen the world."

" Observe those gondoliers," said Candide ; " are they not perpetually singing ? " " You do not see them," answered Martin, " at home with their wives and brats. The dog has his chagrin, gondoliers theirs. Nevertheless, in the main I look upon the gondolier's life as preferable to that of the dog ; but the difference is so trifling that it is not worth the trouble of examining into."

I have heard great talk," said Candide, " of the Senator Pococuranté, who lives in that fine house at the Brenta, where they say he entertains foreigners in the most polite manner. They pretend this man is a perfect stranger to uneasiness." " I should be glad to see so extraordinary a being," said Martin. Candide thereupon sent a messenger to Signor Pococuranté, desiring permission to wait on him the next day.

CHAPTER XXV.

*Candide and Martin pay a visit to Signor Pococuranté,
a noble Venetian.*

CANDIDE and his friend Martin went into a gondola on the Brenta, and arrived at the palace of the noble Pococuranté : the gardens were laid out in elegant taste, and adorned with fine marble statues ; his palace was built after the most approved rules of architecture. The master of the house, who was a man of sixty, and very rich, received our two travellers with great politeness, but without much ceremony, which somewhat disconcerted Candide, but was not at all displeasing to Martin.

As soon as they were seated, two very pretty girls, neatly dressed, brought in chocolate, which was extremely well frothed. Candide could not help making encomiums upon their beauty and graceful carriage. " The creatures are well enough," said the senator. " I make them my companions, for I am heartily tired of the ladies of the town, their coquetry, their jealousy, their quarrels, their humours, their meannesses, their pride, and their folly. I am weary of making sonnets, or of paying for sonnets to be made on them; but after all, these two girls begin to grow very indifferent to me."

After having refreshed himself, Candide walked into a large gallery, where he was struck with the sight of a fine collection of paintings. " Pray," said Candide, " by what master are the two first of these ? " " They are Raphael's," answered the senator. " I gave a great deal of money for them seven years ago, purely out of curiosity, as they were said to be the finest pieces in Italy ; but I cannot say they please me : the colouring is dark and heavy ; the figures do not swell nor come out enough ; and the drapery is very bad. In short, notwithstanding the encomiums lavished upon them, they are not, in my opinion, a true representation of nature. I approve of no paintings but where I think I behold Nature herself ; and there are very few, if any, of that kind to be met with. I have what is called a fine collection, but I take no manner of delight in them."

While dinner was getting ready Pococuranté ordered a concert. Candide praised the music to the skies. " This noise," said the noble Venetian, " may amuse one for a little time, but if it was to last above half-an-hour, it would grow tiresome to everybody, though perhaps no one would care to own it. Music is become the art of executing what is difficult ; now, whatever is difficult cannot be long pleasing.

" I believe I might take more pleasure in an opera, if they had not made such a monster of that species of dramatic entertainment as perfectly shocks me ; and I am amazed how people can bear to see wretched tragedies set to music ; where the scenes are contrived for no other purpose than to lug in, as it were by the ears, three or four ridiculous songs, to give a favourite actress an opportunity of exhibiting her pipe. Let who will or can die away in raptures at the trills of a eunuch quavering the majestic part of Cæsar or Cato, and strutting in a foolish manner upon the stage. For my part, I have long ago renounced these paltry entertainments, which constitute the glory of modern Italy, and are so dearly purchased by crowned heads." Candide opposed these sentiments ; but he did it in a discreet manner. As for Martin, he was entirely of the old senator's opinion.

Dinner being served up, they sat down to table, and after a very hearty repast, returned to the library. Candide observing Homer richly bound, commended the noble Venetian's taste. " This," said he, " is a book that was once the delight of the great Pangloss, the best philosopher in Germany." " Homer is no favourite of mine," answered Pococuranté very coolly. " I was made to believe once that I took a pleasure in reading him ; but his continual repetitions of battles must have all such a resemblance with each other ; his gods that are for ever in a hurry and bustle, without ever doing anything ; his Helen, that is the cause of the war, and yet hardly acts in the whole performance ; his Troy, that holds out so long without being taken ; in short, all these things together make the poem very insipid to me. I have asked some learned men whether they are not in reality as much tired as myself with reading this poet. Those who spoke ingenuously assured me that he had made them fall asleep, and yet that they could not well avoid giving him a place in their libraries ; but that it was merely as they would do an antique, or those rusty medals which are kept only for curiosity, and are of no manner of use in commerce."

" But your excellency does not surely form the same opinion of Virgil ? " said Candide. " Why, I grant," replied Pococuranté, " that the second, third, fourth, and sixth books of his Æneid are excellent ; but as for his pious Æneas, his strong Cloanthus, his friendly Achates, his boy Ascanius, his silly king Latinus, his ill-bred Amata, his insipid Lavinia, and some other characters much in the same strain, I think there cannot in nature be anything more flat and disagreeable. I must confess I prefer Tasso far beyond him; nay, even that sleepy tale-teller Ariosto."

" May I take the liberty to ask if you do not receive great pleasure from reading Horace ? " said Candide. " There are maxims in this writer," replied Pococuranté, " from whence a man of the world may reap some benefit ; and the short measure of the verse makes them more easily to be retained in the memory. But I see nothing extraordinary in his journey to Brundusium, and his account of his bad dinner ; nor in his dirty low quarrel between one Rupilius, whose words, as he expresses it, were full of poisonous filth ; and another, whose language was dipped in vinegar. His indelicate verses against old women and witches have frequently given me great offence ; nor can I discover the great merit of his telling his friend Mæcenas that, if he will but rank him in the class of lyric poets, his lofty head shall touch the stars. Ignorant readers are apt to advance everything by the lump in a writer of reputation. For my part, I read only to please myself. I like nothing but what makes for my purpose." Candide, who had been brought up with a notion of never making use of his own judgment, was astonished at what he heard ; but Martin found there was a good deal of reason in the senator's remarks.

" Oh, here is a Tully ! " said Candide ; " this great man, I fancy, you are never tired of reading." " Indeed, I never read him at all," replied Pococuranté. " What a deuce is it to me whether he pleads for Rabirius or Cluentius ? I try causes enough myself. I had once some liking to his philosophical works ; but when I found he doubted of everything, I thought I knew as much as himself, and had no need of a guide to learn ignorance."

"Ha!" cried Martin, "here are fourscore volumes of the Memoirs of the Academy of Sciences; perhaps there may be something curious and valuable in this collection." "Yes," answered Pococuranté; "so there might, if any one of these compilers of this rubbish had only invented the art of pin-making. But all these volumes are filled with mere chimerical systems, without one single article conducive to real utility."

"I see a prodigious number of plays," said Candide, "in Italian, Spanish, and French." "Yes," replied the Venetian; "there are I think three thousand, and not three dozen of them good for anything. As to those huge volumes of divinity, and those enormous collections of sermons, they are not altogether worth one single page of Seneca; and I fancy you will readily believe that neither myself nor any one else ever looks into them."

Martin, perceiving some shelves filled with English books, said to the senator: "I fancy that a republican must be highly delighted with those books, which are most of them written with a noble spirit of freedom." "It is noble to write as we think," said Pococuranté; "it is the privilege of humanity. Throughout Italy we write only what we do not think; and the present inhabitants of the country of the Cæsars and Antoninuses dare not acquire a single idea without the permission of a Father Dominican. I should be enamoured of the spirit of the English nation did it not utterly frustrate the good effects it would produce by passion and the spirit of party."

Candide, seeing a Milton, asked the senator if he did not think that author a great man. "Who?" said Pococuranté sharply. "That barbarian, who writes a tedious commentary, in ten books of rambling verse, on the first chapter of Genesis! That slovenly imitator of the Greeks, who disfigures the creation by making the Messiah take a pair of compasses from Heaven's armoury to plan the world; whereas Moses represented the Deity as producing the whole universe by his fiat! Can I think you have any esteem for a writer who has spoiled Tasso's hell and the devil; who transforms Lucifer, sometimes into a toad, and at others into a pigmy; who makes him say the same thing over again a hundred times; who metamorphoses him into a school-divine; and who, by an absurdly serious imitation of Ariosto's comic invention of fire-arms, represents the devils and angels cannonading each other in heaven! Neither I, nor any other Italian, can possibly take pleasure in such melancholy reveries. But the marriage of Sin and Death, and snakes issuing from the womb of the former, are enough to make any person sick that is not lost to all sense of delicacy. This obscene, whimsical, and disagreeable poem met with the neglect that it deserved at its first publication; and I only treat the author now as he was treated in his own country by his contemporaries."

Candide was sensibly grieved at this speech, as he had a great respect for Homer and was very fond of Milton. "Alas!" said he softly to Martin, "I am afraid this man holds our German poets in great contempt." "There would be no such great harm in that," said Martin. "Oh, what a surprising man!" said Candide to himself; "what a prodigious genius is this Pococuranté! Nothing can please him."

After finishing their survey of the library they went down into the garden, when Candide commended the several beauties that offered themselves to his view. "I know nothing upon earth laid out in such bad taste," said Pococuranté, "everything about it is childish and trifling; but I shall have another laid out to-morrow upon a nobler plan."

As soon as our two travellers had taken leave of his excellency, "Well," said Candide to Martin, "I hope you will own that this man is the happiest of all mortals, for he is above everything he possesses." "But do not you see," answered Martin, "that he likewise dislikes everything he possesses? It was an observation of Plato long since, that those are not the best stomachs that reject, without distinction, all sorts of aliments." "True," said Candide, "but still there must certainly be a pleasure in criticising everything, and in perceiving faults where others think they see beauties." "That is," replied Martin, "there is a pleasure in having no pleasure." "Well, well," said Candide, "I find that I shall be the only happy man at last, when I am blessed with the sight of my dear Cunegund." "It is good to hope," said Martin.

In the meanwhile, days and weeks passed away, and no news of Cacambo. Candide was so overwhelmed with grief that he did not reflect on the behaviour of Pacquette and Friar Giroflée, who never staid to return him thanks for the presents he had so generously made them.

CHAPTER XXVI.

Candide and Martin sup with six Sharpers ; and who they were.

ONE evening that Candide, with his attendant Martin, were going to sit down to supper with some foreigners who lodged at the same inn where they had taken up their quarters, a man, with a face the colour of soot, came behind him, and taking him by the arm, said, "Hold yourself in readiness to go along with us ; be sure you do not fail." Upon this, turning about to see from whom the above came, he beheld Cacambo. Nothing but the sight of Miss Cunegund could have given greater joy and surprise. He was almost beside himself. After embracing this dear friend, "Cunegund !" said he, "Cunegund has come with you, doubtless ! Where, where is she ? Carry me to her this instant, that I may die with joy in her presence."

"Cunegund is not here," answered Cacambo, "she is at Constantinople." "Good heavens, at Constantinople! But no matter if she were in China, I would fly thither. Quick, quick, dear Cacambo, let us be gone." "Soft and fair," said Cacambo, "stay till you have supped. I cannot at present stay to say anything more to you. I am a slave, and my master waits for me : I must go and attend him at table. But mum! say not a word ; only get your supper, and hold yourself in readiness."

Candide, divided between joy and grief, charmed to have thus met with his faithful agent again, and surprised to hear he was a slave, his heart palpitating, his senses confused, but full of the hopes of recovering his dear Cunegund, sat down to table with Martin, who beheld all these scenes with great unconcern, and with six strangers, who were come to spend the Carnival at Venice.

Cacambo waited at table upon one of those strangers. When supper was nearly over he drew near to his master, and whispered him in the ear, "Sire, your majesty may go when you please ; the ship is ready ;" and so saying he left the room. The guests, surprised at what they had heard, looked at each other without speaking a word, when another servant drawing near to his master, in like manner said, "Sire, your majesty's post-chaise is at Padua, and the bark is ready." The master made him a sign, and he instantly withdrew. The company all stared at each other again, and the general astonishment was increased. A third servant then approached another of the strangers, and said, "Sire, if your majesty will be advised by me, you will not make any longer stay in this place ; I will go and get everything ready," and instantly disappeared.

Candide and Martin then took it for granted that this was some of the diversions of the Carnival, and that these were characters in masquerade. Then a fourth domestic said to the fourth stranger, "Your majesty may set off when

you please ;" saying this, he went away like the rest. A
fifth valet said the same to a fifth master. But the sixth
domestic spoke in a different style to the person on whom
he waited, and who sat near to Candide. "Troth, sir,"
said he, " they will trust your majesty no longer, nor myself
neither, and we may both of us chance to be sent to gaol this
very night ; and therefore I shall e'en take care of myself,
and so adieu." The servants being all gone, the six
strangers, with Candide and Martin, remained in a profound
silence. At length Candide broke it by saying, " Gentlemen, this is a very singular joke, upon my word ; why, how
came you all to be kings? For my part I own frankly that
neither my friend Martin here nor myself have any claim
to royalty.

Cacambo's master then began, with great gravity, to deliver himself thus in Italian : " I am not joking in the least.
My name is Achmet III. I was grand seignor for many
years ; I dethroned my brother, my nephew dethroned me,
my viziers lost their heads, and I am condemned to
end my days in the old seraglio. My nephew, the Grand
Sultan Mahomet, gives me permission to travel sometimes
for my health, and I am come to spend the Carnival at
Venice."

A young man who sat by Achmet spoke next, and said :
" My name is Ivan. I was once Emperor of all the Russias,
but was dethroned in my cradle. My parents were confined, and I was brought up in a prison ; yet I am sometimes allowed to travel, though always with persons to keep
a guard over me, and I am come to spend the Carnival at
Venice."

The third said: "I am Charles-Edward, King of England ;
my father has renounced his right to the throne in my favour.
I have fought in defence of my rights, and near a thousand
of my friends have had their hearts taken out of their
bodies alive, and thrown into their faces. I have myself

been confined in a prison. I am going to Rome to visit
the king my father, who was dethroned as well as myself;
and my grandfather and I are come to spend the Carnival
at Venice."

The fourth spoke thus : " I am the King of Poland ; the
fortune of war has stripped me of my hereditary dominions.
My father experienced the same vicissitudes of fate.   I
resign myself to the will of Providence, in the same manner
as Sultan Achmet, the Emperor Ivan, and King Charles
Edward, whom God long preserve ; and I am come to spend
the Carnival at Venice."

The fifth said : " I am King of Poland also.   I have twice
lost my kingdom ; but Providence has given me other
dominions, where I have done more good than all the
Sarmatian kings put together were ever able to do on the
banks of the Vistula.   I resign myself likewise to Providence ;
and am come to spend the Carnival at Venice."

It now came to the sixth monarch's turn to speak.
"Gentlemen," said he, " I am not so great a prince as the rest
of you, it is true, but I am, however, a crowned head.   I am
Theodore, elected king of Corsica.   I have had the title of
majesty, and am now hardly treated with common civility.
I have coined money, and am not now worth a single ducat.
I have had two secretaries, and am now without a valet.   I
was once seated on a throne, and since that have lain upon
a truss of straw in a common gaol in London, and I very
much fear I shall meet with the same fate here in Venice,
where I come, like your majesties, to divert myself at the
Carnival."

The other five kings listened to this speech with great
attention ; it excited their compassion ; each of them made
the unhappy Theodore a present of twenty sequins, and
Candide gave him a diamond worth just an hundred
times that sum.   " Who can this private person be ? " said
the five princes to one another, " who is able to give,

and has actually given, an hundred times as much as any of us ? "

Just as they rose from table, in came four serene highnesses, who had also been stripped of their territories by the fortune of war, and were come to spend the remainder of the Carnival at Venice. Candide took no manner of notice of them ; for his thoughts were wholly employed on his voyage to Constantinople, whither he intended to go in search of his lovely Miss Cunegund.

CHAPTER XXVII.

Candide's Voyage to Constantinople.

THE trusty Cacambo had already engaged the captain of the Turkish ship, that was to carry Sultan Achmet back to Constantinople, to take Candide and Martin on board. Accordingly they both embarked, after paying their obeisance to his miserable highness. As they were going on board Candide said to Martin : "You see we supped in company with six dethroned kings, and to one of them I gave charity. Perhaps there may be a great many other princes still more unfortunate. For my part, I have lost only a hundred sheep, and am now going to fly to the arms of my charming Miss Cunegund. My dear Martin, I must insist on it that Pangloss was in the right. All is for the best." " I wish it may be so," said Martin. " But this was an odd adventure we met with at Venice. I do not think there ever was an instance before of six dethroned monarchs supping together at a public inn." "This is not more extraordinary," said Martin, "than most of what has happened to us. It is a very common thing for kings to be dethroned ; and as for our having the honour to sup with six of them, it is a mere accident not deserving our attention."

As soon as Candide set his foot on board the vessel he

flew to his old friend and valet, Cacambo; and throwing his arms about his neck, embraced him with transports of joy. "Well," said he, "what news of Miss Cunegund? Does she still continue the paragon of beauty? Does she love me still? How does she do? You have doubtless purchased a superb palace for her at Constantinople?"

"My dear master," replied Cacambo, "Miss Cunegund washes dishes on the banks of the Propontis, in the house of a prince who has very few to wash. She is at present a slave in the family of an ancient sovereign named Ragotsky, whom the Grand Turk allows three crowns a day to maintain him in his exile; but the most melancholy circumstance of all is, that she is turned horribly ugly." "Ugly or handsome," said Candide, "I am a man of honour; and, as such, am obliged to love her still. But how could she possibly have been reduced to so abject a condition when I sent five or six millions to her by you?" "Lord bless me," said Cacambo, "was not I obliged to give two millions to Seignor Don Fernando d'Ibaraa y Fagueora y Mascarenes y Lampourdos y Souza, the Governor of Buenos Ayres, for liberty to take Miss Cunegund away with me? And then did not a brave fellow of a pirate very gallantly strip us of all the rest? And then did not this same pirate carry us with him to Cape Matapan, to Milo, to Nicaria, to Samos, to Petra, to the Dardanelles, to Marmora, to Scutari? Miss Cunegund and the old woman are now servants to the prince I have told you of, and I myself am slave to the dethroned Sultan." "What a chain of shocking accidents!" exclaimed Candide. "But after all, I have still some diamonds left, with which I can easily procure Miss Cunegund's liberty. It is a pity, though, she is grown so very ugly."

Then turning to Martin, "What think you, friend?" said he; "whose condition is most to be pitied, the Emperor Achmet's, the Emperor Ivan's, King Charles Edward's, or mine?" "Faith, I cannot resolve your question," said

Martin, " unless I had been in the breasts of you all."
" Ah !" cried Candide, " were Pangloss here now, he would
have known, and satisfied me at once." "I know not," said
Martin, " in what balance your Pangloss could have weighed
the misfortunes of mankind, and have set a just estimation
on their sufferings. All that I pretend to know of the
matter is, that there are millions of men on the earth, whose
conditions are an hundred times more pitiable than those of
King Charles Edward, the Emperor Ivan, or Sultan Achmet."
" Why, that may be," answered Candide.

In a few days they reached the Bosphorus, and the first
thing Candide did was to pay a very high ransom for
Cacambo ; then, without losing time, he and his companions
went on board a galley in order to search for his Cunegund
on the banks of the Propontis, notwithstanding she was
grown so ugly.

There were two slaves among the crew of the galley, who
rowed very ill, and to whose bare backs the master of the
vessel frequently applied a bull's pizzle. Candide, from
natural sympathy, looked at these two slaves more attentively than at any of the rest, and drew near them with an
eye of pity. Their features, though greatly disfigured,
appeared to him to bear a strong resemblance with those of
Pangloss and the unhappy Baron Jesuit, Miss Cunegund's
brother. This idea affected him with grief and compassion.
He examined them more attentively than before. "In troth,"
said he, turning to Martin, "if I had not seen my Master
Pangloss fairly hanged, and had not myself been unluckly
enough to run the Baron through the body, I should absolutely think those two rowers were the men."

No sooner had Candide uttered the names of the Baron
and Pangloss than the two slaves gave a great cry, ceased
rowing, and let fall their oars out of their hands. The
master of the vessel seeing this, ran up to them, and redoubled the discipline of the bull's pizzle. " Hold, hold,"

cried Candide, " I will give you what money you shall ask
for these two persons." "Good heavens! it is Candide,"
said one of the men. "Candide!" cried the other. " Do
I dream?" said Candide, " or am I awake? Am I actually
on board this galley? Is this my Lord Baron, whom I killed?
and that my Master Pangloss, whom I saw hanged before
my face?"

" It is I! it is I!" cried they both together. " What, is
this your great philosopher?" said Martin. "My dear sir,"
said Candide to the master of the galley, " how much do
you ask for the ransom of the Baron of Thunder-ten-
tronckh, who is one of the first barons of the empire, and
of Mr. Pangloss, the most profound metaphysician in
Germany?" "Why then, Christian cur," replied the Turkish
captain, " since these two dogs of Christian slaves are barons
and metaphysicians, who no doubt are of high rank in their
own country, thou shalt give me fifty thousand sequins."

"You shall have them, sir; carry me back as quick as
thought to Constantinople, and you shall receive the money
immediately. No! carry me me first to Miss. Cunegund."
The captain, upon Candide's first proposal, had already
tacked about, and he made the crew ply their oars so effectually that the vessel flew through the water quicker than
a bird cleaves the air.

Candide bestowed a thousand embraces on the Baron and
Pangloss. " And so then, my dear Baron, I did not kill you?
And you, my dear Pangloss, are come to life again after
your hanging? But how came you slaves on board a
Turkish galley?" " And is it true that my dear sister is
in this country?" said the Baron. " Yes," said Cacambo.
"And do I once again behold my dear Candide?" said
Pangloss. Candide presented Martin and Cacambo to
them. They embraced each other, and all spoke together.
The galley flew like lightning, and now they were got back to
port. Candide instantly sent for a Jew, to whom he sold for

fifty thousand sequins a diamond richly worth one hundred thousand, though the fellow swore to him all the time by Father Abraham that he gave him the most he could possibly afford. He no sooner got the money into his hands than he paid it down for the ransom of the Baron and Pangloss. The latter flung himself at the feet of his deliverer, and bathed him with his tears. The former thanked him with a gracious nod, and promised to return him the money the first opportunity. "But is it possible," said he, "that my sister should be in Turkey?" "Nothing is more possible," answered Cacambo, "for she scours the dishes in the house of a Transylvanian prince." Candide sent directly for two Jews, and sold more diamonds to them. And then he set out with his companions in another galley, to deliver Miss Cunegund from slavery.

CHAPTER XXVIII.

What befell Candide, Cunegund, Pangloss, Martin, etc.

"PARDON," said Candide to the Baron; "once more let me entreat your pardon, reverend father, for running you through the body." "Say no more about it," replied the Baron; "I was a little too hasty, I must own. But as you seem to be desirous to know by what accident I came to be a slave on board the galley where you saw me, I will inform you. After I had been cured of the wound you gave me by the college apothecary, I was attacked and carried off by a party of Spanish troops, who clapped me up in prison in Buenos Ayres, at the very time my sister was setting out from thence. I asked leave to return to Rome, to the general of my order, who appointed me chaplain to the French ambassador at Constantinople. I had not been a week in my new office when I happened to meet one evening with a young Icoglan, extremely handsome and well made. The weather was very hot; the young man had an inclination to bathe. I took the opportunity to bathe likewise. I did not know it was a crime for a Christian to be found naked in company with a young Turk. A cadi ordered me to receive a hundred blows on the soles of my feet, and sent me to the galleys. I do not believe there was ever an act of more flagrant injustice. But I would fain know how my sister came to be a scullion to a Transylvanian prince who had taken refuge among the Turks."

"But **how** happens it that I behold you again, my dear Pangloss?" said Candide. "It is true," answered Pangloss, "you saw me hanged, though I ought properly to have been burnt; but you may remember it that rained extremely hard when they were going to roast me. The storm was so violent that they found it impossible to light the fire, so they e'en hanged me because they could do no better. A surgeon purchased my body, carried it home, and prepared to dissect me. He began by making a crucial incision from my navel to the clavicle. It is impossible for any one to have been more lamely hanged than I had been. The executioner of the holy Inquisition was a sub-deacon, and knew how to burn people very well; but as for hanging, he was a novice at it, being quite out of the way of his practice; the cord being wet and not slipping properly, the noose did not join. In short, I still continued to breathe; the crucial incision made me scream to such a degree that my surgeon fell flat upon his back; and imagining it was the devil he was dissecting, ran away, and in his fright tumbled downstairs. His wife hearing the noise, flew from the next room, and seeing me stretched upon the table with my crucial incis'on, was still more terrified than her husband, and fell upon him. When they had a little recovered themselves, I heard her say to her husband, 'My dear, how could you think of dissecting an heretic? Don't you know that the devil is always in them? I'll run directly to a priest to come and drive the evil spirit out.' I trembled from head to foot at hearing her talk in this manner, and exerted what little strength I had left to cry out, 'Have mercy on me!' At length the Portuguese barber took courage, sewed up my wound, and his wife nursed me: and I was upon my legs in a fortnight's time. The barber got me a place to be lackey to a Knight of Malta, who was going to Venice; but finding my master had no money to pay me my wages, I entered into the service of a Venetian merchant, and went with him to Constantinople.

"One day I happened to enter a mosque, where I saw no one but an old imam and a very pretty young female devotee, who was telling her beads; her neck was quite bare, and in her bosom she had a beautiful nosegay of tulips, roses, anemones, ranunculuses, hyacinths, and auriculas; she let fall her nosegay. I ran immediately to take it up, and presented it to her with the most respectful bow. I was so long in delivering it that the imam began to be angry, and perceiving I was a Christian, he cried out for help; they carried me before the Cadi, who ordered me to receive one hundred bastinadoes and sent me to the galleys. I was chained in the very galley and to the very same bench with the Baron. On board this galley there were four young men belonging to Marseilles, five Neapolitan priests, and two monks of Corfu, who told us that the like adventures happened every day. The Baron pretended that he had been worse used than myself; and insisted that there was far less harm in taking up a nosegay and putting it into a woman's bosom, than to be found stark naked with a young Icoglan. We were continually whipped, and received twenty lashes a day with a bull's pizzle, when the concatenation of sublunary events brought you on board our galley to ransom us from slavery."

"Well, my dear Pangloss," said Candide to them, "when you were hanged, dissected, whipped, and tugging at the oar, did you continue to think that everything in this world happens for the best?" "I have always abided by my first opinion," answered Pangloss; "for, after all, I am a philosopher, and it would not become me to retract my sentiments, especially as Leibnitz could not be in the wrong, and that pre-established harmony is the finest thing in the world, as well as a *plenum* and the *materia subtilis.*"

CHAPTER XXIX.

In what manner Candide found Miss Cunegund and the Old Woman again.

WHILE Candide, the Baron, Pangloss, Martin, and Cacambo were relating their several adventures, and reasoning on the contingent or non-contingent events of this world, on causes and effects, on moral and physical evil, on free-will and necessity, and on the consolation that may be felt by a person when a slave and chained to an oar in a Turkish galley, they arrived at the house of the Transylvanian prince on the coasts of the Propontis. The first objects they beheld there was Miss Cunegund and the old woman, who were hanging some table-cloths on a line to dry.

The Baron turned pale at the sight. Even the tender Candide, that affectionate lover, upon seeing his fair Cunegund all sun-burnt, with blear-eyes, a withered neck, wrinkled face and arms, all covered with a red scurf, started back with horror; but recovering himself, he advanced towards her out of good manners. She embraced Candide and her brother; they embraced the old woman, and Candide ransomed them both.

There was a small farm in the neighbourhood which the old woman proposed to Candide to make a shift with till the company should meet with a more favourable destiny. Cunegund, not knowing that she was grown ugly, as no one had informed her of it, reminded Candide of his promise in so peremptory a manner that the simple lad did not dare to refuse her. He then acquainted the Baron that he was going to marry his sister. "I will never suffer," said the Baron, "my sister to be guilty of an action so derogatory to her birth and family; nor will I bear this insolence on your part; no, I never will be reproached that my nephews are not qualified for the first ecclesiastical dignities in Germany; nor shall a sister of mine ever be the wife of any person below the rank of a baron of the empire." Cunegund flung herself at her brother's feet, and bedewed them with her tears, but he still continued inflexible. "Thou foolish fellow," said Candide, "have I not delivered thee from the galleys, paid thy ransom and thy sister's too, who was a scullion and is very ugly, and yet condescend to marry her; and shalt thou pretend to oppose the match? If I were to listen only to the dictates of my anger, I should kill thee again." "Thou mayest kill me again," said the Baron, "but thou shalt not marry my sister while I am living."

CHAPTER XXX.

Conclusion.

CANDIDE had in truth no great inclination to marry Miss Cunegund; but the extreme impertinence of the Baron determined him to conclude the match; and Cunegund pressed him so warmly that he could not recant. He consulted Pangloss, Martin, and the faithful Cacambo. Pangloss composed a fine memorial, by which he proved that the Baron had no right over his sister; and that she might, according to all the laws of the empire, marry Candide with the left hand. Martin concluded to throw the Baron into the sea; Cacambo decided that he must be delivered to the Turkish captain and sent to the galleys, after which he should be conveyed

by the first ship to the Father-General at Rome.   This
advice was found to be very good : the old woman approved
of it, and not a syllable was said to his sister.   The business
was executed for a little money ; and they had the pleasure
of tricking a Jesuit and punishing the pride of a German
baron.

It was altogether natural to imagine that after undergoing
so many disasters, Candide married to his mistress, and
living with the philosopher Pangloss, the philosopher
Martin, the prudent Cacambo, and the old woman, having
besides brought home so many diamonds from the country
of the ancient Incas, would lead the most agreeable life in
the world.   But he had been so much choused by the Jews
that he had nothing else left but his little farm ; his wife,
every day growing more and more ugly, became headstrong
and insupportable ; the old woman was infirm, and more
ill-natured yet than Cunegund.   Cacambo, who worked in
the garden, and carried the produce of it to sell at Constantinople, was past his labour, and cursed his fate.
Pangloss despaired of making a figure in any of the German
universities.   And as to Martin, he was firmly persuaded
that a person is equally ill-situated everywhere ; he took
things with patience.   Candide, Martin, and Pangloss disputed sometimes about metaphysics and morality.   Boats
were often seen passing under the windows of the farm
fraught with effendis, bashaws, and cadis, that were going
nto banishment to Lemnos, Mytilene, and Erzeroum ; and
other cadis, bashaws, and effendis were seen coming back
to succeed the place of the exiles, and were driven out in
their turns.   They saw several heads very curiously stuck
upon poles, and carry ingas presents to the Sublime Porte.
Such sights gave occasion to frequent dissertations ; and
when no disputes were carried on, the irksomeness was so
excessive, that the old woman ventured one day to tell them,
" I would be glad to know which is worst : to be ravished a

hundred times by negro pirates, to have one buttock cut off, to run the gauntlet among the Bulgarians, to be whipped and hanged at an *auto-da-fé*, to be dissected, to be chained to an oar in a galley ; and, in short, to experience all the miseries through which every one of us has passed, or to remain here doing nothing ? " " This," said Candide, " is a grand question."

This discourse gave birth to new reflexions, and Martin especially concluded that man was born to live in the convulsions of disquiet, or in the lethargy of idleness. Though Candide did not absolutely agree to this, yet he did not determine anything on the head. Pangloss avowed that he had undergone dreadful sufferings ; but having once maintained that everything went on as well as possible, he still maintained it, and at the same time believed nothing of it.

There was one thing which more than ever confirmed Martin in his detestable principles, made Candide hesitate, and embarrassed Pangloss, which was the arrival of Pacquette and Brother Giroflée one day at their farm. This couple had been in the utmost distress ; they had very speedily made away with their three thousand piastres ; they had parted, been reconciled ; quarrelled again, been thrown into prison ; had made their escape, and at last Brother Giroflée turned Turk. Pacquette still continued to follow her trade wherever she came ; but she got little or nothing by it. " I foresaw very well," says Martin to Candide, that your presents would soon be squandered, and only make them more miserable. You and Cacambo have spent millions of piastres, and yet you are not more happy than Brother Giroflée and Pacquette." "Ah !" says Pangloss to Pacquette, " It is heaven who has brought you here among us, my poor child ! Do you know that you have cost me the tip of my nose, one eye and one ear ? What a handsome shape is here ! and what is this world ? " This new adventure en-

gaged them more deeply than ever in philosophical
disputations.

In the neighbourhood lived a very famous dervish who
passed for the best philosopher in Turkey; him they went
to consult. Pangloss, who was their spokesman, addressed
him thus : "Master, we come to entreat you to tell us why
so strange an animal as man has been formed."

"Why do you trouble your head about it?" said the
dervish; "is it any business of yours?" "But my reverend
father," says Candide, "there is a horrible deal of evil on the
earth. "What signifies it," says the dervish, "whether there
is evil or good? When his highness sends a ship to Egypt,
does he trouble his head whether the rats in the vessel are
at their ease or not?" "What must then be done?" says
Pangloss. "Be silent," answers the dervish. "I flattered
myself," replied Pangloss, "to have reasoned a little with you
on the causes and effects, on the best of possible worlds, the
origin of evil, the nature of the soul, and a pre-established
harmony." At these words the dervish shut the door in
their faces.

During this conversation news was spread abroad that
two viziers of the bench and the mufti had been just strangled
at Constantinople, and several of their friends impaled.
This catastrophe made a great noise for some hours. Pangloss, Candide, and Martin, as they were returning to the
little farm, met with a good-looking old man, who was taking
the air at his door under an alcove formed of the boughs of
orange-trees. Pangloss, who was as inquisitive as he was
disputative, asked him what was the name of the mufti who
was lately strangled. "I cannot tell," answered the good
old man; "I never knew the name of any mufti or vizier
breathing. I am entirely ignorant of the event you speak
of; I presume, that in general such as are concerned in
public affairs sometimes come to a miserable end, and that
they deserve it; but I never inquire what is doing at Con-

stantinople. I am contented with sending thither the produce of my garden, which I cultivate with my own hands."
After saying these words, he invited the strangers to come
into his house. His two daughters and two sons presented
them with diverse sorts of sherbet of their own making;
besides caymac heightened with the peels of candied
citrons, oranges, lemons, pine-apples, pistachio-nuts, and
Mocha coffee unadulterated with the bad coffee of Batavia
or the American islands. After which the two daughters of
this good Mussulman perfumed the beards of Candide, Pangloss, and Martin.

" You must certainly have a vast estate," said Candide to
the Turk, who replied, " I have no more than twenty acres
of ground, the whole of which I cultivate myself with the help
of my children, and our labour keeps off from us three great
evils—idleness, vice, and want.'"

Candide as he was returning home made profound
reflections on the Turk's discourse. "This good old man,"
said Martin, "appears to me to have chosen for himself
a lot much preferable to that of the six kings with whom
we had the honour to sup." " Human grandeur," said
Pangloss, "is very dangerous, if we believe the testimonies
of almost all philosophers; for we find Eglon, king of
Moab, was assassinated by Aod; Absalom was hung by the
hair of his head, and run through with three darts; King
Nadab, son of Jeroboam, was slain by Baaza; King Ela by
Zimri; Ahaziah by Jehu; Athalia by Jehoiada; the kings Jehoi-
akim, Jeconiah, and Zedekiah were led into captivity. I need
not tell you what was the fate of Crœsus, Astyages, Darius,
Dionysius of Syracuse, Pyrrhus, Perseus, Hannibal, Jugurtha,
Ariovistus, Cæsar, Pompey, Nero, Otho, Vitellius, Domitian,
Richard II. of England, Edward II., Henry VI., Richard
III., Mary Stuart, Charles I., the three Henrys of France,
and the Emperor Henry IV." " Neither need you tell me,"
said Candide, " that we must take care of our garden." " You

are in the right," said Pangloss; "for when man was put into the garden of Eden, it was with an intent to dress it; and this proves that man was not born to be idle." "Work, then, without disputing," said Martin. "It is the only way to render life supportable."

The little society, one and all, entered into this laudable design, and set themselves to exert their different talents. The little piece of ground yielded them a plentiful crop. Cunegund indeed was very ugly, but she became an excellent hand at pastry-work, Pacquette embroidered, the old woman had the care of the linen. There was none, down to Brother Giroflée, but did some service. He was a very good carpenter, and became an honest man. Pangloss used now and then to say to Candide : "There is a concatenation of all events in the best of possible worlds; for, in short, had you not been kicked out of a fine castle for the love of Miss Cunegund, had you not been put into the Inquisition, had you not travelled over America on foot, had you not run the Baron through the body, and had you not lost all your sheep which you brought from the good country of El Dorado, you would not have been here to eat preserved citrons and pistachio-nuts." "Excellently observed," answered Candide; "but let us take care of our garden."

PART II.

CHAPTER I.

How Candide quitted his Companions, and what happened to him.

WE soon become tired of everything in life : riches fatigue the possessor; ambition, when satisfied, leaves only remorse behind it ; the joys of love are but transient joys ; and Candide, made to experience all the vicissitudes of fortune, was soon disgusted with cultivating his garden. "Mr. Pangloss," said he, "if we are in the best of possible worlds, you will own, to me at least, that this is not enjoying that portion of possible happiness ; but living obscure in a little corner of the Propontis, having no other resource than that of my own manual labour, which may one day fail me ; no other pleasures than what Mrs. Cunegund gives me, who is very ugly, and, which is worse, is my wife ; no other company than yours, which is sometimes irksome to me ; or that of Martin, which makes me melancholy ; or that of Giroflée, who is but very lately become an honest man ; or that of Pacquette, the danger of whose correspondence you have so fully experienced ; or that of the hag who has but one hip, and is constantly repeating old wives' tales."

To this Pangloss made the following reply : "Philosophy teaches us that monads, divisible *in infinitum*, arrange themselves with wonderful sagacity in order to compose the different bodies which we observe in nature. The heavenly bodies are what they ought to be ; they are placed where they should be ; they describe the circles which they ought to do; man follows the bent he ought to follow; he is what he ought to be; he does what he ought to do. You bemoan yourself, O Candide !·because the monad of your soul is disgusted; but disgust is a modification of the soul; and this does not hinder that everything is for the best, both for you and others. When you beheld me covered with sores, I did not maintain my opinion the less for that; for if Miss Pacquette had not made me taste the pleasures of love and its poison, I should not have met with you in Holland; I should not have given the Anabaptist James an opportunity of performing a meritorious act; I should not have been hanged in Lisbon for the edification of my neighbour; I should not have been here to assist you with my advice, and make you live and die in Leibnitz's opinion. Yes, my dear Candide, everything is linked in a chain, everything is necessary in the best of possible worlds. There is a necessity that the burgher of Montauban should instruct kings; that the worm of Quimper-Corentin should carp, carp, carp; that the declaimer against philosophers should occasion his own crucifixion in St. Denis Street; that a rascally recollet and the Archdeacon of St. Malo should diffuse their gall and calumny through their Christian journals; that philosophy should be accused at the tribunal of Melpomene; and that philosophers should continue to enlighten human nature, notwithstanding the croakings of ridiculous animals that flounder in the marshes of learning; and should you be once more driven by a hearty kicking from the finest of all castles, to learn again your exercise among the Bulgarians; should you again suffer the dirty effects of a Dutchwoman's zeal; be half-drowned again before Lisbon; to be unmercifully whipped again by order of the most holy Inquisition; should you run the same risks again among Los Padres, the Oreillons, and the French; should you, in short, suffer every possible calamity, and never understand Leibnitz better than I myself do, you will still maintain that all is well; that all is for the best; that a *plenum*, the *materia subtilis*, a pre-established harmony, and monads, are the finest things in the world ; and that Leibnitz is a great man, even to those who do not comprehend him."

To this fine speech Candide, the mildest being in nature —though he had killed three men, two of whom were priests—answered not a word ; but, weary of the doctor and his society, next morning at break of day, taking a white staff in his hand, he marched off, without knowing whither he was going, but in quest of a place where one does not become disgusted, and where men are not men, as in the good country of El Dorado.

Candide, so much the less unhappy as he had no longer a love for Miss Cunegund, living upon the bounty of different people, who are not Christians but yet give alms, arrived, after a very long and very tiresome journey, at Tauris, upon the frontiers of Persia, a city noted for the cruelties which the Turks and Persians have by turns exercised therein.

Half-dead with fatigue, having hardly more clothes than what were necessary to cover that part which constitutes the man, and which men call shameful, Candide could not well relish Pangloss's opinion, when a Persian accosted him in the most polite manner, beseeching him to ennoble his house with his presence. " You make a jest of me," says Candide to him. " I am a poor devil who have left a miserable dwelling I had in Propontis, because I married Miss Cunegund, because she is grown very ugly, and because I was disgusted. I am not indeed made to ennoble any-body's house ; I am not noble myself, thank God. If I had the honour of being so, Baron Thunder-ten-tronckh should have paid very dearly for the kicks behind with which he favoured me, or I should have died of shame for it, which would have been pretty philosophical. Besides, I have been whipped very ignominiously by the executioners of the most holy Inquisition, and by two thousand heroes at

threepence-halfpenny a day. Give me what you please;
but do not insult my distress with taunts which would de-
prive you of the whole value of your beneficence."   "My
lord," replied the Persian, "you may be a beggar, and this
appears pretty plainly; but my religion obliges me to use
hospitality.   It is sufficient that you are a man, and under
misfortunes, that the apple of my eye should be the path for
your feet. Vouchsafe to ennoble my house with your radiant
presence."   "I will, since you desire it," answered Candide.
"Come then, enter," says the Persian.   They went in
accordingly, and Candide could not forbear admiring the
respectful treatment shown him by his host.   The slaves
prevented his desires; the whole house seemed to be
busied in nothing but contributing to his satisfaction.
"Should this last," said Candide to himself, "all does not
go so badly in this country."   Three days were past, during
which time the kind proceedings of the Persian were all of
a piece; and Candide already cried out, "Master Pangloss,
I always imagined you were in the right, for you are a great
philosopher."

CHAPTER II.

What befell Candide in this House; and how he got out of it.

CANDIDE, being well-fed, well-clothed, and free from chagrin,
soon became again as ruddy, as fresh, and as gay as he
had been in Westphalia.   His host, Ismael Raab, was
pleased to see this change.   He was a man six feet high,
adorned with two small eyes extremely red, and a large
nose full of pimples, which sufficiently declared his in-
fraction of Mahomet's law.   His whiskers were the
most famous in the country; and mothers wished their
sons nothing so much as a like pair.   Raab had
wives, because he was rich.   But he thought in a
manner that is but too common in the East and in

some of our colleges in Europe. "Your excellence is brighter than the stars," says one day the cunning Persian to the brisk Candide, half smiling and half suppressing his words; "you must have captivated a great many hearts; you are formed to give and receive happiness." "Alas!" answered our hero, "I was happy only by halves, behind a screen, where I was but so-so at my ease. Mademoiselle Cunegund was handsome then——" "Mademoiselle Cunegund! poor innocent thing. Follow me, my lord," says the Persian. And Candide followed accordingly. They came to a very agreeable retreat, where silence and pleasure reigned. There Ismael Raab tenderly embraced Candide, and in a few words made a declaration of love like that which the beautiful Alexis expresses with so much pleasure in Virgil's Eclogues. Candide could not recover from his astonishment. "No," cried he, "I can never suffer such infamy! What cause and what horrible effect! I had rather die." "So you shall," says Ismael, enraged; "how, thou Christian dog, because I would politely give you pleasure—resolve directly to satisfy me, or to suffer the most cruel death." Candide did not long hesitate. The cogent reason of the Persian made him tremble, for he feared death like a philosopher.

We accustom ourselves to everything in time. Candide, well-fed, well taken care of, but closely watched, was not absolutely disgusted with his condition. Good cheer, and the different diversions performed by Ismael's slaves gave some respite to his chagrin. He was unhappy only when he thought; and thus it is with the greatest part of mankind.

At that time one of the most staunch supporters of the monkish crew in Persia, the most learned of the Mahometan doctors, who understood Arabic perfectly, and even Greek, as spoken at this day in the country of Demosthenes and Sophocles, the Reverend Ed-Ivan-baal-Denk, returned from

Constantinople, where he had conversed with the Reverend Mamoud-Abram on a very delicate point of doctrine; namely, whether the prophet had plucked from the angel Gabriel's wing the pen which he used for the writing of the Alcoran; or if Gabriel had made him a present of it. They had disputed for three days and three nights with a warmth worthy of the noblest stages of controversy; and the doctor returned home persuaded, like all the disciples of Ali, that Mahomet had plucked the quill; while Mamoud-Abram remained convinced, like the rest of Omar's followers, that the prophet was incapable of committing any such rudeness, and that the angel had very politely made him a present of this quill for his pen.

It is said that there was at Constantinople a certain free-thinker who insinuated that it was necessary to examine first whether the Alcoran was really written with a pen taken from the wing of the angel Gabriel; but he was stoned.

Candide's arrival had made a noise in Tauris: many who had heard him speak of contingent and non-contingent effects, imagined he was a philosoper. The Reverend Ed-Ivan-Baal-Denk was told of him. He had the curiosity to come and see him; and Raab, who could hardly refuse a person of such consequence, sent for Candide to make his appearance. He seemed to be very well pleased with the manner in which Candide spoke of bad physics, bad morals; of agent and actuated. "I understand that you are a philosopher, and that's all. But it is enough, Candide," says the venerable recluse. "It is not right that so great a man as you are should be treated with such indignity, as I am told, in the world. Your are a stranger; Ismael Raab has no right over you. I propose to conduct you to Court; there you shall meet with a favourable reception; the Sophi loves the sciences. Ismael, you must put this young philosopher into my hands, or dread incurring the displeasure of the prince, and drawing upon yourself the vengeance of Heaven, but especially of the monks." These last words frightened the otherwise undaunted Persian, and he consented to everything. Candide, blessing Heaven and the monks, went the same day out of Tauris with the Mahometan doctor. They took the road to Ispahan, where they arrived loaded with the blessings and favours of the people.

CHAPTER III.

Candide's reception at Court, and what followed.

THE reverend Ed-Ivan-Baal-Denk made no delay in presenting Candide to the king. His majesty took a particular pleasure in hearing him. He made him dispute with several learned men of his Court, and those looked upon him as a fool, an ignoramus, and idiot, which very much contributed to persuade his majesty that he was a great man. " Because," said he to them, " you do not comprehend Candide's reasoning, you abuse him ; but I, who also comprehend nothing at all of them, assure you that he is a great philosopher, and I swear to it by my whisker." Upon these words the literati were struck dumb.

Candide had apartments assigned him in the palace. He had slaves to wait on him ; he was dressed in magnificent clothes, and the Sophi commanded that, whatever he should say, no one should dare to assert that he was wrong. His majesty did not stop here. The venerable monk was continually soliciting him in favour of his guest, and his majesty at length resolved to rank him among the number of his most intimate favourites.

" God be praised, and our holy prophet," says the imam, addressing himself to Candide ; " I am come to tell you a very agreeable piece of news : that you are happy, my dear Candide ; that you are going to raise the envy of the world ; you shall swim in opulence ; you may aspire to the most splendid posts in the empire. But do not forget me, my friend. Think that it is I who have procured you the favour you are just upon the point of enjoying : let gaiety reign over the horizon of your countenance. The king grants you a favour which has been sought by many, and you will soon exhibit a sight which the Court has not enjoyed these two years past." "And what are these favours," demanded Candide, "with which the prince intends to honour me?" "This very day," answered the monk, quite overjoyed, "this very day you are to receive fifty strokes with a bull's pizzle on the soles of your feet, in the presence of his majesty. The eunuchs named for perfuming you for the occasion are to be here directly ; prepare yourself to go cheerfully through this little trial, and thereby render yourself worthy of the King of Kings.' " Let the King of Kings," cried Candide in a rage, "keep his favours to himself, if I must receive fifty blows with a bull's pizzle in order to merit them." "It is thus," replied the doctor coldly, "that he deals with those on whom he means to pour down his benefits. I love you too much to regard the little pet which you show on the occasion, and I will make you happy in spite of yourself."

He had not done speaking when the eunuchs arrived, preceded by the executor of his majesty's private pleasures, who was one of the greatest and most robust lords of the Court. Candide in vain remonstrated against their proceedings. They perfumed his legs and feet according to custom. Four eunuchs carried him to the place appointed for the ceremony through the midst of a double file of soldiers, while the trumpets sounded, the cannon fired, and the bells of all the mosques of Ispahan jingled ; the Sophi was ready there, accompanied with his principal officers and most distinguished personages of his Court. In an instant they stretched out Candide upon a little form finely gilt, and the executor of the private pleasures put himself in a posture for entering upon his office. " Oh ! Master Pangloss, Master Pangloss ! were you but here," said Candide, weeping and roaring out with all his force : a circumstance which would have been thought very indecent if the monk had not given the people to understand that his guest had put himself into such violent agitations only the better to divert his majesty. This great king, it is true, laughed like a fool. He even took such delight in the affair, that after the fifty blows had been given, he ordered fifty more to be added. But his first minister having represented to him, with a firmness not very common, that such an unheard-of favour with regard to a stranger might alienate the hearts of his subjects, he revoked that order, and Candide was carried back to his apartments.

They put him to bed, after having bathed his feet with vinegar. The grandees came round him in order to congratulate him on his good fortune. The Sophi then came to assist him in person, and not only gave him his hand to kiss, according to the custom, but likewise honoured him with a great blow of his fist on his mouth. From whence the politicians conjectured that Candide would arrive at extraordinary preferment, and, what is very uncommon, though politicians, they were not deceived.

CHAPTER IV.

Fresh Favours conferred on Candide ; his great Advancement.

As soon as our hero was cured, he was introduced to the king, to return him his thanks. The monarch received him very graciously. He gave him two or three hearty boxes on the ear during their conversation, and conducted him back as far as the guard-room with several sound kicks on the posteriors, at which the courtiers were ready to burst for envy. Since his majesty had been in a drubbing humour, no person had ever received such signal marks of his majesty's favour in this way as Candide.

E

Three days after this interview, our philosopher, who was enraged at the favours he had received, and thought that everything went very bad, was nominated Governor of Chusistan, with an absolute power.   He was decorated with a fur-cap, which is a grand mark of distinction in Persia.   He took his leave of the Sophi, and departed for Sus, the capital of his province.   From the moment that Candide made his appearance at Court, the grandees had conspired his destruction.   The excessive favours which the Sophi had heaped on him, served but to increase the storm ready to burst upon his head.   He, however, applauded himself on his good fortune, and especially his removal from Court; he enjoyed in prospect the pleasures of supreme rank, and he said from the bottom of his heart—

" How blest the subject from his lord removed?"

He had not gone quite twenty miles from Ispahan, before five hundred horsemen, armed *cap-à-pie*, came up with him and his attendants, and discharged a volley of fire-arms upon them.   Candide imagined at first that this was intended to do him an honour; but the ball which broke his leg soon gave him to know what was going on.   His people laid down their arms, and Candide, more dead than alive, was carried to a castle remote from any other dwelling.   His baggage, camels, slaves, white and black eunuchs, with thirty-six women which the Sophi had given him, all became the prey of the conqueror.   Our hero's leg was cut off for fear of a mortification, and care was taken of his life that a more cruel death might be inflicted on him.

"O Pangloss! Pangloss! what would now become of your optimism, if you saw me short of one leg in the hands of my cruellest enemies; just as I was entering upon the path of happiness, and was governor or king, as one may say, of one of the most considerable provinces of the empire of ancient Media; when I had camels, slaves, black and white eunuchs, and thirty-six women for my harem, and of which I had only heard." Thus Candide spoke as soon as he was able to speak.

But while he was thus bemoaning himself everything was going for the best for him. The Ministry, informed of the outrages committed against him, had despatched a body of well-disciplined troops in pursuit of the mutineers, and the monk Ed-Ivan-Baal-Denk took care to publish by means of others of his fraternity, that Candide being the work of the monks, was consequently the work of God. Such as had any knowledge of this atrocious attempt were so much the more ready to discover it, as the ministers of religion gave assurance on the part of Mahomet, that every one who had eaten pork, drunk wine, omitted bathing for any number of days together, or had otherwise acted against the express prohibitions of the Alcoran, should be, *ipso facto*, absolved, upon declaring what they knew concerning the conspiracy. They soon discovered the place of Candide's confinement, which they broke open; and as it was a religious affair, the party worsted were exterminated to a man, agreeably to custom in that case. Candide, marching over a heap of dead bodies, made his escape, triumphed over the greatest peril he had hitherto encountered, and with his attendants resumed the road to his government. He was received there as a favourite who had been honoured with fifty blows of a bull's-pizzle on the soles of his feet in the presence of the King of Kings.

CHAPTER V.

How Candide becomes a very Great Man, and yet is not contented.

THE good of philosophy is its inspiring us with a love for our fellow-creatures. Pascal is almost the only philosopher who seems desirous to make us hate our neighbours. Luckily Candide had not read Pascal, and he loved the poor human race very cordially. This was soon perceived by the upright part of the people. They had always kept at a distance from the pretended legates of heaven, but made no scruple of visiting Candide and assisting him with their counsels. He made several wise regulations for the encouragement of agriculture, population, commerce, and the arts. He rewarded those who had made any useful experiments; and even encouraged such as had produced some essays on literature. "When the people in my province are in general content," said he, with a charming candour, "possibly I shall be so myself." Candide was a stranger to mankind; he saw himself torn to pieces in seditious libels, and calumniated in a work entitled "The Friend to Mankind." He found that, while he was labouring to make people happy, he had only made them ungrateful. "Ah," cried Candide, "how hard it is to govern these beings without feathers, which vegetate on the earth! Why am I not still in Propontis, in the company of Master Pangloss, Miss Cunegund, the daughter of Pope Urban X. with only one buttock, brother Giroflée, and the most luscious Pacquette?"

CHAPTER VI.

The Pleasures of Candide.

CANDIDE, in the bitterness of his grief, wrote a very pathetic letter to the Rev. Ed-Ivan-Baal-Denk. He painted to him in such lively colours the present state of his soul, that Ed-Ivan, greatly affected with it, obtained permission of the Sophi that Candide should resign his employments. His majesty, in recompense of his services, granted him a very considerable pension. Eased from the weight of grandeur, our philosopher immediately sought after Pangloss's optimism in the pleasures of a private life. He till then had lived for the benefit of others, and seemed to have forgotten that he had a seraglio.

He now called it to remembrance with that emotion

which the very name inspires. "Let everything be got ready," says he to his first eunuch, "for my visiting my women." "My lord," answered the shrill-piped slave, "it is now that your excellency deserves the title of wise. The men for whom you have done so much were not worthy of employing your thoughts; but the women——" "That may be," said Candide modestly.

At the bottom of a garden, where art had assisted nature to unfold her beauties, stood a small house, of simple and elegant structure, and by that means alone very different from those which are to be seen in the suburbs of the finest city in Europe. Candide could not approach it without blushing; the air round this charming retreat diffused a delicious perfume; the flowers, amorously intermingled, seemed here to be guided by the instinct of pleasure, and preserved for a long time their various beauties. Here the rose never lost its lovely hue; the view of a rock, from which the waters precipitated themselves with a murmuring and confused noise, invited the soul to that soft melancholy which is ever the forerunner of pleasure. Candide enters trembling into a saloon, where taste and magnificence are united; his senses are drawn by a secret charm; he casts his eyes on young Telemachus, who breathes on the canvas in the midst of the nymphs of Calypso's court. He next turns them to Diana, who flies into the arms of the tender Endymion; his agitation increases at the sight of a Venus, faithfully copied from that of Medicis; his ears on a sudden are struck with a divine harmony; a company of young Circassian females appear covered with their veils; they form round him a sort of dance, agreeably designed, and more just than those trifling jigs that are performed on as trifling stages after the representation of the death of Cæsar and Pompey.

At a signal given they throw off their veils, and discover faces full of expression that lend new life to the diversion.

These beauties studied the most attractive attitude without appearing to intend it : one expressed in her looks a passion without bounds ; another a soft languor, which waits for pleasures without seeking them.   This fair stoops and raises herself precipitately, to give leave to a cursory view of those enchanting charms which the fair sex display in such full scope at Paris ; and that other throws aside a part of her cymar to show a leg which alone is capable of inspiring a mortal of any delicacy.   The dance ceases, and they remain in profound silence.

This pause recalls Candide to himself.   Enthusiasm takes possession of his breast.   He darts the most ardent looks on all around him, and is met by eyes that swim in liquid fire. His eye rests upon forms whiter than alabaster, whose palpitating motion repels the touch ; admires their proportion ; perceives lips like those rosebuds which only wait the genial rays of the sun to unfold them ; he kisses them with rapture.

Our philosopher next admires, for a while, a majestic figure of a fine and delicate shape.   His attention becomes fixed upon one, and he at length throws the handkerchief to a young person whose eyes he had observed to be always fixed upon him.

"O master ! my dear master !" cried Candide, almost beside himself, "everything here is as well as in El Dorado.   I am as happy as it is possible to be.   Leibnitz is in the right, and you are a great philosopher.   For instance, I engage that you, my lovely girl, have always had a bias towards optimism, because you have always been happy." "Alas ! no," answered she, "I do not know what optimism is ; but I swear to you that your slave has not known happiness till to-day.   If my lord is pleased to give me leave, I will convince him of it by a succinct recital of my adventures."   "I am very willing," said Candide ; "I am in a pretty calm situation for hearing an historical detail."   Upon which the fair slave began as follows.

CHAPTER VII.

The History of Zirza.

My father was a Christian, and so likewise am I, as far as I have been told. He had a little hermitage near Cotatis, where, by his fervent devotion, and practising austerities shocking to human nature, he acquired the veneration of the faithful. Crowds came to pay him their homage, and took a particular satisfaction in bathing his posteriors, which he lashed every day with several smart strokes of discipline : doubtless it was to one of the most devout of these visitants that I owe my being. I was brought up in a cave, in the neighbourhood of my father's little cell. I was twelve years of age, and had not yet left this kind of grave, when the earth shook with a dreadful noise ; the arch of the vault fell in, and I was drawn out from under the rubbish half-dead, when light struck my eyes for the first time. My father took me into his hermitage as a pre-destinated child. The whole of this adventure appeared strange to the people ; my father cried it up as a miracle, and so did they.

I was called Zirza, which in Persian signifies *child of providence.* Notice was soon taken of my poor charms : the women already came but seldom to the hermitage, and the men much oftener. One of them tells me that he loved me. "Villain," says my father to him, "hast thou substance sufficient to love her ? This is a deposit which God has entrusted to me : he has made his appearance to me this night under the shape of a venerable hermit, and forbade me to give up the possession thereof out of my hands for less than a thousand sequins. Get thee gone, poor devil, lest thine impure breath should blast her charms." "I have," answered he, "only a heart to offer her. But say, barbarian, dost thou not blush to make sport of the Deity for the gratifying thine avarice? With what front, vile wretch, darest thou pretend that God has spoken to thee? This is throwing the greatest contempt upon the Author of beings, to represent Him conversing with such men as thou art." "O blasphemy!" cried my father in a rage, "God himself has commanded me to stone blasphemers." As he spoke these words, he fell upon my lover, and with repeated blows laid him dead on the ground, and his blood flew in my face. Though I had not yet known what love is, this man had given me concern, and his death threw me into an affliction, so much the greater, as it rendered the sight of my father insupportable to me. I took a resolution to leave him : he perceived it. "Ungrateful," says he to me, "it is to me thou owest thy being. Thou art my daughter, and thou hatest me . but I am going to deserve thy hatred by the most rigorous treatment." He kept his word but too well with me, cruel man ! During five years, which I spent in tears and groans, neither my youth, nor my clouded beauty, could in the least abate his wrath. Sometimes he stuck a thousand pins into all the parts of my body ; at other times, with his discipline, he made the blood trickle down my side." "This," says Candide, "gave you less pain than the pins." "True, my lord," answers Zirza. "At last," continued she, "I fled from my father's habitation ; and not daring to trust myself to anybody, I flung myself into the thickest part of the woods, where I was three days without food, and should have died, were it not for a tiger which I had the happiness to please, and was willing to share with me the prey he caught. But I had many horrors to encounter from this formidable beast; and the brute was very near destroying me. Bad food gave me the scurvy. Scarcely was I cured, before I followed a merchant of slaves, who was going to Teflis; the plague was there then, and I took it. These various misfortunes did not absolutely affect my features, nor hinder the Sophi's messenger from buying me for you.

I have languished in tears these three months that I have been among the number of your women. My companions and I imagined ourselves to be the objects of your contempt. In short, I am not yet eighteen years of age ; and of these I have spent twelve in a frightful cavern ; undergone an earthquake ; been covered with the blood of the first lovely man I had hitherto seen ; endured for the space of four years the most cruel tortures, and have had the scurvy and the plague. Consumed with desires, amidst a crew of black and white monsters, still preserving that which I have saved from the fury of an awkward tiger, and cursing my fate, I have passed three months in this seraglio, where I should have died of the jaundice had not your excellency honoured me at last with your attention." "O heavens !" cried Candide, "is it possible that you have experienced such sensible misfortunes at so tender an age? What would Pangloss say could he hear you? But your misfortunes are at an end, as well as mine. Everything does not go badly now ; is not this true?" Upon that Candide caressed the unfortunate one, and was more than ever confirmed in the belief of Pangloss's system.

CHAPTER VIII.

Candide's disgusts.—An unexpected Meeting.

Our philosopher dried up as he grew happy. Then Zirza's eyes lost all their vivacity in those of Candide ; her complexion, its lustre ; and her lips that pure vermillion which had enchanted him at first sight. He now perceived that she walked badly and had an offensive smell ; he saw, with the greatest disgust, a spot upon the face which he had never observed before to be tainted with any blemish. The vehement ardour of Zirza became burdensome to him : he could see, with great coolness, the faults of his other women, which had escaped him in his first transports of admiration; he saw nothing in them but a barefaced impudence: he was ashamed to have walked in the steps of the wisest of men; and *he found women more bitter than death.*

Candide, always cherishing these Christian sentiments, spent his leisure time in walking over the streets of Sus; when one day a cavalier, in a superb dress, came up to him suddenly, and called him by his name. "Is it possible," cried Candide, "my lord, that you are ——? It is not possible; otherwise you are so very like the Abbé of Perigord ——." I am the very man," answered the Abbé. Upon this Candide started back, and with his usual ingenuousness said, "Are you happy, Mr. Abbé?" "A fine question!" replied the Abbé. "The little deceit which I have put upon you has contributed not a little to gain me credit. The police had employed me for some time, but having fallen out with them, I quitted the ecclesiastical habit, which was no longer of any service to me. I went over into England, where persons of my profession are better paid. I said all I knew, and all I did not know, about the strength and weakness of the country I had lately left. I especially gave bold assurances that the French were the dregs of the world, and that good sense dwelt nowhere but in London. In short, I made a splendid fortune, and have just concluded a treaty at the Court of Persia, which tends to exterminate all the Europeans who come for cotton and silk into the Sophi's dominions, to the detriment of the English." "The object of your mission is very commendable," says our philosopher; "but, Mr. Abbé, you are a cheat. I like not cheats, and I have some credit at Court. Tremble now, your happiness has arrived at its utmost limits: you are just upon the point of suffering the fate you deserve." "My Lord Candide," cried the Abbé, throwing himself on his kness, "have pity on me: I feel myself drawn to evil by an irresistible force, as you find yourself necessitated to the practice of virtue. This fatal propensity I have perceived from the moment I became acquainted with Mr. Wasp, and worked at the *Feuilles.*" "What do you call *Feuilles?*" says Candide. "*Feuilles,*" answered the Abbé, "are sheets of seventy-two pages in print, in which the public are entertained in the strain of calumny, satire, and dulness. An honest man who can read and write, and not being able to continue among the Jesuits so long as he chose, has set himself to compose this pretty little work, that he may have wherewithal to give his wife some lace, and bring up his children in the fear of God ; and there are certain honest people who, for a few pence and some bottles of bad wine, assist the man in carrying on his scheme. This Mr. Wasp is, besides, a member of a curious club, who divert themselves with making poor ignorant people drunk, and setting them to blaspheme ; or in bullying a poor simple devil, and breaking his furniture, and afterwards challenging him. Such little pretty amusements these gentry call mystifications, and richly deserve the attention of the police. In fine, this very honest man, Mr. Wasp, who boasts he never was in the galleys, is troubled with a lethargy, which renders him insensible to the clearest truths, and out of which he can be drawn only by certain violent means, which he sustains with a resignation and courage above conception. I have worked for some time under this celebrated genius ; I am become an eminent writer in my turn, and I had but just quitted Mr. Wasp to do a little for myself, when I had the honour of paying you a visit at Paris." " Though you are a very great cheat, Mr. Abbé, yet your sincerity in this point makes some impression upon me. Go to Court ; ask for the Rev. Ed-Ivan-Baal-Denk ; I shall write to him in your behalf, but upon express condition that you promise me to become an honest man ; and that you will not be the occasion of some thousands having their throats cut for the sake of a little silk and cotton." The Abbé promised all that Candide required, and they parted very good friends.

CHAPTER IX.

Candide's Disgraces, Travels, and Adventures.

No sooner had the Abbé gotten access to Court than he employed all his skill in order to ingratiate himself with the minister and ruin his benefactor. He spread a report that Candide was a traitor, and that he had spoken disrespectfully of the hallowed whiskers of the king of kings. All the courtiers condemned him to be burnt in a slow fire; but the Sophi, more favourable, only sentenced him to perpetual banishment, after having previously kissed the sole of his accuser's foot, according to the usage among the Persians. The Abbé went in person to put the sentence in execution; he found our philosopher in pretty good health, and disposed to become again happy. " My friend," says the English ambassador to him, " I come with regret to let you know that you must quit this kingdom with all expedition, and kiss my feet with a true repentance for your horrid crimes." " Kiss your feet, Mr. Abbé! Certainly you are not in earnest, and I do not understand joking." Upon which some mutes, who had attended the Abbé, entered and took off his shoes, letting poor Candide know by signs that he must submit to this piece of humiliation, or else expect to be impaled. Candide, by virtue of his free will, kissed the Abbé's feet. They put him on a sorry linen robe, and the executioner drove him out of the town, crying all the time, " Behold a traitor who has spoken irreverently of the Sophi's whiskers! Irreverently of the imperial whiskers!"

What did the officious monk while his friend whom he protected was treated thus? I know nothing of that. It is probable that he was tired of protecting Candide. Who can depend on the favour of kings, and especially that of monks?

In the meantime our hero went melancholy on. " I never spoke," said he to himself, " about the King of Persia's whiskers. I am cast in an instant from the pinnacle of happiness into the abyss of misery, because a wretch who has violated all laws accuses me of a pretended crime which I have never committed ; and this wretch, this monster, this persecutor of virtue—he is happy."

Candide, after travelling for some days, found himself upon the frontiers of Turkey. He directed his course towards the Propontis, with a design to settle there again, and pass the rest of his days in the cultivation of his garden. He saw as he entered a little village a great multitude of people tumultuously assembled ; he inquired into the cause of it. "This," says an old man to him, "is an accident pretty singular. It is some time ago since the wealthy Mahomet demanded in marriage the daughter of the janissary Zamoud : he found her not to be honest, and in pursuance of a principle quite natural, and authorized by the laws, he sent her home to her father, after having branded her in the face. Zamoud, exasperated at the disgrace brought on his family, in the first transports of a fury that is very natural, with one stroke of his scimitar clove the disfigured visage of his daughter. His eldest son, who loved his sister passionately—and this is very frequent in nature—flew upon his father, and plunged, quite naturally too, a very sharp poignard to his heart. Afterwards, like a lion who grows more enraged at seeing his own blood flow, the furious Zamoud ran to Mahomet's house, and after striking to the ground some slaves who opposed his passage, murdered Mahomet, his wives, and two children then in the cradle, all of which was very natural, considering the violent situation he then was in. At last, to crown all, he killed himself with the same poignard, reeking with the blood of his father and his enemies, which is also very natural." "What a scene of horrors !" cried Candide. "What would you have said, Master Pangloss, had you found such barbarities in nature ? Would not you acknowledge that nature is corrupted, that all is not." "No," says the old man,

" for the pre-established harmony."   " O heavens ! do ye
not deceive me ?   Is this Pangloss," says Candide, " whom
I again see ? "   " The very same," answered the old man ;
" I knew you, but I was willing to find out your sentiments
before I would discover myself.   Come, let us discourse a
little on contingent effects, and see if you have made any
progress in the art of wisdom."   " Alas ! " says Candide,
" you choose your time improperly ; rather let me know what
is become of Miss Cunegund ; tell me where are Brother
Giroflée, Pacquette, and Pope Urban's daughter."   " I know
nothing of them," says Pangloss ; " it is now two years since
I left our habitation in order to find you out.   I have
travelled over almost all Turkey ; I was upon the point of
setting out for the Court of Persia, where I heard you made
a great figure ; and I only tarried in this little village among
these good people, till I had gathered strength for continuing my journey."   " What is this, I see ? " answered
Candide, quite surprised.   " You want an arm, my dear
doctor."   " That is nothing," says the one-handed and one-
eyed doctor ; " nothing is more common in the best of
worlds than to see persons who want one eye and one arm.
This accident befell me in a journey from Mecca.   Our
caravan was attacked by a troop of Arabs ; our guard
attempted to make resistance, and, according to the rules
of war, the Arabs, who found themselves to be the strongest
side, massacred us all without mercy.   There perished about
five hundred persons in this attack, among whom was about
a dozen of women.   For my part I had only my skull split
and an arm cut off ; I did not die for all this, and I still
found that everything went for the best.   But as for yourself, my dear Candide, whence is it that you have a wooden
leg ? "   Upon this Candide began and gave an account of
his adventures.   Our philosophers turned together towards
the Propontis, and enlivened their journey by discoursing
on physical and moral evil, free-will and predestination,
monads and pre-established harmony.

CHAPTER X.

Candide and Pangloss arrive in the Propontis; what they saw there, and what became of them.

" O CANDIDE!" said Pangloss, " why were you tired of cultivating your garden ? Why did we not still continue to eat
citrons and pistachio-nuts? Why were you weary of your
happiness ? Because everything is necessary in the best of
worlds, there was a necessity that you should undergo the
bastinado in the presence of the King of Persia ; have your
leg cut off in order to make Chusistan happy ; to experience
the ingratitude of men ; and draw down upon the heads of
some atrocious villains the punishment which they had
deserved." With such talk as this they arrived at their old
habitation. The first objects that presented themselves
were Martin and Pacquette in the habit of slaves. " Whence,"
said Candide to them, " is this metamorphosis ? " after embracing them tenderly. " Alas ! " answered they, sobbing,
" you have no more a habitation ; another has undertaken
the labour of cultivating your garden ; he eats your preserved citrons and pistachios, and we are treated like
negroes." " Who," says Candide, " is this other ? " " The
High Admiral," answered they ; " a mortal the least humane
of all mortals. The Sultan, willing to recompense his
services without putting himself to any expense, has confiscated all your goods, under pretext that you had gone over
to his enemies, and condemned us to slavery. Be advised
by me, Candide," added Martin, " and continue your
journey. I always told you everything is for the worst ; the
sum of evil exceeds by much that of good. Begone, and
I do not despair but you may become a Manichæan, if you
are not so already." Pangloss would have begun an argument in form, but Candide interrupted him to ask about Miss
Cunegund, the old woman, Brother Giroflée, and Cacambo.
" Cacambo," answered Martin, " is here ; he is at present

employed about emptying a house of office. The old woman is dead, from a kick given her by a eunuch in the breast. Brother Giroflée has entered among the janissaries. Miss Cunegund has recovered her plumpness and former beauty; she is in our master's seraglio." "What a chain of misfortunes," says Candide. "Was there a necessity for Miss Cunegund to become handsome only to make me miserable?" "It matters little," says Pangloss, "whether Miss Cunegund be beautiful or ugly in your house or that of another; that is nothing to the general system; for my part, I wish her a numerous progeny. Philosophers do not perplex themselves by whom women have children, provided they have them. Population." "Alas!" says Martin, philosophers ought much rather to employ themselves in rendering a few individuals happy, than in engaging them to multiply the number of sufferers." While they were thus arguing a great noise was heard on a sudden; it was the Admiral diverting himself by causing a dozen slaves to be whipped. Pangloss and Candide, both frightened, with tears in their eyes, parted from their friends, and in all haste took the road towards Constantinople.

There they found all the people in a great stir. A fire had broken out in the suburb of Pera; five or six hundred houses were already consumed, and two or three thousand persons perished in the flames. "What a horrible disaster!" cried Candide. "All is well," says Pangloss. "These little accidents happen every year. It is entirely natural for the fire to catch houses built of wood, and for those who are in them to be burnt. Besides, this procures some resources to honest people who languish in misery." "What is this I hear?" says an officer of the Sublime Porte. "How, wretch, darest thou say that all is well when half Constantinople is in flames! Dog, be cursed of our Prophet! Receive the punishment due to thy impudence!" And as he uttered these words he took Pangloss by the middle and flung him headlong into the flames. Candide, half-dead with fright, crept on all-fours as well as he could to a neighbouring quarter, where all was more quiet ; and we shall see what became of him in the next chapter.

CHAPTER XI.

Candide continues his Travels, and in what quality.

"I HAVE nothing left," said our philosopher, "but to make myself either a slave or a Turk. Happiness has forsaken me for ever. A turban would corrupt all my pleasures. I shall be incapable of tasting tranquillity of soul in a religion full of imposture, into which I enter merely from a motive of vile interest. No, I shall never be content if I cease to be an honest man. Let me make myself, then, a slave." Candide had no sooner taken this resolution than he set about putting it into execution. He chose an Armenian merchant for his master, who was a man of a very good character, and passed for virtuous as much as an Armenian can be. He gave Candide two hundred sequins as the price of his liberty. The Armenian was upon the point of departing for Norway. He took Candide with him, in hopes that a philosopher would be of use to him in his traffic. They embarked, and the wind was so favourable for them that they were not above half the usual time in their passage. They even had no occasion for buying a wind from the Lapland witches, and contented themselves with giving them some stock-fish, that they might not disturb their good fortune with their enchantments, which sometimes happens, if we may believe Moreri's Dictionary on this head.

The Armenian no sooner landed than he provided a stock of whale-blubber, and ordered our philosopher to go over all the country to buy him some dried salt fish. He acquitted himself of his commission in the best manner he could, returned with several reindeer loaded with this merchandize, and made profound reflections on the astonishing difference which is to be found between the Laplanders and other men. A very diminutive female Laplander, whose head was a little bigger than her body, her eyes red and full· of fire, a flat nose, and mouth as wide as possible, wished him a good day with an infinite grace. "My little lord," says this being (a foot and ten inches high) to him, "I think you very handsome; do me the favour to love me a little." So saying, she flew to him, and caught him round the neck. Candide pushed her away with horror. She cries out, when in comes her husband with several other Laplanders. "What is the meaning of all this uproar?" say they. "It is," answers the little thing, "that this stranger—— Alas! I am choked with grief; he despises me." "So then," says the Lapland husband, "thou unpolite, dishonest, brutal, infamous, cowardly rascal, thou bringest disgrace upon my house; thou dost me the most sensible injury; thou refusest to admire my wife." "Lo! here's the good of our neighbour," cried our hero; "what would you have said, then, if I had taken your place?" "I would have wished thee all sort of prosperity," says the Laplander to him in wrath, "but thou only deservest my indignation." At uttering this, he discharged on Candide's back a volley of blows with a cudgel. The reindeer were seized by the relations of the offended husband; and Candide, for fear of worse, was forced to betake himself to flight, and renounce for ever his good master; for how dared he present himself before him without money, whale-blubber, or reindeer?

CHAPTER XII.

Candide still continues his Travels.—New Adventures.

CANDIDE travelled a long time without knowing whither he was going; at length he resolved to go to Denmark, where he had heard that everything went pretty well. He had a few pieces of money about him, which the Armenian had made him a present of; and this sum, though inconsiderable, he hoped would carry him to the end of his journey. Hope rendered his misery supportable to him, and he still passed some happy moments. He found himself one day in an inn with three travellers, who talked to him with great warmth about a *plenum* and the *materia subtilis.* "Mighty well," says Candide to himself; "these are philosophers. Gentlemen," says he to them, "a *plenum* is incontestable; there is no vacuum in nature, and the *materia subtilis* is a well-imagined hypothesis." "You are then a Cartesian?" say the three travellers. "Yes," answers Candide, "and a Leibnitzian, which is more." "So much the worse for you," replied the philosophers. "Descartes and Leibnitz had not common sense. We are Newtonians, and we glory in it; if we dispute, it is only the better to confirm ourselves in our opinions, and we all think the same. We search for truth in Newton's track, because we are persuaded that Newton is a great man." "And Descartes too, and Leibnitz and Pangloss likewise," says Candide. "These great men are worth a thousand of yours." "You are a fool, friend," answered the philosophers. "Do you know the laws of refraction, attraction, and motion? Have you read the truths which Dr. Clarke has published, in answer to the reveries of your Leibnitz? Do you know what centrifugal and centripetal force is? and that colours depend on their density? Have you any notion of the theory of light and gravitation? Do you know the period of twenty-five thousand nine hundred and twenty years, which unluckily do not agree with chronology? No; undoubtedly you have but false ideas of all these things. Peace, then, thou contemptible monad, and beware how you insult giants by comparing them to pigmies." "Gentlemen," answered Candide, "were Pangloss here, he would tell you very fine things, for he is a great philosopher. He has a sovereign contempt for your

Newton ; and, as I am his disciple, I likewise make no great account of him." The philosophers, enraged beyond measure, fell upon poor Candide, and drubbed him most philosophically.

Their wrath subsiding, they asked our hero's pardon for their too great warmth. Upon this, one of them began a very fine harangue on mildness and moderation.

While they were talking, they saw a grand burial pass by. Our philosophers from thence took occasion to descant on the foolish vanity of man. " Would it not be more reasonable," says one of them, " that the relations and friends of the deceased should, without pomp and noise, carry the bier themselves? Would not this funereal act, by presenting to them the idea of death, produce an effect the most salutary, the most philosophical? This reflection which would offer itself, namely, *the body I carry is that of my friend, my relation ; he is no more ; and, like him, I must cease to be in this world.* Would not this, I say, be a means of lessening the number of crimes in this vile world, and of bringing back to virtue beings who believe the immortality of the soul? Men are too much inclined to remove from them the thoughts of death for fear of presenting too strong images of it. Whence is it that people keep at a distance from such a spectacle as a mother and a wife in tears? The plaintive accents of nature, the piercing cries of despair, would do much greater honour to the ashes of the dead than all these individuals clad in black from head to foot, together with useless female mourners, and that crowd of ministers who sing in a gay air funeral orations which the deceased do not hear."

" This is extremely well spoken," says Candide, " and did you always speak thus well, without thinking proper to thrash people, you would be a great philosopher."

Our travellers parted with expressions of mutual confidence and friendship. Candide still continued travelling towards Denmark. He plunged into the woods, where, musing deeply on all the misfortunes which had happened to him in the best of worlds, he turned aside from the road and lost himself. The day began to draw towards the evening, when he perceived his mistake. He was seized with dismay, and raising in a melancholy manner his eyes to heaven, and leaning against the trunk of a tree, our hero spoke in the following terms :—" I have gone over half the world, seen fraud and calumny triumphant, have only sought to do service to mankind, and I have been persecuted. A great king honours me with his favour and fifty blows of a bull's pizzle. I arrive with a wooden leg in a very fine province ; there I taste pleasures after having drank deep of mortifications. An abbé comes ; I protect him ; he insinuates himself at Court through my means, and I am obliged to kiss his feet. I meet with my poor Pangloss only to see him burnt. I find myself in company with philosophers, the mildest and most sociable of all the species of animals that are spread over the face of the earth, and they give me an unmerciful drubbing. All must necessarily be for the best, since Pangloss has said it ; but nevertheless I am the most wretched of all possible beings." Here Candide stopped short to listen to the cries of distress, which seemed to come from a place near him. He stepped forward out of curiosity, when he beheld a young woman, who was tearing her hair with all the signs of the greatest despair. " Whoever you are," says she to him, " if you have a heart, follow me." He went with her, but they had not gone many paces before Candide perceived a man and a woman stretched out on the grass. Their faces declared the nobleness of their souls and origin. Their features, though distorted by pain, had something so interesting that Candide could not forbear bemoaning them, and informing himself with a lively eagerness about the cause which reduced them to so miserable a situation. " It is my father and mother whom you see," says the young woman. "Yes, these are the authors of my wretched being," continued she, throwing herself into their arms. "They fled to avoid the rigour of an unjust sentence. I accompanied them in their flight, happy to share in their misfortune, from a thought that in the deserts where we were going to hide ourselves my feeble hands might procure them a necessary subsistence. We have stopped here to take some rest. I discovered that tree which you see, whose fruit has deceived me. Alas! sir, I am a wretch to be detested by the world and myself. Arm your hand to avenge offended virtue, and to punish the parricide. I took this fruit; I presented it to my father and mother; they ate of it with pleasure; I rejoiced to have found the means of quenching the thirst with which they were tormented. Unhappy wretch! it was death I presented to them. This fruit is poison."

This tale made Candide shudder; his hair stood on end, and a cold sweat ran over all his body. He was eager, as much as his present condition could permit, to give some relief to this unfortunate family; but the poison had already made too much progress, and the most efficacious remedies would not have been able to stop its fatal effect.

"Dear child, our only hope!" cried the two unhappy parents; "God pardon thee as we pardon thee; it was the excess of thy tenderness which has robbed us of our lives. Generous stranger, vouchsafe to take care of her; her heart is noble and formed to virtue; she is a deposit which we leave in your hands, that is infinitely more precious to us than our past fortune. Dear Zenoida, receive our last embraces: mingle thy tears with ours. Heavens! how happy are these moments to us! Thou hast opened to us the dreary cave in which we languished for forty years past. Tender Zenoida, we bless thee; mayest thou never forget the lessons which our prudence hath dictated to thee; and may they preserve thee from the abyss which we see ready to swallow thee."

They expired as they pronounced these words. Candide had great difficulty in bringing Zenoida to herself. The moon enlightened the affecting scene : the day appeared, and Zenoida, plunged in sad affliction, had not as yet recovered the use of her senses. As soon as she opened her eyes, she entreated Candide to dig a hole in the ground in order to inter the bodies ; she assisted in the work with an astonishing courage. This duty fulfilled, she gave free scope to her tears. Our philosopher drew her from this fatal place : they travelled a long time without observing any certain route. At length they perceived a little cottage. Two persons in the decline of life dwelt in this desert, who were always ready to give every assistance in their power to fellow-creatures in distress. These old people were such as Philemon and Baucis are described to us. For fifty years they had tasted the soft endearments of marriage, without ever experiencing its bitterness ; an unimpaired health, the fruit of temperance and tranquillity of mind, mild and simple manners; a fund of inexhaustible candour in their character ; all the virtues which man owes to himself, formed the glorious and only fortune which heaven had granted them. They were held in veneration in the neighbouring villages, the inhabitants of which, full of happy rusticity, might have passed for honest people, had they been Catholics. They looked upon it as a duty not to suffer Agaton and Suname (for so the old couple were called) to want for anything. Their charity extended to the new-comers. " Alas ! " said Candide, " it is a great loss, my dear Pangloss, that you were burnt. You were master of sound reason ; but yet in all the parts of Europe and Asia, which I have travelled over in your company, everything is not for the best : it is only in El Dorado, whither no one can go, and in a little cottage situated in the coldest, most barren, and frightful region in the world. What pleasure should I have to hear you

harangue about the pre-established harmony and monads!"
I should be very willing to pass my days among these
honest Lutherans; but I must renounce going to mass, and
resolve to be torn to pieces in the *Journal chrétien.*

Candide was very inquisitive to learn the adventures of
Zenoida, but complaisance withheld him from speaking to
her about it. She perceived the respectful constraint he
put upon himself, and satisfied his impatience in the following terms.

CHAPTER XIII.

*The history of Zenoida. How Candide fell in love with
her, and what followed.*

" I AM come of one of the most ancient families in Denmark.
One of my ancestors perished at that horrid feast which the
wicked Christiern prepared for the destruction of so many
senators. The riches and dignity with which our family has
been distinguished have hitherto served only to make them
more eminently unfortunate. My father had the presumption
to displease a great man in power by boldly telling him the
truth. He was presently accused by suborned witnesses of
a number of crimes which had no foundation. His judges
were deceived. Alas! where is that judge who can always
discover those snares which envy and treachery lay for un-
guarded innocence? My father was sentenced to be be-
headed. He had no way left to avoid his fate but by flight.
Accordingly, he withdrew to the house of an old friend,
whom he thought deserving of that truly noble appellation.
We remained some time concealed in a castle belonging to
him on the seaside, and we might have continued there to
this day had not the base wretch with whom we had taken
refuge attempted to repay himself for the service he did us
in a manner that gave us all reason to detest him. This
infamous monster had conceived a most unnatural passion
towards my mother and myself at the same time. He

attempted our ruin by methods most unworthy of a man of honour; and we were obliged to expose ourselves to the most dreadful dangers to avoid the effects of his brutal passion. In a word, we took to flight a second time, and you know the rest."

In finishing this short narrative, Zenoida burst into tears afresh. Candide wiped them from her eyes, and said to her, by way of consolation, "Madam, everything is for the best. If your father had not died by poison he would infallibly have been discovered, and then his head would have been cut off. The good lady your mother would, in all probability, have died of grief, and we should not have been in this poor hut, where everything is as well as in the finest of possible castles."

"Alas, sir," replied Zenoida, "my father never told me that everything was for the best, but he has often said, 'We are all children of the same Divine Father, who loves us, but who has not exempted us from the most callous sorrows, the most grievous maladies, and an innumerable tribe of miseries that afflict the human race. Poison grows by the side of the salutiferous quinquina in America. The happiest of all mortals has some time or other shed tears. What we call life is a compound of pleasure and pain. It is the passing away of a certain stated portion of time that always appears too long in the sight of the wise man, and which every one ought to employ in doing good to the community in which he is placed; in the enjoyment of the works of Providence, without idly seeking after hidden causes; in squaring his conduct by the rules of conscience; and, above all, in showing a due respect to religion. Happy is he who can follow this unerringly!'

"These things my ever-respected father has frequently inculcated to me. 'Ill-betide those wretched scribblers,' he would say, 'who attempt to pry into the hidden ways of Providence.' From the principle, that God will be honoured from thousands of atoms, mankind have blended the most

absurd chimeras with respectable truths. The Turkish
dervish, the Persian brahmin, the Chinese bonza, and the
Indian talapoin, all worship the Deity in a different manner;
but they enjoy a tranquillity of soul amidst the darkness in
which they are plunged; and he who would endeavour to
enlighten them does them but ill service. It is not loving
mankind to tear the bandage of prejudice from their eyes."

"Why, you talk like a philosopher," said Candide: "may
I ask you, my pretty young lady, of what religion you are?"
"I was brought up in the Lutheran profession," answered
Zenoida. "Every word you have spoken," said Candide,
"has been like a ray of light that has penetrated to my heart,
and I find a sort of esteem and admiration for you, that——
But how, in the name of wonder, came so bright an understanding to be lodged in so beautiful a form? Upon my
word, Miss, I esteem and admire you, as I said before, so
much that——" Candide stammered out a few words more,
when Zenoida, perceiving his confusion, quitted him, and
from that moment carefully avoided all occasions of being
alone with him: and Candide, on his part, sought every
opportunity of being alone with her, or else being by himself. He was buried in a melancholy that to him had
charms, he was deeply enamoured of Zenoida; but endeavoured to conceal his passion from himself: his looks,
however, too plainly evinced the feelings of his heart.
"Alas!" would he often say to himself, "if Master Pangloss
was here he would give me good advice; for he was a
great philosopher."

CHAPTER XIV.

Continuation of the Loves of Candide.

THE only consolation that Candide felt was in conversing with Zenoida in the presence of their hosts.

"How happens it," said he to her one day, "that the monarch to whom you have access has suffered such injustice to be done to your family? Assuredly you have sufficient reason to hate him?"

"How!" said Zenoida, "who can hate the king? who can do otherwise than love that person to whose hand is consigned the keen-edged sword of the laws? Kings are the living images of the Deity, and we ought never to arraign their conduct; obedience and respect is the duty of a subject."

"I admire you more and more," said Candide; "indeed, madam, I do. Pray do you know the great Leibnitz, and the great Pangloss, who was burnt, after having escaped a hanging bout? Are you acquainted with the monads, the *materia subtilis*, and the *vortices?*"

"No, sir," replied Zenoida; "I never heard my father mention any of these; he only gave me a slight tincture of experimental philosophy, and taught me to hold in contempt all those kinds of philosophy that do not directly tend to make mankind happy; that give him false notions of his duty to himself and his neighbour; that do not teach him to regulate his conduct, and fill his mind only with uncouth terms or ill-founded conjectures; that do not give him a clearer idea of the Author of Nature than what he may acquire from his works, and the wonders that are every day passing before our sight."

"Once again, Miss, you enchant me; you ravish me; you are an angel that heaven has sent to remove from before my eyes the mist of Master Pangloss's sophistical arguments. Poor wretch that I was! After having been so heartily kicked, flogged, and bastinadoed; after having been in an earthquake; having seen Doctor Pangloss once hanged, and very lately burnt; after having been ravished by a villainous Persian, who put me to the most excruciating torture; after having been robbed by a decree of the divan, and soundly drubbed by the philosophers; after all these things, I say, to think that everything was for the best! But now, thank heaven, I am disabused. But, truly speaking, nature never appeared half so charming to me as since I have been blessed with the sight of you. The melody of the rural choristers charms my ears with a harmony to which they were till now utter strangers; I breathe a new soul, and the glow of sentiment that enchants me seems imprinted on every object; I do not feel that effeminate languor which I did in the gardens of Sus; the sensation with which you inspire me is wholly different."

"Let us stop here," said Zenoida; "you seem to be running to lengths that may perhaps offend my delicacy, which you ought to respect."

"I will be silent then," said Candide; "but my passion will only burn with the more force." On saying these words he looked stedfastly at Zenoida; he perceived her to blush, and, as a man who was taught by experience, conceived the most flattering hopes from those appearances.

The beautiful Dane continued a long time to shun the pursuits of Candide. One day, as he was walking hastily to and fro in the garden, he cried out in an amorous ecstasy, "Ah! why have I not now my El Dorado sheep? Why have I it not in my power to purchase a small kingdom? Ah! were I but a king——"

"What should I be to you?" said a voice which pierced the heart of our philosopher.

"Is it you, lovely Zenoida?" cried he, falling on his knees. "I thought myself alone. The few words I heard you just now utter seem to promise me the felicity to which my soul aspires. I shall, in all probability, never be a king, nor ever possessed of a fortune ; but if you love me—— Do not turn from me those lovely eyes, but suffer me to read in them a declaration which is alone capable of confirming my happiness. Beauteous Zenoida, I adore you; let your heart be open to compassion. What do I see? You weep! Ah! my happiness is too great."

"Yes, you are happy," said Zenoida ; "nothing can oblige me to disguise my tenderness for a person I think deserving of it. Hitherto you have been attached to my destiny only by the bands of humanity ; it is now time to strengthen those by ties more sacred. I have consulted my heart, reflect maturely in your turn ; but remember, that if you marry me, you become obliged to be my protector : to share with me those misfortunes that fate may yet have in store for me, and to soothe my sorrows."

"Marry you!" said Candide : "those words have shown me all the folly of my conduct. Alas! dear idol of my soul, I am not deserving of the goodness you show towards me. Cunegund is still living."

"Cunegund! Who is that?"

"She is my wife," answered Candide with his usual frankness.

But I will forbear to relate the whole of the interesting conversation, and content myself with saying that the eloquence of Candide, heightened by the warmth of amorous expression, had all the effect that may be imagined on a young sensible female philosopher.

The lovers, who till then had passed their days in tedious melancholy, now counted every hour by a fresh succession of amorous joys. Pleasure flowed through their veins in an uninterrupted current. The gloomy woods, the barren mountains, surrounded by horrid precipices ; the icy plains and dreary fields, covered with snow on all sides, were so many continual mementos to them of the necessity of loving. They determined never to quit that dreadful solitude, but fate was not yet weary of persecuting them, as we shall see in the ensuing chapter.

CHAPTER XV.

The Arrival of Wolhall.—A Journey to Copenhagen.

CANDIDE and Zenoida amused themselves with discoursing on the words of the Deity, the worship which mankind ought to pay Him, the mutual duties they owe to each other, especially that of charity, the most useful of all virtues. They did not confine themselves to frivolous declamations. Candide taught the young men the respect due to the sacred curb of the laws; Zenoida instructed the young women in the duties they owed their parents ; both joined their endeavours to sow the hopeful seeds of religion in their young hearts. One day, as they were busied in those pious offices, Sunama came to tell Zenoida that an old gentleman with several servants was just alighted at their house ; and that, by the description he had given her of a person of whom he was in search, she was certain it could be no other than Zenoida herself. This stranger had followed Sunama close at her heels, and entered, before she had done speaking, into the room where were Candide and Zenoida.

At sight of him Zenoida instantly fainted away; but Wolhall, not in the least affected with the situation he saw her in, took hold of her hand, and pulling her to him with violence, brought her to her senses; which she had no sooner recovered than she burst into a flood of tears.

" So, niece," said he, with a sarcastic smile, " I find you in very good company. I do not wonder you prefer this habitation to the capital, to my house, and the company of your family." " Yes, sir," replied Zenoida, " I do prefer · this place, where dwell simplicity and truth, to the mansions of treason and imposture. I can never behold but with horror that place where first began my misfortunes ; where I have had so many proofs of your black actions, and where I have no other relations but yourself." " Come, madam," said Wolhall, " follow me, if you please ; for you must along, even if you should faint again." Saying this, he dragged her to the door of the house, and made her get into a post-chaise which was waiting for him. She had only time to tell Candide to follow, and to bestow her blessing on her hosts, with promises of rewarding them amply for their generous cares.

A domestic of Wolhall was moved with pity at the grief in which he saw Candide plunged ; he imagined that he felt no other concern for the fair Dane than what unfortunate virtue inspires. He proposed to him taking a journey to Copenhagen, and he facilitated the means for his doing it. He did more ; he insinuated to him that he might be admitted as one of Wolhall's domestics, if he had no other resources than going to service. Candide liked his pro-posal ; and no sooner arrived than his future fellow-servant presented him as one of his relations, for whom he would be answerable. " Rascal," says Wolhall to him, " I consent to grant you the honour of approaching a person of such rank as I am ; never forget the profound respect which you owe to my commands ; prevent them if you have sufficient sagacity for it ; think that a man like me degrades himself in speaking to a wretch such as you." Our philosopher answered with great humility to this impertinent discourse, and from that day he was clad in his master's livery.

It is easy to imagine the joy and surprise that Zenoida felt when she recollected her lover among her uncle's servants. She threw several opportunities in the way of Candide, who knew how to profit by them. They swore eternal constancy. Zenoida had some unhappy moments ; she sometimes reproached herself on account of her love for Candide ; she vexed him sometimes by a few caprices ; but Candide idolized her ; he knew that perfection is not the portion of man, and still less so of woman. Zenoida resumed her good humour. The kind of constraint under which they lay rendered their pleasures more lively. They were still happy.

CHAPTER XVI.

How Candide found his Wife again, and lost his Mistress.

OUR hero had only to bear with the haughty humours of his master, and that was purchasing his mistress's favours at no dear rate. Happy love is not so easily concealed as many imagine. Our lovers betrayed themselves. Their connection was no longer a mystery but to the short-sighted eyes of Wolhall. All the domestics knew it. Candide received congratulations on that head which made him tremble. He expected the storm ready to burst upon his head, and did not doubt but a person who had been dear to him was upon the point of accelerating his misfortune. He had for some days before perceived a face resembling Miss Cunegund ; he again saw the same face in Wolhall's courtyard. The object which struck him was very poorly clothed, and there was no likelihood that a favourite of a great Mahometan should be found in the courtyard of a house at Copenhagen. This disagreeable object, however, looked at Candide very attentively. When coming up to him, and seizing him by the hair, she gave him the smartest blow on the face with her open hand that he had received for some time. " I am not deceived," cried our philosopher. " Oh, heavens ! who would have thought it ? What do you do here after having suffered yourself to be adopted by a follower of Mahomet. Go, perfidious spouse, I know you not." " Thou shalt know me," replied Cunegund, " by my outrageous fury. I know the life thou leadest, thy love for thy master's niece, and thy contempt for me. Alas ! it is now three months since I quitted the seraglio, because I was there good for nothing further. A merchant has bought me to mend his linen ; he takes me along with him when he makes a voyage to this country ; Martin, Cacambo, and Pacquette, whom he has also bought, are with me ; Doctor Pangloss, through the greatest chance in the world, was in the same vessel as a passenger ; we were shipwrecked some miles from hence ; I escaped the danger with the faithful Cacambo, who, I swear to thee, has a skin as firm as thy own. I behold thee again, and find thee false. Tremble, then, and fear everything from a provoked wife."

Candide was quite stupefied at this affecting scene ; he had suffered Cunegund to depart without thinking of the proper measures which are always to be kept with those who know our secrets, when Cacambo presented himself to his sight. They embraced each other with tenderness. Candide informed him of the conversation he had just had ; he was very much afflicted for the loss of the great Pangloss, who, after having been hanged and burnt, was at last unhappily drowned. They spoke with that free effusion of heart which friendship inspires. A little billet thrown in at the window by Zenoida put an end to the conversation. Candide opened it, and found in it these words :—

" Fly, my dear lover ! All is discovered. An innocent inclination, which Nature authorizes, and which hurts no one, is a crime in the eyes of credulous and cruel men. Wolhall has just left my chamber, and has treated me with the utmost inhumanity. He is gone to obtain an order for thee to be clapped into a dungeon, there to perish. Fly, my ever dear lover! Preserve a life which thou canst not pass any longer near me. Those happy moments are no more in which we gave proofs of our reciprocal tenderness. Ah! sad Zenoida, how hast thou offended Heaven to merit so rigorous a fate? But I wander from the purpose. Remember always thy precious, dear Zenoida, and thou, my dear lover, shalt live eternally within my heart. Thou hast never thoroughly understood how much I loved thee. Canst thou receive upon my lips my last adieu? I find myself ready to join my unhappy father in the grave. The light is hateful to me; it serves only to reveal crimes."

Cacambo, always wise and prudent, drew Candide, who no longer was himself, along with him. They made the best of their way out of the city. Candide opened not his mouth, and they were already a good way from Copenhagen before he was roused out of that lethargy in which he was buried. At last he looked at his faithful Cacambo, and spoke in these terms.

CHAPTER XVII.

How Candide had a mind to kill himself, and did not do it. What happened to him at an inn.

"DEAR CACAMBO—formerly my valet, now my equal and always my friend—thou hast borne a share in my misfortunes; thou hast given me salutary advice; and thou hast been witness to my love for Miss Cunegund——" "Alas, my old master," says Cacambo, "it is she who has served you this scurvy trick; it is she who, after having learned from your fellow-servants that your love for Zenoida was as great as hers for you, revealed the whole to the barbarous Wolhall." "If this is so," says Candide, "I have nothing further to do but die." Our philosopher pulled out of his pocket a little knife, and began whetting it with a coolness worthy of an ancient Roman or an Englishman. "What

do you mean to do?" says Cacambo "To cut my throat,"
answers Candide. "A most noble thought!" replied
Cacambo. "But the philosopher ought not to take any resolution but upon reflection. You will always have it in your
power to kill yourself if your mind does not alter. Be advised by me, my dear master. Defer your resolution till
to-morrow. The longer you delay it the more courageous
will the action be." "I perceive the strength of thy reasoning," says Candide. "Besides, if I should cut my throat
immediately, the Gazetteer of Trevoux would insult my
memory. I am determined, therefore, that I will not kill
myself till two or three days hence." As they talked thus they
arrived at Elsinore, a pretty considerable town, not far from
Copenhagen. There they lay that night, and Cacambo
hugged himself for the good effect which sleep had produced
on Candide. They left the town at daybreak. Candide,
still the philosopher (for the prejudices of childhood are
never effaced), entertained his friend Cacambo on the subject of physical good and evil, the discourses of the sage
Zenoida, and the striking truths which he had learned from
her conversation. "Had not Pangloss been dead," said he,
"I should combat his system in a victorious manner. God
keep me from becoming a Manichæan! My mistress taught
me to respect the impenetrable veil with which the Deity
envelopes his manner of operating upon us. It is perhaps
man who precipitates himself into the abyss of misfortunes
under which he groans. Of a frugivorous animal he has
made himself a carnivorous one. The savages which we
have seen eat only Jesuits, and do not live upon bad terms
among themselves. These savages, if there be one scattered
here and there in the woods, only subsisting by acorns and
herbs, are, without doubt, still more happy. Society has
given birth to the greatest crimes. There are men in society
who are necessitated by their condition to wish the death of
others. The shipwreck of a vessel, the burning of a house,

and the loss of a battle, cause sadness in one part of society and give joy to another. All is very bad, my dear Cacambo, and there is nothing left for a philosopher but to cut his own throat with all imaginable calmness." " You are in the right," says Cacambo. " But I perceive an inn ; you must be very dry. Come, my old master ; let us drink one draught, and we will after that continue our philosophical disquisitions."

When they entered the inn they saw a company of country lads and lasses dancing in the midst of the yard to the sound of some wretched instruments. Gaiety and mirth sat in every countenance ; it was a scene worthy the pencil of Watteau. As soon as Candide appeared, a young woman took him by the hand and entreated him to dance. " My pretty maid," answered Candide, " when a person has lost his mistress, found his wife again, and heard that the great Pangloss is dead, he can have little or no inclination to cut capers. Moreover, I am to kill myself to-morrow morning ; and you know that a man who has but a few hours to live ought not to lose them in dancing." Cacambo, hearing Candide talk thus, addressed him in these terms : " A thirst for glory has always been the characteristic of great philosophers. Cato of Utica killed himself after having taken a sound nap ; Socrates drank the hemlock potion after discoursing familiarly with his friends ; many of the English have blown their brains out with a pistol after coming from an entertainment ; but I never yet heard of a great man who cut his own throat after a dancing bout. It is for you, my dear master, that this honour is reserved. Take my advice ; let us dance our fill, and we will kill ourselves to-morrow." " Have you not remarked," answered Candide, " this young country girl ? Is she not a very pretty brunette ? " " She has something very taking in her countenance," says Cacambo. " She has squeezed my hand," replied the philosopher. " Did you mind," says Cacambo, " how that in the hurry of the dance, her handkerchief falling aside, discovered a very pretty neck? I took particular notice of it." "Look you," said Candide, "had I not my heart filled with Miss Zenoida——" The little brunette interrupted him by begging him to take one dance with her. Our hero at length consented and danced with the best grace in the world. The dance finished, he kissed his smart country girl and retired to his seat, without calling out the queen of the ring. Upon this a murmuring arose; every one, as well performers as spectators, appeared greatly incensed at so flagrant a piece of disrespect. Candide never dreamed he had been guilty of any fault, and consequently did not attempt to make any reparation. A rude clown came up to him and gave him a blow with his fist upon the nose. Cacambo returns it to the peasant with a kick. In an instant the musical instruments are all broken; the girls loose their caps; Candide and Cacambo fight like heroes, but at length are obliged to take to their heels, after a very hearty drubbing.

"Everything is embittered to me," said Candide, giving his arm to his friend Cacambo; I have experienced a great many misfortunes, but I did not expect to be thus bruised to a mummy for my dancing with a country girl at her own request.

CHAPTER XVIII.

Candide and Cacambo go into an Hospital, and whom they meet with there.

CACAMBO and his old master were quite dispirited. They began to fall into that sort of malady of the mind which extinguishes all the faculties: they fell into a depression of spirits and despair, when they perceived an hospital which was built for strangers. Cacambo proposed going into it; Candide followed him. There they met with the most obliging reception and charitable treatment. In a little time they were cured of their wounds, but they caught the itch. The cure of this malady did not appear to be the work of a day, the idea of which filled the eyes of our philosopher with tears; and he said, scratching himself, "Thou wouldst not let me cut my throat, my dear Cacambo; thy misplaced counsels have brought me again into disgrace and misfortune; and yet, should I cut my throat now, it will be published in the Journal of Trevoux, and it will be said this man was a poltroon, who killed himself only for having the itch. See what thou hast exposed me to by the mistaken compassion thou hadst for my fate." "Our disasters are not without remedy," answered Cacambo. "If you will but please to listen to me, let us settle here as friars; I understand a little surgery, and I promise you to alleviate and render supportable our wretched condition." "Ah!" says Candide, "may all asses perish, and especially asses of surgeons, who are so dangerous to mankind. I will never suffer that thou shouldst give out thyself to be what thou art not. This is a treachery the consequences of which I dread. Besides, if thou didst but conceive how hard it is, after having been viceroy of a fine province, after having seen one's self rich enough to purchase kingdoms, and after having been the favourite lover of Zenoida, to resolve to serve in quality of friar in an hospital." "I conceive all that you say," replied Cacambo; "but I also conceive that it is very hard to die of hunger. Think, moreover, that the expedient which I propose to you is perhaps the only one which you can take to elude the inquiries of the bloody-minded Wolhall, and avoid the punishment which he is preparing for you."

One of the friars was passing along as they talked in this manner, they put some questions to him, to which he gave satisfactory answers. He assured them that the brothers wanted for nothing, and enjoyed a reasonable liberty. Candide thereupon determined to acquiesce with Cacambo's counsels. They took the habit together, which was granted them upon the first application; and our two poor adventurers now became underlings to those whose duty it was to perform the most servile offices.

One day as Candide was serving the patients with some wretched broth, an old man fixed his eye earnestly upon him. The visage of this poor wretch was livid, his lips were covered with froth, his eyes half turned in his head, and the image of death strongly imprinted on his lean and fallen cheeks. "Poor man," says Candide to him, "I pity you; your sufferings must be horrible." "They are very great indeed," answered the old man with a hollow voice like a ghost; "I am told that I am hectical, phthisicky, asthmatic, and poxed to the bone. If that be the case, I am indeed very ill; yet all does not go so badly, and this gives me comfort." "Ah!" says Candide, "none but Dr. Pangloss, in a case so deplorable, can maintain the doctrine of optimism when all others besides would preach up pessim——" "Do not pronounce that abominable word," cried the poor man; "I am the Pangloss you speak of. Wretch that I am, let me die in peace. All is well, all is for the best." The effort which he made in pronouncing these words cost him the last tooth, which he spat out with a great quantity of corrupted matter, and expired a very few moments after.

Candide lamented him greatly, for he had a good heart. His obstinate perseverance was a source of reflection to our philosopher; he often called to mind all his adventures. Cunegund remained at Copenhagen, he learned that she exercised there the occupation of a mender of old clothes with all possible distinction. The humour of travelling had quite left him. The faithful Cacambo supported him with his counsels and friendship. Candide did not murmur against Providence: "I know," said he at times, "that happiness is not the portion of man : happiness dwells only in the good country of El Dorado, where it is impossible for any one to go."

CHAPTER XIX.

New Discoveries.

CANDIDE was not so unhappy, as he had a true friend. He found in a mongrel valet what the world vainly look for in our quarter of the globe. Perhaps nature, which gives origin to herbs in America that are proper for the maladies of bodies on our continent, has also placed remedies there for the maladies of our hearts and minds. Possibly there are men in the New World of a quite different conformation from us, who are not slaves to personal interests, and are worthy to burn with the noble fire of friendship. How desirable would it be, that instead of bales of indigo and cochineal all covered with blood, some of these men were imported among us! This sort of traffic would be of vast advantage to mankind. Cacambo was of greater value to Candide than a dozen of red sheep loaded with the pebbles of El Dorado. Our philosopher began again to taste the pleasures of life. It was a comfort to him to watch for the conversation of the human species, and not to be a useless member of society. God blessed such pure intentions by giving him, as well as Cacambo, the enjoyment of health. They had got rid of the itch, and fulfilled with cheerfulness the painful functions of their station ; but fortune soon deprived them of the security which they enjoyed. Cunegund, who had set her heart upon tormenting her husband, left Copenhagen to follow his footsteps. Chance brought her to the hospital ; she was accompanied by a man whom Candide knew to be Baron Thunder-ten-tronckh. One may easily imagine what must have been his surprise. The Baron, who saw him, addressed him thus : " I did not tug long at the oar in the Turkish galleys ; the Jesuits heard of my misfortune, and redeemed me for the honour of their society. I have made a journey into Germany, where I received some favours from my father's heirs. I omitted nothing to find my sister; and having learned at Constantinople that she had sailed from thence in a vessel which was shipwrecked on the coasts of Denmark, I disguised myself. I took letters of recommendation to Danish merchants, who have correspondence with the society; and in fine, I found my sister, who still loves you, base and unworthy as you are of her regard; and since you have had the impudence to marry her, I consent to the ratification of the marriage, or rather a new celebration of it, with this express proviso—that my sister shall give you only her left hand, which is very reasonable, since she has seventy-one quarters, and you have never a one." "Alas!" says Candide, "all the quarters of the world without beauty—— Miss Cunegund was very ugly when I had the imprudence to marry her."

"Ungrateful man!" says Cunegund, with the most frightful contortions; "be persuaded, and relent in time. Do not provoke the Baron, who is a priest, to kill us both, to wash out his disgrace with our blood."

This discourse did not make much impression upon Candide. He desired a few hours to take his resolution how to proceed. The Baron granted him two hours, during which time he consulted his friend Cacambo. After having weighed the reasons *pro* and *contra*, they determined to follow the Jesuit and his sister into Germany. They accordingly left the hospital, and set out together on their travels, not on foot, but on good horses hired by the Baron. They arrive on the frontiers of the kingdom. A huge man, of a very villainous aspect, surveys our hero with close attention. "It is the very man," says he, casting his eyes at the same time upon a little bit of paper he had in his hand. "Sir, if I am not too inquisitive, is not your name Candide?" "Yes, sir; so I have always been called." "Sir, I flatter myself you are the very same. You have black eyebrows, eyes level with your head, ears not prominent, of a middling size, and a round, flesh-coloured visage ; to me you plainly appear to be five feet five inches high." "Yes, sir, that is my stature. But what have you to do with my ears and stature?" "Sir, we cannot use too much circumspection in our office. Permit me further to put one single question more to you : Have you not formerly been a servant to Lord Wolhall?" "Sir, upon my word," answered Candide, quite disconcerted, "I know nothing of what you mean." "May be so, sir. But I know for certain that you are the person whose description has been sent to me. Take the trouble, then, to go walk in the guard-house, if you please. Here, soldiers, take care of this gentleman. Get the black hole ready, and let the armourer be sent for to make him a pretty little set of fetters of about thirty or forty pounds weight. Mr. Candide, you have a good horse there. I am in want of such a one ; and I fancy he will answer my purpose. I shall make free with him."

The Baron was afraid to say the horse was his. They carried off poor Candide, and Miss Cunegund wept for a whole quarter of an hour. The Jesuit seemed perfectly unconcerned at this accident. "I should have been obliged to have killed him, or to have made him marry you over again," says he to his sister ; "and, all things considered, what has just happened is much the best for the honour of our family." Cunegund departed with her brother, and only the faithful Cacambo remained, who would not forsake his friend.

CHAPTER XX.

Consequence of Candide's Misfortune. How he found his Mistress again ; and the Fortune that happened to him.

"O PANGLOSS," said Candide, "what a pity it is you perished so miserably ! You have been witness only to a

part of my misfortunes; and I hoped to have prevailed on
you to forsake the ill-founded opinion which you maintained
to your last breath. No man ever suffered greater calamities
than I have done; but there is not a single individual who
has not cursed his existence, as the daughter of Pope Urban
warmly expressed herself. What will become of me, my dear
Cacambo?" "Faith, I cannot tell," said Cacambo; "all
I know is, that I will not forsake you." " But Miss Cunegund has forsaken me," says Candide. "Alas! a wife
is of far less value than a menial servant who is a true
friend."

Candide and Cacambo discoursed thus in the black-hole.
From thence they were taken out to be carried back to
Copenhagen. It was there that our philosopher was to
know his doom. He expected it to be dreadful, and our
readers doubtless expect so to; but Candide was mistaken,
as our readers will be likewise. It was at Copenhagen that
happiness waited to crown all his sufferings. He was hardly
arrived when he understood that Wolhall was dead. This
barbarian had no one to regret him, while everybody
interested themselves for Candide. His irons were knocked
off; and his enlargement gave him so much the more joy as
it was immediately followed by the sight of his dear Zenoida.
He flew to her with the utmost transport; they were a long
time without speaking a word; but their silence was infinitely more expressive than words. They wept; they
embraced each other; they attempted to speak, but tears
stopped their utterance. Cacambo was a pleased spectator
of this scene, so truly interesting to a sensible being; he
shared in the happiness of his friend, and was almost as
much affected as himself. "Dear Cacambo! adorable
Zenoida!" cried Candide; "you efface from my heart the
deep traces of my misfortunes. Love and friendship prepare for me future days of serenity and uninterrupted delight.
Through what a number of trials have I passed to arrive at

this unexpected happiness ! But they are all forgot. Dear Zenoida, I behold you once more; you love me ; everything is for the best in regard to me ; all is good in nature."

By Wolhall's death, Zenoida was left at her own disposal. The Court had given her a pension out of her father's fortune, which had been confiscated ; she shared it with Candide and Cacambo ; she appointed them apartments in her own house, and gave out that she had received several considerable services from these two strangers, which obliged her to procure them all the comforts and pleasures of life, and to repair the injustice which fortune had done them. There were some who saw through the motive of her beneficence ; which was no very hard matter to do, considering the great talk her connection with Candide had formerly occasioned. The greater part blamed her, and her conduct was only approved of by some few who knew how to reflect. Zenoida, who set a proper value on the good opinion even of fools, was nevertheless too happy to repent the loss of it. The news of the death of Miss Cunegund, which was brought by the correspondents of the Jesuit merchants in Copenhagen, procured Zenoida the means of conciliating the minds of people ; she ordered a genealogy to be drawn up for Candide. The author, who was a man of abilities in his way, derived his pedigree from one of the most ancient families in Europe ; he even pretended his true name was Canute, which was that of one of the former kings of Denmark ; which appeared very probable, as *dide* into *ute* is not such a great metamorphosis : and Candide by means of this little change, became a very great lord. He married Zenoida in public; they lived with as much tranquillity as it is possible to do. Cacambo was their common friend ; and Candide said often, " All is not so well as in El Dorado ; but all does not go so badly."

RASSELAS.

Rasselas.

CHAPTER I.

Description of a Palace in a Valley.

YE who listen with credulity to the whispers of fancy, and pursue with eagerness the phantoms of hope ; who expect that age will perform the promises of youth, and that the deficiencies of the present day will be supplied by the morrow, attend to the history of Rasselas, Prince of Abyssinia.

Rasselas was the fourth son of the mighty Emperor in whose dominions the father of waters begins his course— whose bounty pours down the streams of plenty, and scatters over the world the harvests of Egypt.

According to the custom which has descended from age to age among the monarchs of the torrid zone, Rasselas was confined in a private palace, with the other sons and daughters of Abyssinian royalty, till the order of succession should call him to the throne.

The place which the wisdom or policy of antiquity had destined for the residence of the Abyssinian princes was a spacious valley in the kingdom of Amhara, surrounded on every side by mountains, of which the summits overhang the middle part. The only passage by which it could be entered was a cavern that passed under a rock, of which it had long been disputed whether it was the work of nature

or of human industry. The outlet of the cavern was concealed by a thick wood, and the mouth which opened into
the valley was closed with gates of iron, forged by the artificers of ancient days, so massive that no man, without the
help of engines, could open or shut them.

From the mountains on every side rivulets descended
that filled all the valley with verdure and fertility, and
formed a lake in the middle, inhabited by fish of every
species, and frequented by every fowl whom nature has
taught to dip the wing in water. This lake discharged its
superfluities by a stream, which entered a dark cleft of the
mountain on the northern side, and fell with dreadful noise
from precipice to precipice till it was heard no more.

The sides of the mountains were covered with trees, the
banks of the brooks were diversified with flowers ; every
blast shook spices from the rocks, and every month dropped
fruits upon the ground. All animals that bite the grass or
browse the shrubs, whether wild or tame, wandered in this
extensive circuit, secured from beasts of prey by the mountains which confined them. On one part were flocks and
herds feeding in the pastures, on another all the beasts of
chase frisking in the lawns, the sprightly kid was bounding
on the rocks, the subtle monkey frolicking in the trees, and
the solemn elephant reposing in the shade. All the diversities of the world were brought together, the blessings of
nature were collected, and its evils extracted and excluded.

The valley, wide and fruitful, supplied its inhabitants with
all the necessaries of life, and all delights and superfluities
were added at the annual visit which the Emperor paid his
children, when the iron gate was opened to the sound of
music, and during eight days every one that resided in the
valley was required to propose whatever might contribute to
make seclusion pleasant, to fill up the vacancies of attention,
and lessen the tediousness of time. Every desire was immediately granted. All the artificers of pleasure were called to
gladden the festivity ; the musicians exerted the power of

harmony, and the dancers showed their activity before the princes, in hopes that they should pass their lives in blissful captivity, to which those only were admitted whose performance was thought able to add novelty to luxury. Such was the appearance of security and delight which this retirement afforded, that they to whom it was new always desired that it might be perpetual; and as those on whom the iron gate had once closed were never suffered to return, the effect of longer experience could not be known. Thus every year produced new scenes of delight, and new competitors for imprisonment.

The palace stood on an eminence, raised about thirty paces above the surface of the lake. It was divided into many squares or courts, built with greater or less magnificence according to the rank of those for whom they were designed. The roofs were turned into arches of massive stone, joined by a cement that grew harder by time, and the building stood from century to century, deriding the solstitial rains and equinoctial hurricanes, without need of reparation.

This house, which was so large as to be fully known to none but some ancient officers, who successively inherited the secrets of the place, was built as if Suspicion herself had dictated the plan. To every room there was an open and secret passage; every square had a communication with the rest, either from the upper stories by private galleries, or by subterraneous passages from the lower apartments. Many of the columns had unsuspected cavities, in which a long race of monarchs had reposited their treasures. They then closed up the opening with marble, which was never to be removed but in the utmost exigences of the kingdom, and recorded their accumulations in a book, which was itself concealed in a tower, not entered but by the emperor, attended by the prince who stood next in succession.

CHAPTER II.

The Discontent of Rasselas in the Happy Valley.

HERE the sons and daughters of Abyssinia lived only to know the soft vicissitudes of pleasure and repose, attended by all that were skilful to delight, and gratified with whatever the senses can enjoy. They wandered in gardens of fragrance, and slept in the fortresses of security. Every art was practised to make them pleased with their own condition. The sages who instructed them told them of nothing but the miseries of public life, and described all beyond the mountains as regions of calamity, where discord was always raging, and where man preyed upon man. To heighten their opinion of their own felicity, they were daily entertained with songs, the subject of which was the Happy Valley. Their appetites were excited by frequent enumerations of different enjoyments, and revelry and merriment were the business of every hour, from the dawn of morning to the close of the evening.

These methods were generally successful; few of the princes had ever wished to enlarge their bounds, but passed their lives in full conviction that they had all within their reach that art or nature could bestow, and pitied those whom nature had excluded from this seat of tranquillity as the sport of chance and the slaves of misery.

Thus they rose in the morning and lay down at night, pleased with each other and with themselves, all but Rasselas, who, in the twenty-sixth year of his age, began to withdraw himself from the pastimes and assemblies, and to delight in solitary walks and silent meditation. He often sat before tables covered with luxury, and forgot to taste the dainties that were placed before him; he rose abruptly in the midst of the song, and hastily retired beyond the sound of music. His attendants observed the change, and endeavoured to renew his love of pleasure. He neglected their officiousness, repulsed their invitations, and spent day after day on the banks of rivulets sheltered with trees, where he sometimes listened to the birds in the branches, sometimes observed the fish playing in the streams, and anon cast his eyes upon the pastures and mountains filled with animals, of which some were biting the herbage, and some sleeping among the bushes. The singularity of his humour made him much observed. One of the sages, in whose conversation he had formerly delighted, followed him secretly, in hope of discovering the cause of his disquiet. Rasselas, who knew not that any one was near him, having for some time fixed his eyes upon the goats that were browsing among the rocks, began to compare their condition with his own.

"What," said he, "makes the difference between man and all the rest of the animal creation? Every beast that strays beside me has the same corporal necessities with myself: he is hungry, and crops the grass; he is thirsty, and drinks the stream; his thirst and hunger are appeased; he is satisfied, and sleeps; he rises again, and is hungry; he is again fed, and is at rest. I am hungry and thirsty, like him, but when thirst and hunger cease, I am not at rest. I am, like him, pained with want, but am not, like him, satisfied with fulness. The intermediate hours are tedious and gloomy; I long again to be hungry, that I may again quicken the attention. The birds peck the berries or the corn, and fly away to the groves, where they sit in seeming happiness on the branches, and waste their lives in tuning one unvaried series of sounds. I likewise can call the lutist and the singer; but the sounds that pleased me yesterday weary me to-day, and will grow yet more wearisome to-morrow. I can discover in me no power of perception which is not glutted with its proper pleasure, yet I do not feel myself delighted. Man surely has some latent sense for which this place affords no gratification; or he has some desire distinct from sense, which must be satisfied before he can be happy."

After this he lifted up his head, and seeing the moon rising, walked towards the palace. As he passed through the fields, and saw the animals around him, " Ye," said he, " are happy, and need not envy me that walk thus among you, burdened with myself; nor do I, ye gentle beings, envy your felicity ; for it is not the felicity of man.   I have many distresses from which you are free ; I fear pain when I do not feel it; I sometimes shrink at evils recollected, and sometimes start at evils anticipated : surely the equity of Providence has balanced peculiar sufferings with peculiar enjoyments."

With observations like these the Prince amused himself as he returned, uttering them with a plaintive voice, yet with a look that discovered him to feel some complacence in his own perspicacity, and to receive some solace of the miseries of life from consciousness of the delicacy with which he felt and the eloquence with which he bewailed them.   He mingled cheerfully in the diversions of the evening, and all rejoiced to find that his heart was lightened.

CHAPTER III.

The Wants of him that Wants Nothing.

On the next day, his old instructor, imagining that he had now made himself acquainted with his disease of mind, was in hope of curing it by counsel, and officiously sought an opportunity of conference, which the Prince, having long considered him as one whose intellects were exhausted, was not very willing to afford.   " Why," said he, " does this man thus intrude upon me ? Shall I never be suffered to forget these lectures, which pleased only while they were new, and to become new again, must be forgotten ? "   He then walked into the wood, and composed himself to his usual meditations; when, before his thoughts had taken any settled form, he perceived his pursuer at his side, and was at first prompted by his impatience to go hastily away; but being unwilling to offend a man whom he had once reverenced and still loved, he invited him to sit down with him on the bank.

The old man, thus encouraged, began to lament the change which had been lately observed in the Prince, and to inquire why he so often retired from the pleasures of the palace to loneliness and silence. " I fly from pleasure," said the Prince, " because pleasure has ceased to please : I am lonely because I am miserable, and am unwilling to cloud with my presence the happiness of others." " You, sir," said the sage, "are the first who has complained of misery in the Happy Valley. I hope to convince you that your complaints have no real cause. You are here in full possession of all the Emperor of Abyssinia can bestow ; here is neither labour to be endured nor danger to be dreaded, yet here is all that labour or danger can procure or purchase. Look round and tell me which of your wants is without supply : if you want nothing, how are you unhappy ? "

" That I want nothing," said the Prince, " or that I know not what I want, is the cause of my complaint : if I had any known want, I should have a certain wish ; that wish would excite endeavour, and I should not then repine to see the sun move so slowly towards the western mountains, or to lament when the day breaks, and sleep will no longer hide me from myself. When I see the kids and the lambs chasing one another, I fancy that I should be happy if I had something to pursue. But, possessing all that I can want, I find one day and one hour exactly like another, except that the latter is still more tedious than the former. Let your experience inform me how the day may now seem as short as in my childhood, while nature was yet fresh, and every moment showed me what I never had observed before.

I have already enjoyed too much : give me something to desire." The old man was surprised at this new species of affliction, and knew not what to reply, yet was unwilling to be silent. "Sir," said he, "if you had seen the miseries of the world, you would know how to value your present state." "Now," said the Prince, "you have given me something to desire. I shall long to see the miseries of the world, since the sight of them is necessary to happiness."

CHAPTER IV.

The Prince continues to Grieve and Muse.

At this time the sound of music proclaimed the hour of repast, and the conversation was concluded. The old man went away sufficiently discontented to find that his reasonings had produced the only conclusion which they were intended to prevent. But in the decline of life, shame and grief are of short duration : whether it be that we bear easily what we have borne long ; or that, finding ourselves in age less regarded, we less regard others ; or, that we look with slight regard upon afflictions to which we know that the hand of death is about to put an end.

The Prince, whose views were extended to a wider space, could not speedily quiet his emotions. He had been before terrified at the length of life which nature promised him, because he considered that in a long time much must be endured : he now rejoiced in his youth, because in many years much might be done. The first beam of hope that had been ever darted into his mind rekindled youth in his cheeks, and doubled the lustre of his eyes. He was fired with the desire of doing something, though he knew not yet, with distinctness, either end or means. He was now no longer gloomy and unsocial ; but considering himself as master of a secret stock of happiness, which he could only enjoy by concealing it, he affected to be busy in all the schemes of diversion, and endeavoured to make others pleased with the state of which he himself was weary. But pleasures can never be so multiplied or continued as not to leave much of life unemployed ; there were many hours, both of the night and day, which he could spend without suspicion in solitary thought. The load of life was much lightened; he went eagerly into the assemblies, because he supposed the frequency of his presence necessary to the success of his purposes ; he retired gladly to privacy, because he had now a subject of thought. His chief amusement was to picture to himself that world which he had never seen, to place himself in various conditions, to be entangled in imaginary difficulties, and to be engaged in wild adventures ; but his benevolence always terminated his projects in the relief of distress, the detection of fraud, the defeat of oppression, and the diffusion of happiness.

Thus passed twenty months of the life of Rasselas. He busied himself so intensely in visionary bustle that he forgot his real solitude ; and amidst hourly preparations for the various incidents of human affairs, neglected to consider by what means he should mingle with mankind.

One day, as he was sitting on a bank, he feigned to himself an orphan virgin robbed of her little portion by a treacherous lover, and crying after him for restitution. So strongly was the image impressed upon his mind, that he started up in the maid's defence, and ran forward to seize the plunderer with all the eagerness of real pursuit. Fear naturally quickens the flight of guilt. Rasselas could not catch the fugitive with his utmost efforts ; but, resolving to weary by perseverance him whom he could not surpass in speed, he pressed on till the foot of the mountain stopped his course.

Here he recollected himself, and smiled at his own useless impetuosity. Then raising his eyes to the mountain, " This," said he, " is the fatal obstacle that hinders at once the enjoyment of pleasure and the exercise of virtue. How long is it that my hopes and wishes have flown beyond this boundary of my life, which yet I never have attempted to surmount?" Struck with this reflection, he sat down to muse, and remembered that since he first resolved to escape from his confinement, the sun had passed twice over him in his annual course. He now felt a degree of regret with which he had never been before acquainted. He considered how much might have been done in the time which had passed, and left nothing real behind it. He compared twenty months with the life of man. "In life," said he, "is not to be counted the ignorance of infancy or imbecility of age. We are long before we are able to think, and we soon cease from the power of acting. The true period of human existence may be reasonably estimated at forty years, of which I have mused away the four-and-twentieth part. What I have lost was certain, for I have certainly possessed it; but of twenty months to come, who can assure me?"

The consciousness of his own folly pierced him deeply, and he was long before he could be reconciled to himself. "The rest of my time," said he, "has been lost by the crime or folly of my ancestors, and the absurd institutions of my country; I remember it with disgust, yet without remorse: but the months that have passed since new light darted into my soul, since I formed a scheme of reasonable felicity, have been squandered by my own fault. I have lost that which can never be restored; I have seen the sun rise and set for twenty months, an idle gazer on the light of heaven; in this time the birds have left the nest of their mother, and committed themselves to the woods and to the skies; the kid has forsaken the teat, and learned by degrees to climb the rocks in quest of independent sustenance. I only have made no advances, but am still helpless and ignorant. The moon, by more than twenty changes, admonished me of the flux of life; the stream that rolled before my feet upbraided my inactivity. I sat feasting on intellectual luxury, regardless alike of the examples of the earth and the instructions of the planets. Twenty months are passed : who shall restore them ? "

These sorrowful meditations fastened upon his mind ; he passed four months in resolving to lose no more time in idle resolves, and was awakened to more vigorous exertion by hearing a maid, who had broken a porcelain cup, remark that what cannot be repaired is not to be regretted.

This was obvious ; and Rasselas reproached himself that he had not discovered it ; having not known, or not considered, how many useful hints are obtained by chance, and how often the mind, hurried by her own ardour to distant views, neglects the truths that lie open before her. He for a few hours regretted his regret, and from that time bent his whole mind upon the means of escaping from the Valley of Happiness.

CHAPTER V.

The Prince meditates his Escape.

HE now found that it would be very difficult to effect that which it was very easy to suppose effected. When he looked round about him, he saw himself confined by the bars of nature, which had never yet been broken, and by the gate through which none that once had passed it were ever able to return. He was now impatient as an eagle in a grate. He passed week after week in clambering the mountains, to see if there was any aperture which the bushes might conceal, but found all the summits inaccessible by their prominence. The iron gate he despaired to open, for it was not only secured with all the power of art, but was always watched by successive sentinels, and was, by its position, exposed to the perpetual observation of all the inhabitants.

He then examined the cavern through which the waters of the lake were discharged ; and, looking down at a time when the sun shone strongly upon its mouth, he discovered it to be full of broken rocks, which, though they permitted the stream to flow through many narrow passages, would stop any body of solid bulk. He returned, discouraged and dejected: but having now known the blessing of hope, resolved never to despair.

In these fruitless researches he spent ten months. The time, however, passed cheerfully away: in the morning he rose with new hope, in the evening applauded his own diligence, and in the night slept soundly after his fatigue. He met a thousand amusements, which beguiled his labour and diversified his thoughts. He discerned the various instincts of animals and properties of plants, and found the place replete with wonders, of which he proposed to solace himself with the contemplation, if he should never be able to accomplish his flight; rejoicing that his endeavours, though yet unsuccessful, had supplied him with a source of inexhaustible inquiry.

But his original curiosity was not yet abated: he resolved to obtain some knowledge of the ways of men. His wish still continued, but his hope grew less. He ceased to survey any longer the walls of his prison, and spared to search by new toils for interstices which he knew could not be found, yet determined to keep his design always in view, and lay hold on any expedient that time should offer.

CHAPTER VI.

A Dissertation on the Art of Flying.

AMONG the artists that had been allured into the Happy Valley, to labour for the accommodation and pleasure of its inhabitants, was a man eminent for his knowledge of the mechanic powers, who had contrived many engines both of use and recreation. By a wheel which the stream turned, he forced the water into a tower, whence it was distributed to all the apartments of the palace. He erected a pavilion in the garden, around which he kept the air always cool by artificial showers. One of the groves, appropriated to the ladies, was ventilated by fans, to which the rivulets that ran through it gave a constant motion ; and instruments of soft music were played at proper distances, of which some played by the impulse of the wind, and some by the power of the stream.

This artist was sometimes visited by Rasselas, who was pleased with every kind of knowledge, imagining that the time would come when all his acquisitions should be of use to him in the open world. He came one day to amuse himself in his usual manner, and found the master busy in building a sailing chariot. He saw that the design was practicable upon a level surface, and with expressions of great esteem solicited its completion. The workman was pleased to find himself so much regarded by the Prince, and resolved to gain yet higher honours. " Sir," said he, " you have seen but a small part of what the mechanic sciences can perform. I have been long of opinion that, instead of the tardy conveyance of ships and chariots, man might use the swifter migration of wings; that the fields of air are open to knowledge, and that only ignorance and idleness need crawl upon the ground."

This hint rekindled the Prince's desire of passing the mountains. Having seen what the mechanist had already performed, he was willing to fancy that he could do more ; yet resolved to inquire further before he suffered hope to afflict him by disappointment. " I am afraid," said he to the artist, "that your imagination prevails over your skill, and that you now tell me rather what you wish than what you know. Every animal has his element assigned him ; the birds have the air, and man and beasts the earth." "So," replied the mechanist, "fishes have the water, in which yet beasts can swim by nature and man by art. He that can swim needs not despair to fly ; to swim is to fly in a grosser fluid, and to fly is to swim in a subtler. We are only to proportion our power of resistance to the different density of matter through which we are to pass. You will be necessarily upborne by the air if you can renew any impulse upon it faster than the air can recede from the pressure."

"But the exercise of swimming," said the Prince, "is very laborious; the strongest limbs are soon wearied. I am afraid the act of flying will be yet more violent; and wings will be of no great use unless we can fly further than we can swim."

"The labour of rising from the ground," said the artist, "will be great, as we see it in the heavier domestic fowls; but as we mount higher the earth's attraction and the body's gravity will be gradually diminished, till we shall arrive at a region where the man shall float in the air without any tendency to fall; no care will then be necessary but to move forward, which the gentlest impulse will effect. You, sir, whose curiosity is so extensive, will easily conceive with what pleasure a philosopher, furnished with wings and hovering in the sky, would see the earth and all its inhabitants rolling beneath him, and presenting to him successively, by its diurnal motion, all the countries within the same parallel. How must it amuse the pendent spectator to see the moving scene of land and ocean, cities and deserts; to survey with equal security the marts of trade and the fields of battle; mountains infested by barbarians, and fruitful regions gladdened by plenty and lulled by peace. How easily shall we then trace the Nile through all his passages, pass over to distant regions, and examine the face of nature from one extremity of the earth to the other."

"All this," said the Prince, "is much to be desired, but I am afraid that no man will be able to breathe in these regions of speculation and tranquillity. I have been told that respiration is difficult upon lofty mountains; yet from these precipices, though so high as to produce great tenuity of air, it is very easy to fall; therefore I suspect that from any height where life can be supported, there may be danger of too quick descent."

" Nothing," replied the artist, " will ever be attempted if all possible objections must be first overcome. If you will favour my project, I will try the first flight at my own hazard. I have considered the structure of all volant animals, and find the folding continuity of the bat's wings most easily accommodated to the human form. Upon this model I shall begin my task to-morrow; and in a year expect to tower into the air beyond the malice and pursuit of man. But I will work only on this condition : that the art shall not be divulged, and that you shall not require me to make wings for any but ourselves."

" Why," said Rasselas, " should you envy others so great an advantage? All skill ought to be exerted for universal good ; every man has owed much to others, and ought to repay the kindness that he has received."

" If men were all virtuous," returned the artist, " I should with great alacrity teach them to fly. But what would be the security of the good if the bad could at pleasure invade them from the sky? Against an army sailing through the clouds, neither walls, mountains, nor seas, could afford security. A flight of northern savages might hover in the wind, and light with irresistible violence upon the capital of a fruitful region. Even this valley, the retreat of princes, the abode of happiness, might be violated by the sudden descent of some of the naked nations that swarm on the coast of the southern sea ! "

The Prince promised secrecy, and waited for the performance, not wholly hopeless of success. He visited the work from time to time, observed its progress, and remarked many ingenious contrivances to facilitate motion, and unite levity with strength. The artist was every day more certain that he should leave vultures and eagles behind him, and the contagion of his confidence seized upon the Prince. In a year the wings were finished; and on a morning appointed the maker appeared, furnished for flight, on a little promontory: he waved his pinions a while to gather air, then leaped from his stand, and in an instant dropped into the lake. His wings, which were of no use in the air, sustained him in the water; and the Prince drew him to land half dead with terror and vexation.

CHAPTER VII.

The Prince finds a Man of Learning.

THE Prince was not much afflicted by this disaster, having suffered himself to hope for a happier event only because he had no other means of escape in view. He still persisted in his design to leave the Happy Valley by the first opportunity.

His imagination was now at a stand; he had no prospect of entering into the world; and notwithstanding all his endeavours to support himself, discontent by degrees preyed upon him; and he began again to lose his thoughts in sadness when the rainy season, which in these countries is periodical, made it inconvenient to wander in the woods.

The rain continued longer and with more violence than had ever been known: the clouds broke on the surrounding mountains, and the torrents streamed into the plain on every side, till the cavern was too narrow to discharge the water. The lake overflowed its banks, and all the level of the valley was covered with the inundation. The eminence on which the palace was built, and some other spots of rising ground, were all that the eye could now discover. The herds and flocks left the pasture, and both the wild beasts and the tame retreated to the mountains.

This inundation confined all the princes to domestic amusements; and the attention of Rasselas was particularly seized by a poem, which Imlac rehearsed, upon the various

conditions of humanity. He commanded the poet to attend
him in his apartment, and recite his verses a second time;
then entering into familiar talk, he thought himself happy
in having found a man who knew the world so well, and
could so skilfully paint the scenes of life. He asked a
thousand questions about things, to which, though common
to all other mortals, his confinement from childhood had
kept him a stranger. The poet pitied his ignorance, and
loved his curiosity, and entertained him from day to day
with novelty and instruction, so that the Prince regretted the
necessity of sleep, and longed till the morning should renew
his pleasure.

As they were sitting together, the Prince commanded
Imlac to relate his history, and to tell by what accident he
was forced, or by what motive induced, to close his life in
the Happy Valley. As he was going to begin his narrative,
Rasselas was called to a concert, and obliged to restrain
his curiosity till the evening.

CHAPTER VIII.

The History of Imlac.

THE close of the day is, in the regions of the torrid zone,
the only season of diversion and entertainment, and it was
therefore midnight before the music ceased and the
princesses retired. Rasselas then called for his companion,
and required him to begin the story of his life.

" Sir," said Imlac, " my history will not be long: the life
that is devoted to knowledge passes silently away, and is
very little diversified by events. To talk in public, to think
in solitude, to read and to hear, to inquire and answer inquiries, is the business of a scholar. He wanders about the
world without pomp or terror, and is neither known nor
valued but by men like himself.

" I was born in the kingdom of Goiama, at no great dis-

tance from the fountain of the Nile. My father was a
wealthy merchant, who traded between the inland countries
of Africa and the ports of the Red Sea.   He was honest,
frugal, and diligent, but of mean sentiments and narrow
comprehension ; he desired only to be rich, and to conceal
his riches, lest he should be spoiled by the governors of the
province."

"Surely," said the Prince, "my father must be negligent
of his charge if any man in his dominions dares take that
which belongs to another.   Does he not know that kings
are accountable for injustice permitted as well as done ?   If
I were emperor, not the meanest of my subjects should be
oppressed with impunity.   My blood boils when I am told
that a merchant durst not enjoy his honest gains for fear of
losing them by the rapacity of power.   Name the governor
who robbed the people, that I may declare his crimes to the
Emperor ! "

"Sir," said Imlac, "your ardour is the natural effect of
virtue animated by youth.   The time will come when you
will acquit your father, and perhaps hear with less impatience
of the governor.   Oppression is, in the Abyssinian dominions,
neither frequent nor tolerated ; but no form of government
has been yet discovered by which cruelty can be wholly
prevented.   Subordination supposes power on one part and
subjection on the other ; and if power be in the hands of
men it will sometimes be abused.   The vigilance of the
supreme magistrate may do much, but much will still remain
undone.   He can never know all the crimes that are committed, and can seldom punish all that he knows."

"This," said the Prince, "I do not understand ; but I
had rather hear thee than dispute.   Continue thy narration."

"My father," proceeded Imlac, "originally intended that
I should have no other education than such as might qualify
me for commerce ; and discovering in me great strength
of memory and quickness of apprehension, often declared

his hope that I should be some time the richest man in Abyssinia."

"Why," said the Prince, "did thy father desire the increase of his wealth when it was already greater than he durst discover or enjoy? I am unwilling to doubt thy veracity, yet inconsistencies cannot both be true."

"Inconsistencies," answered Imlac, "cannot both be right; but, imputed to man, they may both be true. Yet diversity is not inconsistency. My father might expect a time of greater security. However, some desire is necessary to keep life in motion; and he whose real wants are supplied must admit those of fancy."

"This," said the Prince, "I can in some measure conceive. I repent that I interrupted thee."

"With this hope," proceeded Imlac, "he sent me to school. But when I had once found the delight of knowledge, and felt the pleasure of intelligence and the pride of invention, I began silently to despise riches, and determined to disappoint the purposes of my father, whose grossness of conception raised my pity. I was twenty years old before his tenderness would expose me to the fatigue of travel; in which time I had been instructed, by successive masters, in all the literature of my native country. As every hour taught me something new, I lived in a continual course of gratification; but as I advanced towards manhood, I lost much of the reverence with which I had been used to look on my instructors; because when the lessons were ended I did not find them wiser or better than common men.

"At length my father resolved to initiate me in commerce; and, opening one of his subterranean treasuries, counted out ten thousand pieces of gold. 'This, young man,' said he, 'is the stock with which you must negotiate. I began with less than a fifth part, and you see how diligence and parsimony have increased it. This is your own, to waste or to improve. If you squander it by negligence or caprice, you must wait for my death before you will be rich; if in four years you double your stock, we will thenceforward let subordination cease, and live together as friends and partners, for he shall be always equal with me who is equally skilled in the art of growing rich.'

"We laid out our money upon camels, concealed in bales of cheap goods, and travelled to the shore of the Red Sea. When I cast my eye on the expanse of waters, my heart bounded like that of a prisoner escaped. I felt an inextinguishable curiosity kindle in my mind, and resolved to snatch this opportunity of seeing the manners of other nations, and of learning sciences unknown in Abyssinia.

"I remembered that my father had obliged me to the improvement of my stock, not by a promise, which I ought not to violate, but by a penalty, which I was at liberty to incur; and therefore determined to gratify my predominant desire, and, by drinking at the fountain of knowledge, to quench the thirst of curiosity.

"As I was supposed to trade without connection with my father, it was easy for me to become acquainted with the master of a ship, and procure a passage to some other country. I had no motives of choice to regulate my voyage. It was sufficient for me that, wherever I wandered, I should see a country which I had not seen before. I therefore entered a ship bound for Surat, having left a letter for my father declaring my intention."

CHAPTER IX.

The History of Imlac (continued).

"WHEN I first entered upon the world of waters, and lost sight of land, I looked round about me in pleasing terror, and thinking my soul enlarged by the boundless prospect, imagined that I could gaze around me for ever without satiety; but in a short time I grew weary of looking on barren uniformity, where I could only see again what I had already seen. I then descended into the ship, and doubted for a while whether all my future pleasures would not end, like this, in disgust and disappointment. 'Yet surely,' said I, 'the ocean and the land are very different. The only variety of water is rest and motion. But the earth has mountains and valleys, deserts and cities; it is inhabited by men of different customs and contrary opinions; and I may hope to find variety in life, though I should miss it in nature.'

"With this thought I quieted my mind: and amused myself during the voyage, sometimes by learning from the sailors the art of navigation, which I have never practised, and sometimes by forming schemes for my conduct in different situations, in not one of which I have been ever placed.

"I was almost weary of my naval amusements when we safely landed at Surat. I secured my money, and purchasing some commodities for show, joined myself to a caravan that was passing into the inland country. My companions, for some reason or other, conjecturing that I was rich, and, by my inquiries and admiration, finding that I was ignorant, considered me as a novice whom they had a right to cheat, and who was to learn, at the usual expense, the art of fraud. They exposed me to the theft of servants and the exaction of officers, and saw me plundered upon false pretences, without any advantage to themselves but that of rejoicing in the superiority of their own knowledge."

"Stop a moment," said the Prince; "is there such depravity in man as that he should injure another without benefit to himself? I can easily conceive that all are pleased with superiority; but your ignorance was merely accidental, which, being neither your crime nor your folly, could afford them no reason to applaud themselves; and the knowledge which they had, and which you wanted, they might as effectually have shown by warning as betraying you."

"Pride," said Imlac, "is seldom delicate; it will please

itself with very mean advantages; and envy feels not its own happiness but when it may be compared with the misery of others. They were my enemies because they grieved to think me rich, and my oppressors because they delighted to find me weak."

" Proceed," said the Prince : " I doubt not of the facts which you relate, but imagine that you impute them to mistaken motives."

" In this company," said Imlac, " I arrived at Agra, the capital of Hindostan, the city in which the Great Mogul commonly resides. I applied myself to the language of the country, and in a few months was able to converse with the learned men ; some of whom I found morose and reserved, and others easy and communicative : some were unwilling to teach another what they had with difficulty learned themselves ; and some showed that the end of their studies was to gain the dignity of instructing.

'To the tutor of the young princes I recommended myself so much that I was presented to the Emperor as a man of uncommon knowledge. The Emperor asked me many questions concerning my country and my travels; and though I cannot now recollect anything that he uttered above the power of a common man, he dismissed me, astonished at his wisdom and enamoured of his goodness.

" My credit was now so high that the merchants with whom I had travelled applied to me for recommendations to the ladies of the Court. I was surprised at their confidence of solicitation, and greatly reproached them with their practices on the road. They heard me with cold indifference, and showed no tokens of shame or sorrow.

" They then urged their request with the offer of a bribe ; but what I would not do for kindness, I would not do for money, and refused them ; not because they had injured me, but because I would not enable them to injure others ; for I knew they would have made use of my credit to cheat those who should buy their wares.

"Having resided at Agra till there was no more to be learned, I travelled into Persia, where I saw many remains of ancient magnificence, and observed many new accommodations of life. The Persians are a nation eminently social, and their assemblies afforded me daily opportunities of remarking characters and manners, and of tracing human nature through all its variations.

' From Persia I passed into Arabia, where I saw a nation pastoral and warlike, who lived without any settled habitation, whose wealth is their flocks and herds, and who have carried on through ages an hereditary war with mankind, though they neither covet nor envy their possessions."

CHAPTER X.

Imlac's History (continued). A Dissertation upon Poetry.

" WHEREVER I went I found that poetry was considered as the highest learning, and regarded with a veneration somewhat approaching to that which man would pay to angelic nature. And yet it fills me with wonder, that in almost all countries the most ancient poets are considered as the best; whether it be that every other kind of knowledge is an acquisition gradually attained, and poetry is a gift conferred at once; or that the first poetry of every nation surprised them as a novelty, and retained the credit by consent which it received by accident at first; or whether, as the province of poetry is to describe nature and passion, which are always the same, the first writers took possession of the most striking objects for description and the most probable occurrences for fiction, and left nothing to those that followed them but transcription of the same events and new combinations of the same images. Whatever be the reason, it is commonly observed that the early writers are in possession of nature, and their followers of art; that the first excel in strength and invention, and the latter in elegance and refinement.

" I was desirous to add my name to this illustrious fraternity. I read all the poets of Persia and Arabia, and was able
to repeat by memory the volumes that are suspended in the
mosque of Mecca. But I soon found that no man was ever
great by imitation. My desire of excellence impelled me to
transfer my attention to nature and to life. Nature was to
be my subject, and men to be my auditors. I could never
describe what I had not seen. I could not hope to move
those with delight or terror whose interests and opinions I
did not understand.

" Being now resolved to be a poet, I saw everything with
a new purpose ; my sphere of attention was suddenly mag-
nified ; no kind of knowledge was to be overlooked. I
ranged mountains and deserts for images and resemblances,
and pictured upon my mind every tree of the forest and
flower of the valley. I observed with equal care the
crags of the rock and the pinnacles of the palace. Sometimes I wandered along the mazes of the rivulet, and sometimes watched the changes of the summer clouds. To a
poet nothing can be useless. Whatever is beautiful and
whatever is dreadful must be familiar to his imagination ;
he must be conversant with all that is awfully vast or
elegantly little. The plants of the garden, the animals of
the wood, the minerals of the earth, and meteors of the sky,
must all concur to store his mind with inexhaustible variety ;
for every idea is useful for the enforcement or decoration
of moral or religious truth, and he who knows most will
have most power of diversifying his scenes and of gratifying his reader with remote allusions and unexpected
instruction.

" All the appearances of nature I was therefore careful to
study, and every country which I have surveyed has contributed something to my poetical powers."

" In so wide a survey," said the Prince, " you must
surely have left much unobserved. I have lived till now
within the circuit of the mountains, and yet cannot walk

abroad without the sight of something which I had never beheld before, or never heeded."

"This business of a poet," said Imlac, "is to examine, not the individual, but the species; to remark general properties and large appearances. He does not number the streaks of the tulip, or describe the different shades of the verdure of the forest. He is to exhibit in his portraits of nature such prominent and striking features as recall the original to every mind, and must neglect the minuter discriminations, which one may have remarked and another have neglected, for those characteristics which are alike obvious to vigilance and carelessness.

"But the knowledge of nature is only half the task of a poet; he must be acquainted likewise with all the modes of life. His character requires that he estimate the happiness and misery of every condition, observe the power of all the passions in all their combinations, and trace the changes of the human mind, as they are modified by various institutions and accidental influences of climate or custom, from the sprightliness of infancy to the despondence of decrepitude. He must divest himself of the prejudices of his age and country; he must consider right and wrong in their abstracted and invariable state; he must disregard present laws and opinions, and rise to general and transcendental truths, which will always be the same. He must, therefore, content himself with the slow progress of his name, contemn the praise of his own time, and commit his claims to the justice of posterity. He must write as the interpreter of nature and the legislator of mankind, and consider himself as presiding over the thoughts and manners of future generations, as a being superior to time and place.

"His labour is not yet at an end. He must know many languages and many sciences, and, that his style may be worthy of his thoughts, must by incessant practice familiarize to himself every delicacy of speech and grace of harmony."

CHAPTER XI.

Imlac's Narrative (continued).   A Hint on Pilgrimage.

IMLAC now felt the enthusiastic fit, and was proceeding to aggrandize his own profession, when the Prince cried out : " Enough ! thou hast convinced me that no human being can ever be a poet.   Proceed with thy narration."

" To be a poet," said Imlac, " is indeed very difficult." "So difficult," returned the Prince, " that I will at present hear no more of his labours.   Tell me whither you went when you had seen Persia."

" From Persia," said the poet, " I travelled through Syria, and for three years resided in Palestine, where I conversed with great numbers of the northern and western nations of Europe ; the nations which are now in possession of all power and all knowledge, whose armies are irresistible, and whose fleets command th eremotest parts of the globe. When I compared these men with the natives of our own kingdom and those that surround us, they appeared almost another order of beings.   In their countries it is difficult to wish for anything that may not be obtained : a thousand arts, of which we never heard, are continually labouring for their convenience and pleasure ; and whatever their own climate has denied them is supplied by their commerce."

" By what means," said the Prince, " are the Europeans thus powerful ? or why, since they can so easily visit Asia and Africa for trade or conquest, cannot the Asiatics and Africans invade their coast, plant colonies in their ports, and give laws to their natural princes? The same wind that carries them back would bring us thither."

" They are more powerful, sir, than we," answered Imlac, "because they are wiser ; knowledge will always predominate over ignorance, as man governs the other animals. But why their knowledge is more than ours, I know not what reason can be given but the unsearchable will of the Supreme Being."

"When," said the Prince with a sigh, " shall I be able to visit Palestine, and mingle with this mighty confluence of nations? Till that happy moment shall arrive, let me fill up the time with such representations as thou canst give me. I am not ignorant of the motive that assembles such numbers in that place, and cannot but consider it as the centre of wisdom and piety, to which the best and wisest men of every land must be continually resorting."

"There are some nations," said Imlac, " that send few visitants to Palestine : for many numerous and learned sects in Europe concur to censure pilgrimage as superstitious, or deride it as ridiculous."

"You know," said the Prince, "how little my life has made me acquainted with diversity of opinions ; it will be too long to hear the arguments on both sides ; you, that have considered them, tell me the result."

"Pilgrimage," said Imlac, " like many other acts of piety, may be reasonable or superstitious, according to the principles upon which it is performed. Long journeys in search of truth are not commanded. Truth, such as is necessary to the regulation of life, is always found where it is honestly sought. Change of place is no natural cause of the increase of piety, for it inevitably produces dissipation of mind. Yet, since men go every day to view the fields where great actions have been performed, and return with stronger impressions of the event, curiosity of the same kind may naturally dispose us to view that country whence our religion had its beginning, and I believe no man surveys those awful scenes without some confirmation of holy resolutions. That the Supreme Being may be more easily propitiated in one place than in another, is the dream of idle superstition ; but that some places may operate upon our own minds in an uncommon manner, is an opinion which hourly experience will justify. He who supposes that his vices may be more successfully combated

in Palestine will perhaps find himself mistaken.; yet he may
go thither without folly: he who thinks they will be more
freely pardoned, dishonours at once his reason and religion."

"These," said the Prince, "are European distinctions. I
will consider them another time. What have you found to
be the effect of knowledge? Are those nations happier than
we?"

"There is so much infelicity," said the poet, "in the world,
that scarce any man has leisure from his own distresses to
estimate the comparative happiness of others. Knowledge
is certainly one of the means of pleasure, as is confessed by
the natural desire which every mind feels of increasing its
ideas. Ignorance is mere privation, by which nothing can
be produced; it is a vacuity in which the soul sits motion-
less and torpid for want of attraction; and, without knowing
why, we always rejoice when we learn, and grieve when we
forget. I am therefore inclined to conclude that if nothing
counteracts the natural consequence of learning, we grow
more happy as our minds take a wider range.

"In enumerating the particular comforts of life we shall
find many advantages on the side of the Europeans. They
cure wounds and diseases with which we languish and perish.
We suffer inclemencies of weather which they can obviate.
They have engines for the despatch of many laborious works,
which we must perform by manual industry. There is such
communication between distant places, that one friend can
hardly be said to be absent from another. Their policy
removes all public inconveniences: they have roads cut
through the mountains, and bridges laid over their rivers.
And, if we descend to the privacies of life, their habitations
are more commodious, and their possessions are more secure."

"They are surely happy," said the Prince, "who have all
these conveniences, of which I envy none so much as the
facility with which separated friends interchange their
thoughts."

"The Europeans," answered Imlac, "are less unhappy

than we, but they are not happy. Human life is everywhere a state in which much is to be endured and little to
be enjoyed."

CHAPTER XII.

The Story of Imlac (continued).

"I AM not willing," said the Prince, "to suppose that
happiness is so parsimoniously distributed to mortals ; nor
can I believe but that, if I had the choice of life, I should
be able to fill every day with pleasure. I would injure no
man, and should provoke no resentments : I would relieve
every distress, and should enjoy the benedictions of gratitude. I would choose my friends among the wise, and my
wife among the virtuous; and therefore should be in no
danger from treachery or unkindness. My children should
by my care be learned and pious, and would repay to my
age what their childhood had received. What would dare
to molest him who might call on every side to thousands
enriched by his bounty or assisted by his power? And
why should not life glide away in the soft reciprocation of
protection and reverence? All this may be done without
the help of European refinements, which appear by their
effects to be rather specious than useful. Let us leave
them, and pursue our journey."

"From Palestine," said Imlac, "I passed through many
regions of Asia ; in the more civilized kingdoms as a trader,
and among the barbarians of the mountains as a pilgrim.
At last I began to long for my native country, that I might
repose, after my travels and fatigues, in the places where I
had spent my earliest years, and gladden my old companions
with the recital of my adventures. Often did I figure to
myself those with whom I had sported away the gay hours
of dawning life, sitting round me in its evening, wondering
at my tales and listening to my counsels.

"When this thought had taken possession of my mind I

considered every moment as wasted which did not bring me
nearer to Abyssinia. I hastened into Egypt, and, notwithstanding my impatience, was detained ten months in the
contemplation of its ancient magnificence, and in inquiries
after the remains of its ancient learning. I found in Cairo
a mixture of all nations ; some brought thither by the love
of knowledge, some by the hope of gain, many by the desire
of living after their own manner without observation, and
of lying hid in the obscurity of multitudes : for in a city
populous as Cairo it is possible to obtain at the same time
the gratifications of society and the secrecy of solitude.

" From Cairo I travelled to Suez, and embarked on the
Red Sea, passing along the coast till I arrived at the port
from which I had departed twenty years before. Here I
joined myself to a caravan, and re-entered my native
country.

" I now expected the caresses of my kinsmen and the
congratulations of my friends ; and was not without hope
that my father, whatever value he had set upon riches,
would own with gladness and pride a son who was able to
add to the felicity and honour of the nation. But I was
soon convinced that my thoughts were vain. My father
had been dead fourteen years, having divided his wealth
among my brothers, who were removed to some other
provinces. Of my companions, the greater part was in the
grave ; of the rest, some could with difficulty remember me,
and some considered me as one corrupted by foreign
manners.

" A man used to vicissitudes is not easily dejected. I
forgot, after a time, my disappointment, and endeavoured
to recommend myself to the nobles of the kingdom : they
admitted me to their tables, heard my story, and dismissed
me. I opened a school, and was prohibited to teach. I
then resolved to sit down in the quiet of domestic life, and
addressed a lady that was fond of my conversation, but
rejected my suit because my father was a merchant.

"Wearied at last with solicitation and repulses, I resolved to hide myself for ever from the world, and depend no longer on the opinion or caprice of others. I waited for the time when the gate of the Happy Valley should open, that I might bid farewell to hope and fear : the day came ; my performance was distinguished with favour, and I resigned myself with joy to perpetual confinement."

"Hast thou here found happiness at last?" said Rasselas. "Tell me without reserve : art thou content with thy condition? or dost thou wish to be again wandering and inquiring? All the inhabitants of this valley celebrate their lot, and at the annual visit of the Emperor invite others to partake of their felicity."

"Great Prince," said Imlac, "I shall speak the truth : I know not one of all your attendants who does not lament the hour when he entered this retreat. I am less unhappy than the rest, because I have a mind replete with images, which I can vary and combine at pleasure. I can amuse my solitude by the renovation of the knowledge which begins to fade from my memory, and by recollection of the accidents of my past life. Yet all this ends in the sorrowful consideration that my acquirements are now useless, and that none of my pleasures can be again enjoyed. The rest, whose minds have no impression but of the present moment, are either corroded by malignant passions, or sit stupid in the gloom of perpetual vacancy."

"What passions can infest those," said the Prince, "who have no rivals? We are in a place where impotence precludes malice, and where all envy is repressed by community of enjoyments."

"There may be community," said Imlac, "of material possessions, but there can never be community of love or of esteem. It must happen that one will please more than another : he that knows himself despised will always be envious ; and still more envious and malevolent if he is condemned to live in the presence of those who despise him.

The invitations by which they allure others to a state which they feel to be wretched proceed from the natural malignity of hopeless misery. They are weary of themselves and of each other, and expect to find relief in new companions. They envy the liberty which their folly has forfeited, and would gladly see all mankind imprisoned like themselves.

" From this crime, however, I am wholly free. No man can say that he is wretched by my persuasion. I look with pity on the crowds who are annually soliciting admission to captivity, and wish that it were lawful for me to warn them of their danger."

"My dear Imlac," said the Prince, " I will open to thee my whole heart. I have long meditated an escape from the Happy Valley. I have examined the mountain on every side, but find myself insuperably barred : teach me the way to break my prison ; thou shalt be the companion of my flight, the guide of my rambles, the partner of my fortune, and my sole director in the *choice of life*."

"Sir," answered the poet, "your escape will be difficult, and perhaps you may soon repent your curiosity. The world, which you figure to yourself smooth and quiet as the lake in the valley, you will find a sea foaming with tempests and boiling with whirlpools ; you will be sometimes overwhelmed by the waves of violence, and sometimes dashed against the rocks of treachery. Amidst wrongs and frauds, competitions and anxieties, you will wish a thousand times for these seats of quiet, and willingly quit hope to be free from fear."

" Do not seek to deter me from my purpose," said the Prince. " I am impatient to see what thou hast seen ; and since thou art thyself weary of the valley, it is evident that thy former state was better than this. Whatever be the consequence of my experiment, I am resolved to judge with mine own eyes of the various conditions of men, and then to make deliberately my *choice of life*."

" I am afraid," said Imlac, " you are hindered by stronger restraints than my persuasions ; yet, if your determination is fixed, I do not counsel you to despair. Few things are impossible to diligence and skill."

CHAPTER XIII.

Rasselas discovers the Means of Escape.

THE Prince now dismissed his favourite to rest; but the narrative of wonders and novelties filled his mind with perturbation. He revolved all that he had heard, and prepared innumerable questions for the morning.

Much of his uneasiness was now removed. He had a friend to whom he could impart his thoughts, and whose experience could assist him in his designs. His heart was no longer condemned to swell with silent vexation. He thought that even the Happy Valley might be endured with such a companion, and that if they could range the world together, he should have nothing further to desire.

In a few days the water was discharged, and the ground dried. The Prince and Imlac then walked out together, to converse without the notice of the rest. The Prince, whose thoughts were always on the wing, as he passed by the gate said, with a countenance of sorrow, " Why art thou so strong, and why is man so weak ? "

" Man is not weak," answered his companion; "knowledge is more than equivalent to force. The master of mechanics laughs at strength. I can burst the gate, but cannot do it secretly. Some other expedient must be tried."

As they were walking on the side of the mountain they observed that the coneys, which the rain had driven from their burrows, had taken shelter among the bushes, and formed holes behind them, tending upwards in an oblique line. " It has been the opinion of antiquity," said Imlac, "that human reason borrowed many arts from the instinct of animals; let us therefore not think ourselves degraded by learning from the coney. We may escape by piercing the mountain in the same direction. We will begin where the summit hangs over the middle part, and labour upward till we shall issue out beyond the prominence."

The eyes of the Prince, when he heard this proposal, sparkled with joy. The execution was easy and the success certain.

No time was now lost. They hastened early in the morning to choose a place proper for their mine. They clambered with great fatigue among crags and brambles, and returned without having discovered any part that favoured their design. The second and the third day were spent in the same manner, and with the same frustration; but on the fourth they found a small cavern concealed by a thicket, where they resolved to make their experiment.

Imlac procured instruments proper to hew stone and remove earth, and they fell to their work on the next day with more eagerness than vigour. They were presently exhausted by their efforts, and sat down to pant upon the grass. The Prince for a moment appeared to be discouraged. "Sir," said his companion, "practice will enable us to continue our labour for a longer time. Mark, however, how far we have advanced, and ye will find that our toil will sometime have an end. Great works are performed not by strength, but perseverance; yonder palace was raised by single stones, yet you see its height and spaciousness. He that shall walk with vigour three hours a day will pass in seven years a space equal to the circumference of the globe."

They returned to their work day after day, and in a short time found a fissure in the rock, which enabled them to pass far with very little obstruction. This Rasselas considered as a good omen. "Do not disturb your mind," said Imlac, "with other hopes or fears than reason may suggest: if you are pleased with the prognostics of good, you will be terrified likewise with tokens of evil, and your whole life will be a prey to superstition. Whatever facilitates our work is more than an omen; it is a cause of success. This is one of those pleasing surprises which often happen to active resolution. Many things difficult to design prove easy to performance."

CHAPTER XIV.

Rasselas and Imlac receive an Unexpected Visit.

THEY had now wrought their way to the middle, and solaced their toil with the approach of liberty, when the Prince, coming down to refresh himself with air, found his sister Nekayah standing at the mouth of the cavity. He started, and stood confused, afraid to tell his design, and yet hopeless to conceal it. A few moments determined him to repose on her fidelity, and secure her secrecy by a declaration without reserve.

" Do not imagine," said the Princess, " that I came hither as a spy. I had long observed from my window that you and Imlac directed your walk every day towards the same point, but I did not suppose you had any better reason for the preference than a cooler shade or more fragrant bank, nor followed you with any other design than to partake of your conversation. Since, then, not suspicion but fondness has detected you, let me not lose the advantage of my discovery. I am equally weary of confinement with yourself, and not less desirous of knowing what is done or suffered in the world. Permit me to fly with you from this tasteless tranquillity, which will yet grow more loathsome when you have left me. You may deny me to accompany you, but cannot hinder me from following."

The Prince, who loved Nekayah above his other sisters, had no inclination to refuse her request, and grieved that he had lost an opportunity of showing his confidence by a voluntary communication. It was therefore agreed that she should leave the valley with them; and that in the meantime she should watch, lest any other straggler should, by chance or curiosity, follow them to the mountain.

At length their labour was at an end. They saw light

beyond the prominence, and issuing to the top of the mountain, beheld the Nile, yet a narrow current, wandering beneath them.

The Prince looked round with rapture, anticipated all the pleasures of travel, and in thought was already transported beyond his father's dominions. Imlac, though very joyful at his escape, had less expectation of pleasure in the world, which he had before tried and of which he had been weary.

Rasselas was so much delighted with a wider horizon that he could not soon be persuaded to return into the valley. He informed his sister that the way was now open, and that nothing now remained but to prepare for their departure.

CHAPTER XV.

The Prince and Princess leave the Valley, and see many Wonders.

THE Prince and Princess had jewels sufficient to make them rich whenever they came into a place of commerce, which, by Imlac's direction, they hid in their clothes, and on the night of the next full moon all left the valley. The Princess was followed only by a single favourite, who did not know whither she was going.

They clambered through the cavity, and began to go down on the other side. The Princess and her maid turned their eyes toward every part, and seeing nothing to bound their prospect, considered themselves in danger of being lost in a dreary vacuity. They stopped and trembled. " I am almost afraid," said the Princess, " to begin a journey of which I cannot perceive an end, and to venture into this immense plain, where I may be approached on every side by men whom I never saw." The Prince felt nearly the same emotions, though he thought it more manly to conceal them.

Imlac smiled at their terrors, and encouraged them to proceed. But the Princess continued irresolute till she had been imperceptibly drawn forward too far to return.

In the morning they found some shepherds in the field, who set some milk and fruits before them. The Princess wondered that she did not see a palace ready for her reception and a table spread·with delicacies ; but being faint and hungry, she drank the milk and ate the fruits, and thought them of a higher flavour than the products of the valley.

They travelled forward by easy journeys, being all unaccustomed to toil and difficulty, and knowing that, though they might be missed, they could not be pursued. In a few days they came into a more populous region, where Imlac was diverted with the admiration which his companions expressed at the diversity of manners, stations, and employments. Their dress was such as might not bring • upon them the suspicion of having anything to conceal ; yet the Prince, wherever he came, expected to be obeyed, and the Princess was frighted because those who came into her presence did not prostrate themselves. Imlac was forced to observe them with great vigilance, lest they should betray their rank by their unusual behaviour, and detained them several weeks in the first village to accustom them to the sight of common mortals.

By degrees the royal wanderers were taught to understand that they had for a time laid aside their dignity, and were to expect only such regard as liberality and courtesy could procure. And Imlac having by many admonitions prepared them to endure the tumults of a·port and the ruggedness of the commercial race, brought them down to the sea-coast.

The Prince and his sister, to whom everything was new, were gratified equally at all places, and therefore remained for some months at the port without any inclination to ·pass further. Imlac was content with their stay, because he did not think it safe to expose them, unpractised in the world, to the hazards of a foreign country.

At last he began to fear lest they should be discovered, and proposed to fix a day for their departure. They had no pretensions to judge for themselves, and referred the whole scheme to his direction. He therefore took passage in a ship to Suez, and, when the time came, with great difficulty prevailed on the Princess to enter the vessel. They had a quick and prosperous voyage, and from Suez travelled by land to Cairo.

CHAPTER XVI.

They enter Cairo, and find every Man happy.

As they approached the city, which filled the strangers with astonishment, " This," said Imlac to the Prince, " is the place where travellers and merchants assemble from all corners of the earth. You will here find men of every cha- racter and every occupation. Commerce is here honour- able. I will act as a merchant, and you shall live as strangers who have no other end of travel than curiosity; it will soon be observed that we are rich. Our reputation will procure us access to all whom we shall desire to know ; you shall see all the conditions of humanity, and enable yourselves at leisure to make your *choice of life.*"

They now entered the town, stunned by the noise and offended by the crowds. Instruction had not yet so pre- vailed over habit but that they wondered to see themselves pass undistinguished along the streets, and met by the lowest of the people without reverence or notice. The Princess could not at first bear the thought of being levelled with the vulgar, and for some time continued in her chamber, where she was served by her favourite Pekuah, as in the palace of the valley.

Imlac, who understood traffic, sold part of the jewels the next day, and hired a house, which he adorned with such magnificence that he was immediately considered as a merchant of great wealth. His politeness attracted many acquaintances, and his generosity made him courted by many dependants. His companions, not being able to mix in the conversation, could make no discovery of their ignorance or surprise, and were gradually initiated in the world as they gained knowledge of the language.

The Prince had by frequent lectures been taught the use and nature of money; but the ladies could not for a long time comprehend what the merchants did with small pieces of gold and silver, or why things of so little use should be received as an equivalent to the necessaries of life.

They studied the language two years, while Imlac was preparing to set before them the various ranks and conditions of mankind. He grew acquainted with all who had anything uncommon in their fortune or conduct. He frequented the voluptuous and the frugal, the idle and the busy, the merchants and the men of learning.

The Prince now being able to converse with fluency, and having learned the caution necessary to be observed in his intercourse with strangers, began to accompany Imlac to places of resort, and to enter into all assemblies, that he might make his *choice of life.*

For some time he thought choice needless, because all appeared to him really happy. Wherever he went he met gaiety and kindness, and heard the song of joy or the laugh of carelessness. He began to believe that the world overflowed with universal plenty, and that nothing was withheld either from want or merit; that every hand showered liberality and every heart melted with benevolence: "And who then," says he, "will be suffered to be wretched?"

Imlac permitted the pleasing delusion, and was unwilling to crush the hope of inexperience: till one day, having sat a while silent, "I know not," said the Prince, "what can be the reason that I am more unhappy than any of our friends. I see them perpetually and unalterably cheerful, but feel my own mind restless and uneasy. I am unsatisfied with those pleasures which I seem most to court. I live in the crowds of jollity, not so much to enjoy company as to shun myself, and am only loud and merry to conceal my sadness."

"Every man," said Imlac, "may by examining his own

mind guess what passes in the minds of others. When you feel that your own gaiety is counterfeit, it may justly lead you to suspect that of your companions not to be sincere. Envy is commonly reciprocal. We are long before we are convinced that happiness is never to be found, and each believes it possessed by others, to keep alive the hope of obtaining it for himself. In the assembly where you passed the last night there appeared such sprightliness of air and volatility of fancy as might have suited beings of a higher order, formed to inhabit serener regions, inaccessible to care or sorrow; yet, believe me, Prince, there was not one who did not dread the moment when solitude should deliver him to the tyranny of reflection."

"This," said the Prince, "may be true of others since it is true of me; yet, whatever be the general infelicity of man, one condition is more happy than another, and wisdom surely directs us to take the least evil in the *choice of life.*"

"The causes of good and evil," answered Imlac, "are so various and uncertain, so often entangled with each other, so diversified by various relations, and so much subject to accidents which cannot be foreseen, that he who would fix his condition upon incontestible reasons of preference must live and die inquiring and deliberating."

"But, surely," said Rasselas, "the wise men, to whom we listen with reverence and wonder, chose that mode of life for themselves which they thought most likely to make them happy."

"Very few," said the poet, "live by choice. Every man is placed in the present condition by causes which acted without his foresight, and with which he did not always willingly co-operate; and therefore you will rarely meet one who does not think the lot of his neighbour better than his own."

"I am pleased to think," said the Prince, "that my birth has given me at least one advantage over others by enabling me to determine for myself. I have here the world before

me. I will review it at leisure : surely happiness is somewhere to be found."

CHAPTER XVII.

The Prince associates with Young Men of Spirit and Gaiety.

RASSELAS rose next day, and resolved to begin his experiments upon life. " Youth," cried he, " is the time of gladness : I will join myself to the young men whose only
business is to gratify their desires, and whose time is all
spent in a succession of enjoyments."

To such societies he was readily admitted, but a few days
brought him back weary and disgusted. Their mirth was
without images, their laughter without motive; their pleasures
were gross and sensual, in which the mind had no part ;
their conduct was at once wild and mean—they laughed at
order and at law, but the frown of power dejected and the
eye of wisdom abashed them.

The Prince soon concluded that he should never be
happy in a course of life of which he was ashamed. He
thought it unsuitable to a reasonable being to act without a
plan, and to be sad or cheerful only by chance. " Happiness," said he, " must be something solid and permanent,
without fear and without uncertainty."

But his young companions had gained so much of his regard by their frankness and courtesy that he could not leave
them without warning and remonstrance. " My friends,"
said he, " I have seriously considered our manners and our
prospects, and find that we have mistaken our own interest.
The first years of man must make provision for the last. He
that never thinks, never can be wise. Perpetual levity must
end in ignorance, and intemperance, though it may fire the
spirits for an hour, will make life short or miserable. Let us
consider that youth is of no long duration, and that in
mature age, when the enchantments of fancy shall cease, and
phantoms of delight dance no more about us, we shall have

no comforts but the esteem of wise men and the means of doing good. Let us therefore stop while to stop is in our power : let us live as men who are some time to grow old, and to whom it will be the most dreadful of all evils to count their past years by follies, and to be reminded of their former luxuriance of health only by the maladies which riot has produced."

They stared awhile in silence one upon another, and at last drove him away by a general chorus of continued laughter.

The consciousness that his sentiments were just and his intention kind was scarcely sufficient to support him against the horror of derision. But he recovered his tranquillity and pursued his search.

CHAPTER XVIII.

The Prince finds a Wise and Happy Man.

As he was one day walking in the street he saw a spacious building which all were by the open doors invited to enter. He followed the stream of people, and found it a hall or school of declamation, in which professors read lectures to their auditory. He fixed his eye upon a sage raised above the rest, who discoursed with great energy on the government of the passions. His look was venerable, his action graceful, his pronunciation clear, and his diction elegant. He showed with great strength of sentiment and variety of illustration that human nature is degraded and debased when the lower faculties predominate over the higher; that when fancy, the parent of passion, usurps the dominion of the mind, nothing ensues but the natural effect of unlawful government, perturbation, and confusion ; that she betrays the fortresses of the intellect to rebels, and excites her children to sedition against their lawful sovereign. He compared reason to the sun, of which the light is constant, uniform, and lasting ; and fancy to a meteor, of bright but transitory lustre, irregular in its motion and delusive in its direction,

He then communicated the various precepts given from time to time for the conquest of passion, and displayed the happiness of those who had obtained the important victory, after which man is no longer the slave of fear nor the fool of hope ; is no more emaciated by envy, inflamed by anger, emasculated by tenderness, or depressed by grief; but walks on calmly through the tumults or privacies of life, as the sun pursues alike his course through the calm or the stormy sky.

He enumerated many examples of heroes immovable by pain or pleasure, who looked with indifference on those modes or accidents to which the vulgar give the names of good and evil. He exhorted his hearers to lay aside their prejudices, and arm themselves against the shafts of malice or misfortune, by invulnerable patience : concluding that this state only was happiness, and that this happiness was in every one's power.

Rasselas listened to him with the veneration due to the instructions of a superior being, and waiting for him at the door, humbly implored the liberty of visiting so great a master of true wisdom. The lecturer hesitated a moment, when Rasselas put a purse of gold into his hand, which he received with a mixture of joy and wonder.

"I have found," said the Prince at his return to Imlac, "a man who can teach all that is necessary to be known ; who, from the unshaken throne of rational fortitude, looks down on the scenes of life changing beneath him. He speaks, and attention watches his lips. He reasons, and conviction closes his periods. This man shall be my future guide : I will learn his doctrines and imitate his life."

"Be not too hasty," said Imlac, "to trust or to admire the teachers of morality : they discourse like angels, but they live like men."

Rasselas, who could not conceive how any man could reason so forcibly without feeling the cogency of his own arguments, paid his visit in a few days, and was denied admission. He had now learned the power of money, and made his way by a piece of gold to the inner apartment, where he found the philosopher in a room half darkened, with his eyes misty and his face pale. "Sir," said he, "you are come at a time when all human friendship is useless; what I suffer cannot be remedied, what I have lost cannot be supplied. My daughter, my only daughter, from whose tenderness I expected all the comforts of my age, died last night of a fever. My views, my purposes, my hopes are at an end: I am now a lonely being, disunited from society."

"Sir," said the Prince, "mortality is an event by which a wise man can never be surprised: we know that death is always near, and it should therefore always be expected." "Young man," answered the philosopher, "you speak like one that has never felt the pangs of separation." "Have you then forgot the precepts," said Rasselas, "which you so powerfully enforced? Has wisdom no strength to arm the heart against calamity? Consider that external things are naturally variable, but truth and reason are always the same." "What comfort," said the mourner, "can truth and reason afford me? Of what effect are they now, but to tell me that my daughter will not be restored?"

The Prince, whose humanity would not suffer him to insult misery with reproof, went away, convinced of the emptiness of rhetorical sounds, and the inefficacy of polished periods and studied sentences.

CHAPTER XIX.

A Glimpse of Pastoral Life.

He was still eager upon the same inquiry; and having heard of a hermit that lived near the lowest cataract of the Nile, and filled the whole country with the fame of his sanctity, resolved to visit his retreat, and inquire whether that felicity which public life could not afford was to be found in solitude, and whether a man whose age and virtue made him venerable could teach any peculiar art of shunning evils or enduring them.

Imlac and the Princess agreed to accompany him, and after the necessary preparations, they began their journey. Their way lay through the fields, where shepherds tended their flocks and the lambs were playing upon the pasture. "This," said the poet, "is the life which has been often celebrated for its innocence and quiet; let us pass the heat of the day among the shepherds' tents, and know whether all our searches are not to terminate in pastoral simplicity."

The proposal pleased them; and they induced the shepherds, by small presents and familiar questions, to tell the opinion of their own state. They were so rude and ignorant, so little able to compare the good with the evil of the occupation, and so indistinct in their narratives and descriptions, that very little could be learned from them. But it was evident that their hearts were cankered with discontent; that they considered themselves as condemned to labour for the luxury of the rich, and looked up with stupid malevolence towards those that were placed above them.

The Princess pronounced with vehemence that she would never suffer these envious savages to be her companions, and that she should not soon be desirous of seeing any more specimens of rustic happiness; but could not believe that all the accounts of primeval pleasures were fabulous, and was in doubt whether life had anything that could be justly preferred to the placid gratification of fields and woods. She hoped that the time would come when, with a few virtuous and elegant companions, she should gather flowers planted by her own hands, fondle the lambs of her own ewe, and listen without care, among brooks and breezes, to one of her maidens reading in the shade.

CHAPTER XX.

The Danger of Prosperity.

ON the next day they continued their journey till the heat compelled them to look round for shelter. At a small distance they saw a thick wood, which they no sooner entered than they perceived that they were approaching the habitations of men. The shrubs were diligently cut away to open walks where the shades were darkest; the boughs of opposite trees were artificially interwoven; seats of flowery turf were raised in vacant spaces; and a rivulet that wantoned along the side of a winding path had its banks sometimes opened into small basins, and its stream sometimes obstructed by little mounds of stone heaped together to increase its murmurs.

They passed slowly through the wood, delighted with such unexpected accommodations, and entertained each other with conjecturing what or who he could be that in those rude and unfrequented regions had leisure and art for such harmless luxury.

As they advanced they heard the sound of music, and saw youths and virgins dancing in the grove; and going still farther beheld a stately palace built upon a hill surrounded by woods. The laws of Eastern hospitality allowed them to enter, and the master welcomed them like a man liberal and wealthy.

He was skilful enough in appearances soon to discern that they were no common guests, and spread his table with magnificence. The eloquence of Imlac caught his attention, and the lofty courtesy of the Princess excited his respect. When they offered to depart, he entreated their stay, and was the next day more unwilling to dismiss them than before. They were easily persuaded to stop, and civility grew up in time to freedom and confidence.

The Prince now saw all the domestics cheerful and all the face of nature smiling round the place, and could not forbear to hope that he should find here what he was seeking; but when he was congratulating the master upon his possessions he answered with a sigh, "My condition has indeed the appearance of happiness, but appearances are delusive. My prosperity puts my life in danger; the Bassa of Egypt is my enemy, incensed only by my wealth and popularity. I have been hitherto protected against him by the princes of the country; but as the favour of the great is uncertain, I know not how soon my defenders may be persuaded to share the plunder with the Bassa. I have sent my treasures into a distant country, and upon the first alarm am prepared to follow them. Then will my enemies riot in my mansion, and enjoy the gardens which I have planted."

They all joined in lamenting his danger and deprecating his exile; and the Princess was so much disturbed with the tumult of grief and indignation that she retired to her apartment. They continued with their kind inviter a few days longer, and then went to find the hermit.

CHAPTER XXI.

The Happiness of Solitude. The Hermit's History.

THEY came on the third day, by the direction of the peasants, to the hermit's cell. It was a cavern in the side of a mountain, overshadowed with palm trees, at such a distance from the cataract that nothing more was heard than a gentle uniform murmur, such as composes the mind to pensive meditation, especially when it was assisted by the wind whistling among the branches. The first rude essay of nature had been so much improved by human labour that the cave contained several apartments appropriated to different uses, and often afforded lodging to travellers whom darkness or tempests happened to overtake.

The hermit sat on a bench at the door, to enjoy the coolness of the evening. On one side lay a book with pens and paper, on the other mechanical instruments of various kinds. As they approached him unregarded, the Princess observed that he had not the countenance of a man that had found or could teach the way to happiness.

They saluted him with great respect, which he repaid like a man not unaccustomed to the forms of Courts. "My children," said he, "if you have lost your way, you shall be willingly supplied with such conveniences for the night as this cavern will afford. I have all that nature requires, and you will not expect delicacies in a hermit's cell."

They thanked him; and, entering, were pleased with the neatness and regularity of the place. The hermit set flesh and wine before them, though he fed only upon fruits and water. His discourse was cheerful without levity, and pious without enthusiasm. He soon gained the esteem of his guests, and the Princess repented her hasty censure.

At last Imlac began thus: "I do not now wonder that your reputation is so far extended: we have heard at Cairo of your wisdom, and came hither to implore your direction for this young man and maiden in the *choice of life.*"

"To him that lives well," answered the hermit, "every form of life is good; nor can I give any other rule for choice than to remove all apparent evil."

"He will most certainly remove from evil," said the Prince, "who shall devote himself to that solitude which you have recommended by your example."

"I have indeed lived fifteen years in solitude," said the hermit, "but have no desire that my example should gain any imitators. In my youth I professed arms, and was raised by degrees to the highest military rank. I have traversed wide countries at the head of my troops, and seen many battles and sieges. At last, being disgusted by the preferments of a younger officer, and feeling that my vigour was beginning to decay, I resolved to close my life in peace, having found the world full of snares, discord, and misery. I had once escaped from the pursuit of the enemy by the shelter of this cavern, and therefore chose it for my final residence. I employed artificers to form it into chambers, and stored it with all that I was likely to want.

"For some time after my retreat I rejoiced like a tempest-beaten sailor at his entrance into the harbour, being delighted with the sudden change of the noise and hurry of war to stillness and repose. When the pleasure of novelty went away, I employed my hours in examining the plants which grow in the valley, and the minerals which I collected from the rocks. But that inquiry is now grown tasteless and irksome. I have been for some time unsettled and distracted: my mind is disturbed with a thousand perplexities of doubt and vanities of imagination, which hourly prevail upon me, because I have no opportunities of relaxation or diversion. I am sometimes ashamed to think that I could not secure myself from vice but by retiring from the exercise of virtue, and begin to suspect that I was rather impelled by resentment than led by devotion into solitude. My fancy riots in scenes of folly, and I lament that I have lost so much, and have gained so little. In solitude, if I escape the example of bad men, I want likewise the counsel and conversation of the good. I have been long comparing the evils with the advantages of society, and resolve to return into the world to-morrow. The life of a solitary man will be certainly miserable, but not certainly devout."

They heard his resolution with surprise, but after a short pause offered to conduct him to Cairo. He dug up a considerable treasure which he had hid among the rocks, and accompanied them to the city, on which, as he approached it, he gazed with rapture.

CHAPTER XXII.

The Happiness of a Life led according to Nature.

RASSELAS went often to an assembly of learned men, who met at stated times to unbend their minds and compare their opinions. Their manners were somewhat coarse, but their conversation was instructive, and their disputations acute, though sometimes too violent, and often continued till neither controvertist remembered upon what question he began. Some faults were almost general among them : every one was pleased to hear the genius or knowledge of another depreciated.

In this assembly Rasselas was relating his interview with the hermit, and the wonder with which he heard him censure a course of life which he had so deliberately chosen and so laudably followed. The sentiments of the hearers were various. Some were of opinion that the folly of his choice had been justly punished by condemnation to perpetual perseverance. One of the youngest among them, with great vehemence, pronounced him a hypocrite. Some talked of the right of society to the labour of individuals, and considered retirement as a desertion of duty. Others readily allowed that there was a time when the claims of the public were satisfied, and when a man might properly sequester himself, to review his life and purify his heart.

One, who appeared more affected with the narrative than the rest, thought it likely that the hermit would in a few years go back to his retreat, and perhaps, if shame did not restrain or death intercept him, return once more from his retreat into the world. " For the hope of happiness," said he, " is so strongly impressed, that the longest experience is not able to efface it. Of the present state, whatever it be, we feel and are forced to confess the misery ; yet when the same state is again at a distance, imagination paints it as desirable. But the time will surely come when desire will no longer be our torment, and no man shall be wretched but by his own fault.

" This," said a philosopher who had heard him with tokens of great impatience, " is the present condition of a wise man. The time is already come when none are wretched but by their own fault. Nothing is more idle than to inquire after happiness which nature has kindly placed within our reach. The way to be happy is to live according to nature, in obedience to that universal and unalterable law with which every heart is originally impressed; which is not written on it by precept, but engraven by destiny; not instilled by education, but infused at our nativity. He that lives according to nature will suffer nothing from the delusions of hope or importunities of desire; he will receive and reject with equability of temper; and act or suffer as the reason of things shall alternately prescribe. Other men may amuse themselves with subtle definitions or intricate ratiocination. Let them learn to be wise by easier means: let them observe the hind of the forest and the linnet of the grove: let them consider the life of animals, whose motions are regulated by instinct; they obey their guide, and are happy. Let us therefore at length cease to dispute, and learn to live: throw away the encumbrance of precepts, which they who utter them with so much pride and pomp do not understand, and carry with us this simple and intelligible maxim: that deviation from nature is deviation from happiness."

When he had spoken he looked round him with a placid air, and enjoyed the consciousness of his own beneficence.

"Sir," said the Prince with great modesty, "as I, like all the rest of mankind, am desirous of felicity, my closest attention has been fixed upon your discourse: I doubt not the truth of a position which a man so learned has so confidently advanced. Let me only know what it is to live according to nature."

"When I find young men so humble and so docile," said the philosopher, "I can deny them no information which my studies have enabled me to afford. To live according to nature is to act always with due regard to the fitness arising from the relations and qualities of causes and effects; to concur with the great and unchangeable scheme of universal felicity; to co-operate with the general disposition and tendency of the present system of things."

H

The Prince soon found that this was one of the sages whom he should understand less as he heard him longer. He therefore bowed and was silent ; and the philosopher, supposing him satisfied and the rest vanquished, rose up and departed with the air of a man that had co-operated with the present system.

CHAPTER XXIII.

The Prince and his Sister divide between them the Work of Observation.

RASSELAS returned home full of reflections, doubting how to direct his future steps. Of the way to happiness he found the learned and simple equally ignorant ; but as he was yet young, he flattered himself that he had time remaining for more experiments and further inquiries. He communicated to Imlac his observations and his doubts, but was answered by him with new doubts and remarks that gave him no comfort. He therefore discoursed more frequently and freely with his sister, who had yet the same hope with himself, and always assisted him to give some reason why, though he had been hitherto frustrated, he might succeed at last.

"We have hitherto," said she, " known but little of the world ; we have never yet been either great or mean. In our own country, though we had royalty, we had no power ; and in this we have not yet seen the private recesses of domestic peace. Imlac favours not our search, lest we should in time find him mistaken. We will divide the task between us ; you shall try what is to be found in the splendour of Courts, and I will range the shades of humbler life. Perhaps command and authority may be the supreme blessings, as they afford the most opportunities of doing good; or perhaps what this world can give may be found in the modest habitations of middle fortune—too low for great designs, and too high for penury and distress."

CHAPTER XXIV.

The Prince examines the Happiness of high Stations.

RASSELAS applauded the design, and appeared next day with a splendid retinue at the Court of the Bassa. He was soon distinguished for his magnificence, and admitted, as a Prince whose curiosity had brought him from distant countries, to an intimacy with the great officers and frequent conversation with the Bassa himself.

He was at first inclined to believe that the man must be pleased with his own condition whom all approached with reverence and heard with obedience, and who had the power to extend his edicts to a whole kingdom. "There can be no pleasure," said he, "equal to that of feeling at once the joy of thousands all made happy by wise administration. Yet, since by the law of subordination this sublime delight can be in one nation but the lot of one, it is surely reasonable to think that there is some satisfaction more popular and accessible, and that millions can hardly be subjected to the will of a single man, only to fill his particular breast with incommunicable content."

These thoughts were often in his mind, and he found no solution of the difficulty. But as presents and civilities gained him more familiarity, he found that almost every man who stood high in his employment hated all the rest and was hated by them, and that their lives were a continual succession of plots and detections, stratagems and escapes, faction and treachery. Many of those who surrounded the Bassa were sent only to watch and report his conduct: every tongue was muttering censure, and every eye was searching for a fault.

At last the letters of revocation arrived: the Bassa was carried in chains to Constantinople, and his name was mentioned no more.

"What are we now to think of the prerogatives of power?" said Rasselas to his sister: "is it without efficacy to good?

or is the subordinate degree only dangerous, and the supreme safe and glorious? Is the Sultan the only happy man in his dominions? or is the Sultan himself subject to the torments of suspicion and the dread of enemies?"

In a short time the second Bassa was deposed. The Sultan that had advanced him was murdered by the Janissaries, and his successor had other views or different favourites.

CHAPTER XXV.

The Princess pursues her Inquiry with more Diligence than Success.

THE Princess in the meantime insinuated herself into many families; for there are few doors through which liberality, joined with good humour, cannot find its way. The daughters of many houses were airy and cheerful; but Nekayah had been too long accustomed to the conversation of Imlac and her brother to be much pleased with childish levity and prattle which had no meaning. She found their thoughts narrow, their wishes low, and their merriment often artificial. Their pleasures, poor as they were, could not be preserved pure, but were embittered by petty competitions and worthless emulation. They were always jealous of the beauty of each other, of a quality to which solicitude can add nothing, and from which detraction can take nothing away. Many were in love with triflers like themselves, and many fancied that they were in love when in truth they were only idle. Their affection was not fixed on sense or virtue, and therefore seldom ended but in vexation. Their grief, however, like their joy, was transient; everything floated in their mind unconnected with the past or future, so that one desire easily gave way to another, as a second stone, cast into the water, effaces and confounds the circles of the first.

With these girls she played as with inoffensive animals, and found them proud of her countenance and weary of her company.

But her purpose was to examine more deeply, and her affability easily persuaded the hearts that were swelling with sorrow to discharge their secrets in her ear, and those whom hope flattered or prosperity delighted often courted her to partake their pleasure.

The Princess and her brother commonly met in the evening in a private summer-house on the banks of the Nile, and related to each other the occurrences of the day. As they were sitting together the Princess cast her eyes upon the river that flowed before her. "Answer," said she, "great father of waters, thou that rollest thy floods through eighty nations, to the invocations of the daughter of thy native king. Tell me if thou waterest through all thy course a single habitation from which thou dost not hear the murmurs of complaint."

"You are then," said Rasselas, not more successful in private houses than I have been in Courts." "I have, since the last partition of our provinces," said the Princess, "enabled myself to enter familiarly into many families, where there was the fairest show of prosperity and peace, and know not one house that is not haunted by some fury that destroys their quiet.

"I did not seek ease among the poor, because I concluded that there it could not be found. But I saw many poor whom I had supposed to live in affluence. Poverty has in large cities very different appearances. It is often concealed iu splendour and often in extravagance. It is the care of a very great part of mankind to conceal their indigence from the rest. They support themselves by temporary expedients, and every day is lost in contriving for the morrow.

"This, however, was an evil which, though frequent, I saw with less pain, because I could relieve it. Yet some have refused my bounties, more offended with my quickness to detect their wants than pleased with my readiness to succour them ; and others, whose exigences compelled them to admit my kindness, have never been able to forgive their benefactress. Many, however, have been sincerely grateful without the ostentation of gratitude or the hope of other favours."

CHAPTER XXVI.

The Princess continues her Remarks upon Private Life.

NEKAYAH, perceiving her brother's attention fixed, proceeded in her narrative.

" In families where there is or is not poverty there is commonly discord. If a kingdom be, as Imlac tells us, a great family, a family likewise is a little kingdom, torn with factions and exposed to revolutions. An unpractised observer expects the love of parents and children to be constant and equal. But this kindness seldom continues beyond the years of infancy ; in a short time the children become rivals to their parents. Benefits are allowed by reproaches, and gratitude debased by envy.

" Parents and children seldom act in concert; each child endeavours to appropriate the esteem or the fondness of the parents ; and the parents, with yet less temptation, betray each other to their children. Thus some place their confidence in the father and some in the mother, and by degrees the house is filled with artifices and feuds.

" The opinions of children and parents, of the young and the old, are naturally opposite, by the contrary effects of hope and despondency, of expectation and experience, without crime or folly on either side. The colours of life in youth and age appear different, as the face of nature in spring and winter. And how can children credit the assertions of parents which their own eyes show them to be false ?

" Few parents act in such a manner as much to enforce their maxims by the credit of their lives. The old man trusts wholly to slow contrivance and gradual progression ; the youth expects to force his way by genius, vigour, and precipitance. The old man pays regard to riches, and the youth reverences virtue. The old man deifies prudence ;

the youth commits himself to magnanimity and chance. The young man, who intends no ill, believes that none is intended, and therefore acts with openness and candour; but his father, having suffered the injuries of fraud, is impelled to suspect and too often allured to practise it. Age looks with anger on the temerity of youth, and youth with contempt on the scrupulosity of age. Thus parents and children for the greatest part live on to love less and less; and if those whom nature has thus closely united are the torments of each other, where shall we look for tenderness and consolation?"

"Surely," said the Prince, "you must have been unfortunate in your choice of acquaintance. I am unwilling to believe that the most tender of all relations is thus impeded in its effects by natural necessity."

"Domestic discord," answered she, "is not inevitably and fatally necessary; but yet it is not easily avoided. We seldom see that a whole family is virtuous: the good and the evil cannot well agree, and the evil can yet less agree with one another. Even the virtuous fall sometimes to variance, when their virtues are of different kinds and tending to extremes. In general, those parents have most reverence who most deserve it; for he that lives well cannot be despised.

"Many other evils infest private life. Some are the slaves of servants whom they have trusted with their affairs. Some are kept in continual anxiety by the caprice of rich relations, whom they cannot please and dare not offend. Some husbands are imperious, and some wives perverse; and, as it is always more easy to do evil than good, though the wisdom or virtue of one can very rarely make many happy, the folly or vice of one makes many miserable."

"If such be the general effect of marriage," said the Prince, "I shall for the future think it dangerous to connect my interest with that of another, lest I should be unhappy by my partner's fault."

"I have met," said the Princess, "with many who live
single for that reason; but I never found that their prudence ought to raise envy. They dream away their time
without friendship, without fondness, and are driven to rid
themselves of the day, for which they have no use, by
childish amusements or vicious delights. They act as beings
under the constant sense of some known inferiority, that fills
their minds with rancour and their tongues with censure.
They are peevish at home and malevolent abroad ; and, as
the outlaws of human nature, make it their business and
their pleasure to disturb that society which debars them from
its privileges. To live without feeling or exciting sympathy,
to be fortunate without adding to the felicity of others, or
afflicted without tasting the balm of pity, is a state more
gloomy than solitude ; it is not retreat but exclusion from
mankind. Marriage has many pains, but celibacy has no
pleasures."

"What then is to be done?" said Rasselas. "The more
we inquire the less we can resolve. Surely he is most
likely to please himself that has no other inclination to
regard."

CHAPTER XXVII.

Disquisition upon Greatness.

THE conversation had a short pause. The Prince, having
considered his sister's observation, told her that she had
surveyed life with prejudice, and supposed misery where she
did not find it. "Your narrative," says he, "throws yet a
darker gloom upon the prospects of futurity. The predic-
tions of Imlac were but faint sketches of the evils painted by
Nekayah. I have been lately convinced that quiet is not
the daughter of grandeur or of power ; that her presence is
not to be bought by wealth nor enforced by conquest. It
is evident that as any man acts in a wider compass, he must
be more exposed to opposition from enmity, or miscarriage
from chance. Whoever has many to please or to govern

must use the ministry of many agents, some of wnom will be wicked and some ignorant ; by some he will be misled and by others betrayed. If he gratifies one, he will offend another; those that are not favoured will think themselves injured ; and since favours can be conferred but upon few, the greater number will be always discontented."

"The discontent," said the Princess, "which is thus unreasonable, I hope that I shall always have spirit to despise and you power to repress."

"Discontent," answered Rasselas, will not always be without reason under the most just and vigilant administration of public affairs. None, however attentive, can always discover that merit which indigence or faction may happen to obscure ; and none, however powerful, can always reward it. Yet, he that sees inferior desert advanced above him will naturally impute that preference to partiality or caprice, and indeed it can scarcely he hoped that any man, however magnanimous by nature or exalted by condition, will be able to persist for ever in fixed and inexorable justice of distribution ; he will sometimes indulge his own affections, and sometimes those of his favourites; he will permit some to please him who can never serve him ; he will discover in those whom he loves qualities which in reality they do not possess ; and to those from whom he receives pleasure he will in his turn endeavour to give it. Thus will recommendations sometimes prevail which were purchased by money, or by the more destructive bribery of flattery and servility.

" He that hath much to do will do something wrong, and of that wrong must suffer the consequences ; and if it were · possible that he should always act rightly, yet when such numbers are to judge of his conduct, the bad will censure and obstruct him by malevolence, and the good sometimes by mistake.

"The highest stations cannot therefore hope to be the abodes of happiness, which I would willingly believe to have fled from thrones and palaces to seats of humble privacy and placid obscurity.   For what can hinder the satisfaction or intercept the expectations of him whose abilities are adequate to his employments, who sees with his own eyes the whole circuit of his influence, who chooses by his own knowledge all whom he trusts, and whom none are tempted to deceive by hope or fear?   Surely he has nothing to do but to love and to be loved, to be virtuous and to be happy."

" Whether perfect happiness would be procured by perfect goodness," said Nekayah, " this world will never afford an opportunity of deciding.   But this, at least, may be maintained, that we do not always find visible happiness in proportion to visible virtue.   All natural and almost all political evils are incident alike to the bad and good : they are confounded in the misery of a famine, and not much distinguished in the fury of a faction ; they sink together in a tempest, and are driven together from their country by invaders.   All that virtue can afford is quietness of conscience, and a steady prospect of a happier state : this may enable us to endure calamity with patience, but remember that patience must suppose pain."

CHAPTER XXVIII.

Rasselas and Nekayah continue their Conversation.

" DEAR PRINCESS," said Rasselas, "you fall into the common errors of exaggeratory declamation, by producing in a familiar disquisition examples of national calamities and scenes of extensive misery which are found in books rather than in the world, and which, as they are horrid, are ordained to be rare.   Let us not imagine evils which we do not feel, nor injure life by misrepresentations.   I cannot bear that querulous eloquence which threatens every city with a siege like that of Jerusalem, that makes famine attend on every flight of locusts, and suspends pestilence on the wing of every blast that issues from the south.

" On necessary and inevitable evils which overwhelm kingdoms at once, all disputation is vain : when they happen they must be endured. But it is evident that these bursts of universal distress are more dreaded than felt : thousands and tens of thousands flourish in youth and wither in age, without the knowledge of any other than domestic evils, and share the same pleasures and vexations, whether their kings are mild or cruel, whether the armies of their country pursue their enemies or retreat before them. While courts are disturbed with intestine competitions, and ambassadors are negotiating in foreign countries, the smith still plies his anvil, and the husbandman drives his plough forward; the necessaries of life are required and obtained, and the successive business of the season continues to make its wonted revolutions.

" Let us cease to consider what perhaps may never happen, and what, when it shall happen, will laugh at human speculation. We will not endeavour to modify the motions of the elements or to fix the destiny of kingdoms. It is our business to consider what beings like us may perform, each labouring for his own happiness, by promoting within his circle, however narrow, the happiness of others.

" Marriage is evidently the dictate of nature ; men and women were made to be the companions of each other ; and therefore I cannot be persuaded but that marriage is one of the means of happiness."

" I know not," said the Princess, " whether marriage be more than one of the innumerable modes of human misery. When I see and reckon the various forms of connubial infelicity, the unexpected causes of lasting discord, the diversities of temper, the oppositions of opinion, the rude collisions of contrary desire where both are urged by violent impulses, the obstinate contest of disagreeing virtues where both are supported by consciousness of good intention, I am sometimes disposed to think, with the severer casuists of most nations, that marriage is rather permitted than approved, and that none, but by the instigation of a passion too much indulged, entangle themselves with indissoluble compact."

"You seem to forget," replied Rasselas, "that you have, even now, represented celibacy as less happy than marriage. Both conditions may be bad, but they cannot both be worse. Thus it happens, when wrong opinions are entertained, that they mutually destroy each other, and leave the mind open to truth."

"I did not expect," answered the Princess, "to hear that imputed to falsehood which is the consequence only of frailty. To the mind, as to the eye, it is difficult to compare with exactness objects vast in their extent and various in their parts. When we see or conceive the whole at once, we readily note the discriminations and decide the preference; but of two systems, of which neither can be surveyed by any human being in its full compass of magnitude and multiplicity of complication, where is the wonder that, judging of the whole by parts, I am alternately affected by one and the other as either presses on my memory or fancy? We differ from ourselves just as we differ from each other when we see only part of the question, as in the multifarious relations of politics and morality; but when we perceive the whole at once, as in numerical computations, all agree in one judgment, and none ever varies in his opinion."

"Let us not add," said the Prince, "to the other evils of life the bitterness of controversy, nor endeavour to vie with each other in subtilties of argument. We are employed in a search of which both are equally to enjoy the success or suffer by the miscarriage; it is therefore fit that we assist each other. You surely conclude too hastily from the infelicity of marriage against its institution; will not the misery of life prove equally that life cannot be the gift of Heaven? The world must be peopled by marriage or peopled without it."

"How the world is to be peopled," returned Nekayah,

"is not my care, and need not be yours. I see no danger that the present generation should omit to leave successors behind them; we are not now inquiring for the world, but for ourselves."

CHAPTER XXIX.

The Debate on Marriage (continued).

"THE good of the whole," says Rasselas, "is the same with the good of all its parts. If marriage be best for mankind, it must be evidently best for individuals; or a permanent and necessary duty must be the cause of evil, and some must be inevitably sacrificed to the convenience of others. In the estimate which you have made of the two states it appears that the incommodities of a single life are in a great measure necessary and certain, but those of the conjugal state accidental and avoidable. I cannot forbear to flatter myself that prudence and benevolence will make marriage happy. The general folly of mankind is the cause of general complaint. What can be expected but disappointment and repentance from a choice made in the immaturity of youth, in the ardour of desire, without judgment, without foresight, without inquiry after conformity of opinions, similarity of manners, rectitude of judgment, or purity of sentiment?

"Such is the common process of marriage. A youth and maiden, meeting by chance or brought together by artifice, exchange glances, reciprocate civilities, go home and dream of one another. Having little to divert attention or diversify thought, they find themselves uneasy when they are apart, and therefore conclude that they shall be happy together. They marry, and discover what nothing but voluntary blindness before had concealed; they wear out life in altercations, and charge nature with cruelty.

" From those early marriages proceeds likewise the rivalry of parents and children: the son is eager to enjoy the world before the father is willing to forsake it, and there is hardly room at once for two generations. The daughter begins to bloom before the mother can be content to fade, and neither can forbear to wish for the absence of the other.

"Surely all these evils may be avoided by that deliberation and delay which prudence prescribes to irrevocable choice. In the variety and jollity of youthful pleasures, life may be well enough supported without the help of a partner. Longer time will increase experience, and wider views will allow better opportunities of inquiry and selection : one ad· vantage at least will be certain, the parents will be visibly older than their children."

" What reason cannot collect," said Nekayah, " and what experiment has not yet taught, can be known only from the report of others. I have been told that late marriages are not eminently happy. This is a question too important to be neglected ; and I have often proposed it to those whose accuracy of remark and comprehensiveness of knowledge made their suffrages worthy of regard. They have generally determined that it is dangerous for a man and woman to suspend their fate upon each other at a time when opinions are fixed and habits are established, when friendships have been contracted on both sides, when life has been planned into method, and the mind has long enjoyed the contemplation of its own prospects.

"It is scarcely possible that two travelling through the world under the conduct of chance should have been both directed to the same path, and it will not often happen that either will quit the track which custom has made pleasing. When the desultory levity of youth has settled into regularity, it is soon succeeded by pride ashamed to yield, or obstinacy delighting to contend. And even though mutual esteem produces mutual desire to please, time itself, as it modifies unchangeably the external mien, determines likewise the direction of the passions and gives an inflexible rigidity to the manners. Long customs are not easily broken ; he that attempts to change the course of his own life very often labours in vain, and how shall we do that for others which we are seldom able to do for ourselves?"

"But surely," interposed the Prince, "you suppose the chief motive of choice forgotten or neglected. Whenever I shall seek a wife, it shall be my first question whether she be willing to be led by reason?"

"Thus it is," said Nekayah, "that philosophers are deceived. There are a thousand familiar disputes which reason never can decide; questions that elude investigation, and make logic ridiculous; cases where something must be done, and where little can be said. Consider the state of mankind, and inquire how few can be supposed to act upon any occasions, whether small or great, with all the reasons of action present to their minds. Wretched would be the pair, above all names of wretchedness, who should be doomed to adjust by reason, every morning, all the minute details of a domestic day.

"Those who marry at an advanced age will probably escape the encroachments of their children, but in the diminution of this advantage they will be likely to leave them, ignorant and helpless, to a guardian's mercy; or if that should not happen, they must at least go out of the world before they see those whom they love best either wise or great.

"From their children, if they have less to fear, they have less also to hope; and they lose without equivalent the joys of early love, and the convenience of uniting with manners pliant and minds susceptible of new impressions, which might wear away their dissimilitudes by long cohabitation, as soft bodies by continual attrition conform their surfaces to each other.

"I believe it will be found that those who marry late are best pleased with their children, and those who marry early with their partners."

"The union of these two affections," said Rasselas, "would produce all that could be wished. Perhaps there is a time when marriage might unite them—a time neither too early for the father nor too late for the husband."

" Every hour," answered the Princess, "confirms my prejudice in favour of the position so often uttered by the mouth of Imlac, that 'Nature sets her gifts on the right hand and on the left.' Those conditions which flatter hope and attract desire are so constituted that as we approach one we recede from another. There are goods so opposed that we cannot seize both, but by too much prudence may pass between them at too great a distance to reach either. This is often the fate of long consideration : he does nothing who endeavours to do more than is allowed to humanity. Flatter not yourself with contrarieties of pleasure. Of the blessings set before you make your choice, and be content. No man can taste the fruits of autumn while he is delighting his scent with the flowers of the spring ; no man can at the same time fill his cup from the source and from the mouth of the Nile."

CHAPTER XXX.

Imlac enters, and changes the Conversation.

HERE Imlac entered, and interrupted them. " Imlac," said Rasselas, " I have been taking from the Princess the dismal history of private life, and am almost discouraged from further search."

" It seems to me," said Imlac, "that while you are making the choice of life you neglect to live. You wander about a single city, which, however large and diversified, can now afford few novelties, and forget that you are in a country famous among the earliest monarchies for the power and wisdom of its inhabitants ; a country where the sciences first dawned that illuminate the world, and beyond which the arts cannot be traced of civil society or domestic life.

"The old Egyptians have left behind them monuments of industry and power before which all European magnificence is confessed to fade away. The ruins of their architecture

are the schools of modern builders, and from the wonders
which time has spared we may conjecture, though uncer-
tainly, what it has destroyed."

" My curiosity," said Rasselas, "does not very strongly
lead me to survey piles of stone or mounds of earth. My
business is with man. I came hither, not to measure frag-
ments of temples or trace choked aqueducts, but to look
upon the various scenes of the present world."

" The things that are now before us," said the Princess,
require attention, and deserve it. What have I to do with
the heroes or the monuments of ancient times—with times
which can never return, and heroes whose form of life was
different from all that the present condition of mankind
requires or allows ? "

" To know anything," returned the poet, " we must know
its effects; to see men, we must see their works, that we
may learn what reason has dictated or passion has excited,
and find what are the most powerful motives of action. To
judge rightly of the present, we must oppose it to the past ;
for all judgment is comparative, and of the future nothing
can be known. The truth is, that no mind is much employed
upon the present : recollection and anticipation fill up almost
all our moments. Our passions are joy and grief, love and
hatred, hope and fear. Of joy and grief the past is the
object ; and the future, of hope and fear : even love and
hatred respect the past, for the cause must have been before
the effect.

" The present state of things is the consequence of the
former ; and it is natural to inquire what were the sources
of the good that we enjoy, or the evils that we suffer. If
we act only for ourselves, to neglect the study of history is
not prudent. If we are entrusted with the care of others, it
is not just. Ignorance, when it is voluntary, is criminal ;
and he may properly be charged with evil who refused to
learn how he might prevent it.

" There is no part of history so generally useful as that

which relates to the progress of the human mind, the gradual improvement of reason, the successive advances of science, the vicissitudes of learning and ignorance, which are the light and darkness of thinking beings, the extinction and resuscitation of arts, and the revolutions of the intellectual world. If accounts of battles and invasions are peculiarly the business of princes, the useful or elegant arts are not to be neglected ; those who have kingdoms to govern have understandings to cultivate.

" Example is always more efficacious than precept. A soldier is formed in war, and a painter must copy pictures. In this, contemplative life has the advantage. Great actions are seldom seen, but the labours of art are always at hand for those who desire to· know what art has been able to perform.

"When the eye or the imagination is struck with any uncommon work, the next transition of an active mind is to the means by which it was performed. Here begins the true use of such contemplation. We enlarge our comprehension by new ideas, and perhaps recover some art lost to mankind, or learn what is less perfectly known in our own country. At least we compare our own with former times, and either rejoice at our improvements, or, what is the first motion towards good, discover our defects."

" I am willing," said the Prince, " to see all that can deserve my search." " And I," said the Princess, " shall rejoice to learn something of the manners of antiquity."

" The most pompous monument of Egyptian greatness, and one of the most bulky works of manual industry," said Imlac, " are the Pyramids : fabrics raised before the time of history, and of which the earliest narratives afford us only uncertain traditions. Of these the greatest is still standing, very little injured by time."

" Let us visit them to-morrow," said Nekayah. " I have often heard of the Pyramids, and shall not rest till I have seen them, within and without, with my own eyes."

CHAPTER XXXI.

They visit the Pyramids.

THE resolution being thus taken, they set out the next day. They laid tents upon their camels, being resolved to stay among the Pyramids till their curiosity was fully satisfied. They travelled gently, turned aside to everything remarkable, stopped from time to time and conversed with the inhabitants, and observed the various appearances of towns ruined and inhabited, of wild and cultivated nature.

When they came to the Great Pyramid they were astonished at the extent of the base and the height of the top. Imlac explained to them the principles upon which the pyramidal form was chosen for a fabric intended to co-extend its duration with that of the world: he showed that its gradual diminution gave it such stability as defeated all the common attacks of the elements, and could scarcely be overthrown by earthquakes themselves, the least resistible of natural violence. A concussion that should shatter the pyramid would threaten the dissolution of the continent.

They measured all its dimensions, and pitched their tents at its foot. Next day they prepared to enter its interior apartments, and having hired the common guides, climbed up to the first passage; when the favourite of the Princess, looking into the cavity, stepped back and trembled. "Pekuah," said the Princess, "of what art thou afraid?"

"Of the narrow entrance," answered the lady, "and of the dreadful gloom. I dare not enter a place which must surely be inhabited by unquiet souls. The original possessors of these dreadful vaults will start up before us, and perhaps shut us in for ever." She spoke, and threw her arms round the neck of her mistress.

"If all your fear be of apparitions," said the Prince, "I will promise you safety. There is no danger from the dead: he that is once buried will be seen no more."

"That the dead are seen no more," said Imlac, "I will

not undertake to maintain against the concurrent and unvaried testimony of all ages and of all nations. There is no people, rude or learned, among whom apparitions of the dead are not related and believed. This opinion, which perhaps prevails as far as human nature is diffused, could become universal only by its truth : those that never heard of one another would not have agreed in a tale which nothing but experience can make credible. That it is doubted by single cavillers can very little weaken the general evidence, and some who deny it with their tongues confess it by their fears.

"Yet I do not mean to add new terrors to those which have already seized upon Pekuah. There can be no reason why spectres should haunt the Pyramid more than other places, or why they should have power or will to hurt innocence and purity. Our entrance is no violation of their privileges : we can take nothing from them ; how, then, can we offend them ? "

"My dear Pekuah," said the Princess, "I will always go before you, and Imlac shall follow you. Remember that you are the companion of the Princess of Abyssinia."

"If the Princess is pleased that her servant should die," returned the lady, "let her command some death less dreadful than enclosure in this horrid cavern. You know I dare not disobey you—I must go if you command me ; but if I once enter, I never shall come back."

The Princess saw that her fear was too strong for expostulation or reproof, and, embracing her, told her that she should stay in the tent till their return. Pekuah was not yet satisfied, but entreated the Princess not to pursue so dreadful a purpose as that of entering the recesses of the Pyramids. "Though I cannot teach courage," said Nekayah, "I must not learn cowardice, nor leave at last undone what I came hither only to do."

CHAPTER XXXII.

They enter the Pyramid.

PEKUAH descended to the tents, and the rest entered the Pyramid. They passed through the galleries, surveyed the vaults of marble, and examined the chest in which the body of the founder is supposed to have been deposited. They then sat down in one of the most spacious chambers to rest awhile, before they attempted to return.

"We have now," said Imlac, "gratified our minds with an exact view of the greatest work of man, except the wall of China.

"Of the wall it is very easy to assign the motive. It secured a wealthy and timorous nation from the incursions of barbarians, whose unskilfulness in the arts made it easier for them to supply their wants by rapine than by industry, and who from time to time poured in upon the inhabitants of peaceful commerce as vultures descend upon domestic fowl. Their celerity and fierceness made the wall necessary, and their ignorance made it efficacious.

"But for the Pyramids no reason has ever been given adequate to the cost and labour of the work. The narrowness of the chambers proves that it could afford no retreat from enemies, and treasures might have been reposited at far less expense with equal security. It seems to have been erected only in compliance with that hunger of imagination which preys incessantly upon life, and must be always appeased by some employment. Those who have already all that they can enjoy must enlarge their desires. He that has built for use till use is supplied, must begin to build for vanity, and extend his plan to the utmost power of human performance that he may not be soon reduced to form another wish.

"I consider this mighty structure as a monument of the insufficiency of human enjoyments. A king whose power is unlimited, and whose treasures surmount all real and imaginary wants, is compelled to solace, by the erection of a pyramid, the satiety of dominion and tastelessness of pleasures, and to amuse the tediousness of declining life by seeing thousands labouring without end, and one stone, for no purpose, laid upon another. Whoever thou art that, not content with a moderate condition, imaginest happiness in royal magnificence, and dreamest that command or riches can feed the appetite of novelty with perpetual gratifications, survey the Pyramids, and confess thy folly ! "

CHAPTER XXXIII.

The Princess meets with an unexpected Misfortune.

THEY rose up, and returned through the cavity at which they had entered; and the Princess prepared for her favourite a long narrative of dark labyrinths and costly rooms, and of the different impressions which the varieties of the way had made upon her. But when they came to their train, they found every one silent and dejected: the men discovered shame and fear in their countenances, and the women were weeping in their tents.

What had happened they did not try to conjecture, but immediately inquired. "You had scarcely entered into the Pyramid," said one of the attendants, "when a troop of Arabs rushed upon us: we were too few to resist them, and too slow to escape. They were about to search the tents, set us on our camels, and drive us along before them, when the approach of some Turkish horsemen put them to flight: but they seized the Lady Pekuah with her two maids, and carried them away: the Turks are now pursuing them by our instigation, but I fear they will not be able to overtake them."

The Princess was overpowered with surprise and grief. Rasselas, in the first heat of his resentment, ordered his servants to follow him, and prepared to pursue the robbers with his sabre in his hand. "Sir," said Imlac, "what can you hope from violence or valour? The Arabs are mounted on horses trained to battle and retreat; we have only beasts of burden. By leaving our present station we may lose the Princess, but cannot hope to regain Pekuah."

In a short time the Turks returned, having not been able to reach the enemy. The Princess burst out into new lamentations, and Rasselas could scarcely forbear to reproach them with cowardice; but Imlac was of opinion that the escape of the Arabs was no addition to their misfortune, for perhaps they would have killed their captives rather than have resigned them.

CHAPTER XXXIV.

They return to Cairo without Pekuah.

THERE was nothing to be hoped from longer stay. They returned to Cairo, repenting of their curiosity, censuring the negligence of the government, lamenting their own rashness, which had neglected to procure a guard, imagining many expedients by which the loss of Pekuah might have been prevented, and resolving to do something for her recovery, though none could find anything proper to be done.

Nekayah retired to her chamber, where her women attempted to comfort her by telling her that all had their troubles, and that Lady Pekuah had enjoyed much happiness in the world for a long time, and might reasonably expect a change of fortune. They hoped that some good would befall her wheresoever she was, and that their mistress would find another friend who might supply her place.

The Princess made them no answer; and they continued the form of condolence, not much grieved in their hearts that the favourite was lost.

Next day the Prince presented to the Bassa a memorial of the wrong which he had suffered, and a petition for redress. The Bassa threatened to punish the robbers, but did not attempt to catch them; nor indeed could any account or description be given by which he might direct the pursuit.

It soon appeared that nothing would be done by authority. Governors being accustomed to hear of more crimes than they can punish, and more wrongs than they can redress, set themselves at ease by indiscriminate negligence, and presently forget the request when they lose sight of the petitioner.

Imlac then endeavoured to gain some intelligence by private agents. He found many who pretended to an exact knowledge of all the haunts of the Arabs, and to regular correspondence with their chiefs, and who readily undertook the recovery of Pekuah. Of these, some were furnished with money for their journey, and came back no more; some were liberally paid for accounts which a few days discovered to be false. But the Princess would not suffer any means, however improbable, to be left untried. While she was doing something, she kept her hope alive. As one expedient failed, another was suggested; when one messenger returned unsuccessful, another was despatched to a different quarter.

Two months had now passed, and of Pekuah nothing had been heard; the hopes which they had endeavoured to raise in each other grew more languid; and the Princess, when she saw nothing more to be tried, sunk down inconsolable in hopeless dejection. A thousand times she reproached herself with the easy compliance by which she permitted her favourite to stay behind her. "Had not my fondness," said she, "lessened my authority, Pekuah had not dared to talk of her terrors. She ought to have feared me more than spectres. A severe look would have overpowered her; a peremptory command would have compelled obedience. Why did foolish indulgence prevail upon me? Why did I not speak, and refuse to hear?"

"Great Princess," said Imlac, "do not reproach yourself for your virtue, or consider that as blameable by which evil has accidentally been caused. Your tenderness for the timidity of Pekuah was generous and kind. When we act according to our duty, we commit the events to Him by whose laws our actions are governed, and who will suffer none to be finally punished for obedience. When, in prospect of some good, whether natural or moral, we break the rules prescribed us, we withdraw from the direction of superior wisdom, and take all consequences upon ourselves. Man cannot so far know the connection of causes and events as that he may venture to do wrong in order to do right. When we pursue our end by lawful means, we may always console our miscarriage by the hope of future recompense. When we consult only our own policy, and attempt to find a nearer way to good by overleaping the settled boundaries of right and wrong, we cannot be happy even by success, because we cannot escape the consciousness of our fault; but if we miscarry, the disappointment is irremediably embittered. How comfortless is the sorrow of him who feels at once the pangs of guilt and the vexation of calamity which guilt has brought upon him.

" Consider, Princess, what would have been your condition if the Lady Pekuah had entreated to accompany you, and, being compelled to stay in the tents, had been carried away; or how would you have borne the thought if you had forced her into the Pyramid, and she had died before you in agonies of terror? "

" Had either happened," said Nekayah, " I could not have endured life till now; I should have been tortured to madness by the remembrance of such cruelty, or must have pined away in abhorrence of myself."

"This, at least," said Imlac, " is the present reward of virtuous conduct, that no unlucky consequence can oblige us to repent it."

CHAPTER XXXV.

The Princess languishes for want of Pekuah.

NEKAYAH, being thus reconciled to herself, found that no evil is insupportable but that which is accompanied with consciousness of wrong. She was from that time delivered from the violence of tempestuous sorrow, and sunk into silent pensiveness and gloomy tranquillity. She sat from morning to evening recollecting all that had been done or said by her Pekuah, treasured up with care every trifle on which Pekuah had set an accidental value, and which might recall to mind any little incident or careless conversation. The sentiments of her whom she now expected to see no more were treasured in her memory as rules of life, and she deliberated to no other end than to conjecture on any occasion what would have been the opinion and counsel of Pekuah.

The women by whom she was attended knew nothing of her real condition, and therefore she could not talk to them but with caution and reserve. She began to remit her curiosity, having no great desire to collect notions which she had no convenience of uttering. Rasselas endeavoured first to comfort and afterwards to divert her; he hired musicians, to whom she seemed to listen, but did not hear them; and procured masters to instruct her in various arts, whose lectures, when they visited her again, were again to be repeated. She had lost her taste of pleasure and her ambition of excellence; and her mind, though forced into short excursions, always recurred to the image of her friend.

Imlac was every morning earnestly enjoined to renew his inquiries, and was asked every night whether he had yet heard of Pekuah; till, not being able to return the Princess the answer that she desired, he was less and less willing to come into her presence. She observed his backwardness, and commanded him to attend her. "You are not," said she, "to confound impatience with resentment, or to suppose that I charge you with negligence because I repine at your unsuccessfulness. I do not much wonder at your absence. I know that the unhappy are never pleasing, and that all naturally avoid the contagion of misery. To hear complaints is wearisome alike to the wretched and the happy; for who would cloud by adventitious grief the short gleams of gaiety which life allows us? or who that is struggling under his own evils will add to them the miseries of another?

" The time is at hand when none shall be disturbed any longer by the sighs of Nekayah : my search after happiness is now at an end. I am resolved to retire from the world, with all its flatteries and deceits, and will hide myself in solitude, without any other care than to compose my thoughts and regulate my hours by a constant succession of innocent occupations, till, with a mind purified from earthly desires, I shall enter into that state to which all are hastening, and in which I hope again to enjoy the friendship of Pekuah."

" Do not entangle your mind," said Imlac, by irrevocable determinations, nor increase the burden of life by a voluntary accumulation of misery. The weariness of retirement will continue to increase when the loss of Pekuah is forgot. That you have been deprived of one pleasure is no very good reason for rejection of the rest."

" Since Pekuah was taken from me," said the Princess, "I have no pleasure to reject or to retain. She that has no one to love or trust has little to hope. She wants the radical principle of happiness. We may perhaps allow that what satisfaction this world can afford must arise from the conjunction of wealth, knowledge, and goodness. Wealth is nothing but as it is bestowed, and knowledge nothing but as it is communicated. They must therefore be imparted to others, and to whom could I now delight to impart them ? Goodness affords the only comfort which can be enjoyed without a partner, and goodness may be practised in retirement.

"How far solitude may admit goodness or advance it, I shall not," replied Imlac, "dispute at present. Remember the confession of the pious hermit. You will wish to return into the world when the image of your companion has left your thoughts." "That time," said Nekayah, "will never come. The generous frankness, the modest obsequiousness, and the faithful secrecy of my dear Pekuah will always be more missed as I shall live longer to see vice and folly."

"The state of a mind oppressed with a sudden calamity," said Imlac, "is like that of the fabulous inhabitants of the new-created earth, who, when the first night came upon them, supposed that day would never return. When the clouds of sorrow gather over us, we see nothing beyond them, nor can imagine how they will be dispelled; yet a new day succeeded to the night, and sorrow is never long without a dawn of ease. But they who restrain themselves from receiving comfort do as the savages would have done had they put out their eyes when it was dark. Our minds, like our bodies, are in continual flux; something is hourly lost, and something acquired. To lose much at once is inconvenient to either, but while the vital power remains uninjured, nature will find the means of reparation. Distance has the same effect on the mind as on the eye: and while we glide along the stream of time, whatever we leave behind us is always lessening, and that which we approach increasing in magnitude. Do not suffer life to stagnate: it will grow muddy for want of motion; commit yourself again to the current of the world; Pekuah will vanish by degrees; you will meet in your way some other favourite, or learn to diffuse yourself in general conversation."

"At least," said the Prince, "do not despair before all remedies have been tried. The inquiry after the unfortunate lady is still continued, and shall be carried on with yet greater diligence, on condition that you will promise to wait a year for the event, without any unalterable resolution."

Nekayah thought this a reasonable demand, and made the

promise to her brother, who had been obliged by Imlac to require it. Imlac had, indeed, no great hope of regaining Pekuah ; but he supposed that if he could secure the interval of a year, the Princess would be then in no danger of a cloister.

CHAPTER XXXVI.

Pekuah is still remembered. The Progress of Sorrow.

NEKAYAH, seeing that nothing was omitted for the recovery of her favourite, and having by her promise set her intention of retirement at a distance, began imperceptibly to return to common cares and common pleasures. She rejoiced without her own consent at the suspension of her sorrows, and sometimes caught herself with indignation in the act of turning away her mind from the remembrance of her whom yet she resolved never to forget.

She then appointed a certain hour of the day for meditation on the merits and fondness of Pekuah, and for some weeks retired constantly at the time fixed, and returned with her eyes swollen and her countenance clouded. By degrees she grew less scrupulous, and suffered any important and pressing avocation to delay the tribute of daily tears. She then yielded to less occasions, and sometimes forgot what she was indeed afraid to remember, and at last wholly released herself from the duty of periodical affliction.

Her real love of Pekuah was not yet diminished. A thousand occurrences brought her back to memory, and a thousand wants, which nothing but the confidence of friendship can supply, made her frequently regretted. She therefore solicited Imlac never to desist from inquiry, and to leave no art of intelligence untried, that at least she might have the comfort of knowing that she did not suffer by negligence or sluggishness. " Yet what," said she, " is to be expected from our pursuit of happiness, when we find the state of life to be such that happiness itself is the cause of misery ? Why should we endeavour to attain that of which the possession cannot be secured? I shall henceforward fear to yield my heart to excellence, however bright, or to fondness, however tender, lest I should lose again what I have lost in Pekuah."

CHAPTER XXXVII.

The Princess hears News of Pekuah.

IN seven months one of the messengers who had been sent away upon the day when the promise was drawn from the Princess, returned, after many unsuccessful rambles, from the borders of Nubia, with an account that Pekuah was in the hands of an Arab chief, who possessed a castle or fortress on the extremity of Egypt. The Arab, whose revenue was plunder, was willing to restore her, with her two attendants, for two hundred ounces of gold.

The price was no subject of debate. The Princess was in ecstacies when she heard that her favourite was alive, and might so cheaply be ransomed. She could not think of delaying for a moment Pekuah's happiness or her own, but entreated her brother to send back the messenger with the sum required. Imlac being consulted, was not very confident of the veracity of the relater, and was still more doubtful of the Arab's faith, who might, if he were too liberally trusted, detain at once the money and the captives. He thought it dangerous to put themselves in the power of the Arab by going into his district; and could not expect that the rover would so much expose himself as to come into the lower country, where he might be seized by the forces of the Bassa.

It is difficult to negotiate where neither will trust. But Imlac, after some deliberation, directed the messenger to propose that Pekuah should be conducted by ten horsemen to the monastery of St. Anthony, which is situated in the deserts of Upper Egypt, where she should be met by the same number, and her ransom should be paid.

That no time might be lost, as they expected that the proposal would not be refused, they immediately began their journey to the monastery; and when they arrived, Imlac went forward with the former messenger to the Arab's fortress. Rasselas was desirous to go with them; but neither his sister nor Imlac would consent. The Arab, according to the custom of his nation, observed the laws of hospitality with great exactness to those who put themselves into his power, and in a few days brought Pekuah with her maids, by easy journeys, to the place appointed, where, receiving the stipulated price, he restored her, with great respect, to liberty and her friends, and undertook to conduct them back towards Cairo beyond all danger of robbery or violence.

The Princess and her favourite embraced each other with transport too violent to be expressed, and went out together to pour the tears of tenderness in secret, and exchange professions of kindness and gratitude. After a few hours they returned into the refectory of the convent, where, in the presence of the prior and his brethren, the Prince required of Pekuah the history of her adventures.

CHAPTER XXXVIII.

The Adventures of the Lady Pekuah.

"AT what time and in what manner I was forced away," said Pekuah, "your servants have told you. The suddenness of the event struck me with surprise, and I was at first rather stupefied than agitated with any passion of either fear or sorrow. My confusion was increased by the speed and tumult of our flight, while we were followed by the Turks, who, as it seemed, soon despaired to overtake us, or were afraid of those whom they made a show of menacing.

"When the Arabs saw themselves out of danger, they slackened their course; and as I was less harassed by external violence, I began to feel more uneasiness in my mind.

After some time, we stopped near a spring shaded with trees, in a pleasant meadow, where we were set upon the ground, and offered such refreshments as our masters were partaking. I was suffered to sit with my maids apart from the rest, and none attempted to comfort or insult us. Here I first began to feel the full weight of my misery. The girls sat weeping in silence, and from time to time looked on me for succour. I knew not to what condition we were doomed, nor could conjecture where would be the place of our captivity, or whence to draw any hope of deliverance. I was in the hands of robbers and savages, and had no reason to suppose that their pity was more than their justice, or that they would forbear the gratification of any ardour of desire or caprice of cruelty. I, however, kissed my maids, and endeavoured to pacify them by remarking that we were yet treated with decency, and that since we were now carried beyond pursuit, there was no danger of violence to our lives.

" When we were to be set again on horseback, my maids clung round me, and refused to be parted; but I commanded them not to irritate those who had us in their power. We travelled the remaining part of the day through an unfrequented and pathless country, and came by moonlight to the side of a hill, where the rest of the troop was stationed. Their tents were pitched and their fires kindled, and our chief was welcomed as a man much beloved by his dependants.

"We were received into a large tent, where we found women who had attended their husbands in the expedition. They set before us the supper which they had provided, and I ate it rather to encourage my maids than to comply with any appetite of my own. When the meat was taken away, they spread the carpets for repose. I was weary, and hoped to find in sleep that remission of distress which nature seldom denies. Ordering myself, therefore, to be undressed, I observed that the women looked very earnestly upon me, not expecting, I suppose, to see me so submissively attended. When my upper vest was taken off, they were apparently struck with the splendour of my clothes, and one of them timorously laid her hand upon the embroidery. She then went out, and in a short time came back with another woman, who seemed to be of higher rank and greater authority. She did, at her entrance, the usual act of reverence, and taking me by the hand placed me in a smaller tent, spread with finer carpets, where I spent the night quietly with my maids.

" In the morning, as I was sitting on the grass, the chief of the troop came towards me. I rose up to receive him, and he bowed with great respect. 'Illustrious lady,' said he, ' my fortune is better than I had presumed to hope : I am told by my women that I have a princess in my camp.' ' Sir,' answered I, ' your women have deceived themselves and you ; I am not a princess, but an unhappy stranger who intended soon to have left this country, in which I am now to be imprisoned for ever.' 'Whoever or whencesoever you are,' returned the Arab, ' your dress and that of your servants show your rank to be high and your wealth to be great. Why should you, who can so easily procure your ransom, think yourself in danger of perpetual captivity? The purpose of my incursions is to increase my riches, or, more properly, to gather tribute. The sons of Ishmael are the natural and hereditary lords of this part of the continent, which is usurped by late invaders and low-born tyrants, from whom we are compelled to take by the sword what is denied to justice. The violence of war admits no distinction : the lance that is lifted at guilt and power will sometimes fall on innocence and gentleness.'

" ' How little,' said I, ' did I expect that yesterday it should have fallen upon me.'

" ' Misfortunes,' answered the Arab, ' should always be expected. If the eye of hostility could learn reverence or pity, excellence like yours had been exempt from injury. But the angels of affliction spread their toils alike' for the virtuous and the wicked, for the mighty and the mean. Do

I

not be disconsolate; I am not one of the lawless and cruel rovers of the desert; I know the rules of civil life; I will fix your ransom, give a passport to your messenger, and perform my stipulation with nice punctuality.'

"You will easily believe that I was pleased with his courtesy, and finding that his predominant passion was desire for money, I began now to think my danger less, for I knew that no sum would be thought too great for the release of Pekuah. I told him that he should have no reason to charge me with ingratitude if I was used with kindness, and that any ransom which could be expected for a maid of common rank would be paid, but that he must not persist to rate me as a princess. He said he would consider what he should demand, and then, smiling, bowed and retired.

"Soon after the women came about me, each contending to be more officious than the other, and my maids themselves were served with reverence. We travelled onward by short journeys. On the fourth day the chief told me that my ransom must be two hundred ounces of gold, which I not only promised him, but told him that I would add fifty more if I and my maids were honourably treated.

"I never knew the power of gold before. From that time I was the leader of the troop. The march of every day was longer or shorter as I commanded, and the tents were pitched where I chose to rest. We now had camels and other conveniences for travel; my own women were always at my side, and I amused myself with observing the manners of the vagrant nations, and with viewing remains of ancient edifices with which these deserted countries appear to have been in some distant age lavishly embellished.

"The chief of the band was a man far from illiterate: he was able to travel by the stars or the compass, and had marked in his erratic expeditions such places as are most worthy the notice of a passenger. He observed to me that buildings are always best preserved in places little frequented and difficult of access; for when once a country declines from its primitive splendour, the more inhabitants are left, the quicker ruin will be made. Walls supply stones more easily than quarries : and palaces and temples will be demolished to make stables of granite and cottages of porphyry.' "

CHAPTER XXXIX.

The Adventures of Pekuah (continued).

" WE wandered about in this manner for some weeks, either, as our chief pretended, for my gratification, or, as I rather suspected, for some convenience of his own. I endeavoured to appear contented where sullenness and resentment would have been of no use, and that endeavour conduced much to the calmness of my mind ; but my heart was always with Nekayah, and the troubles of the night much overbalanced the amusements of the day. My women, who threw all their cares upon their mistress, set their minds at ease from the time when they saw me treated with respect, and gave themselves up to the incidental alleviations of our fatigue without solicitude or sorrow. I was pleased with their pleasure, and animated with their confidence. My condition had lost much of its terror, since I found that the Arab ranged the country merely to get riches. Avarice is a uniform and tractable vice : other intellectual distempers are different in different constitutions of mind ; that which soothes the pride of one will offend the pride of another ; but to the favour of the covetous there is a ready way—bring money, and nothing is denied.

" At last we came to the dwelling of our chief; a strong and spacious house, built with stone in an island of the Nile, which lies, as I was told, under the tropic. 'Lady, said the Arab, ' you shall rest after your journey a few weeks in this place, where you are to consider yourself as sovereign. My occupation is war : I have therefore chosen this obscure residence, from which I can issue unexpected, and to which I can retire unpursued. You may now repose in security:

here are few pleasures, but here is no danger.' He then led me into the inner apartments, and seating me on the richest couch, bowed to the ground.

"His women, who considered me as a rival, looked on me with malignity; but being soon informed that I was a great lady detained only for my ransom, they began to vie with each other in obsequiousness and reverence.

"Being again comforted with new assurances of speedy liberty, I was for some days diverted from impatience by the novelty of the place. The turrets overlooked the country to a great distance, and afforded a view of many windings of the stream. In the day I wandered from one place to another, as the course of the sun varied the splendour of the prospect, and saw many things which I had never seen before. The crocodiles and river horses are common in this unpeopled region; and I often looked upon them with terror, though I knew they could not hurt me. For some time I expected to see mermaids and tritons, which, as Imlac has told me, the European travellers have stationed in the Nile; but no such beings ever appeared, and the Arab, when I inquired after them, laughed at my credulity.

"At night the Arab always attended me to a tower set apart for celestial observations, where he endeavoured to teach me the names and courses of the stars. I had no great inclination to this study; but an appearance of attention was necessary to please my instructor, who valued himself for his skill, and in a little while I found some employment requisite to beguile the tediousness of time, which was to be passed always amidst the same objects. I was weary of looking in the morning on things from which I had turned away weary in the evening: I therefore was at last willing to observe the stars rather than do nothing, but could not always compose my thoughts, and was very often thinking on Nekayah when others imagined me contemplating the sky. Soon after the Arab went upon another expedition, and then my only pleasure was to talk with my maids about the accident by which we were carried away, and the happiness we should all enjoy at the end of our captivity."

"There were women in your Arab's fortress," said the Princess; "why did you not make them your companions, enjoy their conversation, and partake their diversions? In a place where they found business or amusement, why should you alone sit corroded with idle melancholy? or why could not you bear for a few months that condition to which they were condemned for life?"

"The diversions of the women," answered Pekuah, "were only childish play, by which the mind, accustomed to stronger operations, could not be kept busy. I could do all which they delighted in doing by powers merely sensitive, while my intellectual faculties were flown to Cairo. They ran from room to room, as a bird hops from wire to wire in his cage. They danced for the sake of motion, as lambs frisk in a meadow. One sometimes pretended to be hurt that the rest might be alarmed, or hid herself that another might seek her. Part of their time passed in watching the progress of light bodies that floated on the river, and part in marking the various forms into which clouds broke in the sky.

"Their business was only needlework, in which I and my maids sometimes helped them; but you know that the mind will easily straggle from the fingers, nor will you suspect that captivity and absence from Nekayah could receive solace from silken flowers.

"Nor was much satisfaction to be hoped from their conversation: for of what could they be expected to talk? They had seen nothing, for they had lived from early youth in that narrow spot: of what they had not seen they could have no knowledge, for they could not read. They had no idea but of the few things that were within their view, and had hardly names for anything but their clothes and their food. As I bore a superior character, I was often called to

terminate their quarrels, which I decided as equitably as I
could.   If it could have amused me to hear the complaints
of each against the rest, I might have been often detained
by long stories ; but the motives of their animosity were so
small that I could not listen without interrupting the tale."

"How," said Rasselas, "can the Arab, whom you represented as a man of more than common accomplishments,
take any pleasure in his seraglio, when it is filled only with
women like these?   Are they exquisitely beautiful?"

"They do not," said Pekuah, "want that unaffecting and
ignoble beauty which may subsist without sprightliness or
sublimity, without energy of thought or dignity of virtue.
But to a man like the Arab such beauty was only a flower
casually plucked and carelessly thrown away.   Whatever
pleasures he might find among them, they were not those
of friendship or society.   When they were playing about
him, he looked on them with inattentive superiority : when
they vied for his regard, he sometimes turned away disgusted.
As they had no knowledge, their talk could take nothing
from the tediousness of life : as they had no choice, their
fondness, or appearance of fondness, excited in him neither
pride nor gratitude.   He was not exalted in his own esteem
by the smiles of a woman who saw no other man, nor was
much obliged by that regard of which he could never know
the sincerity, and which he might often perceive to be exerted
not so much to delight him as to pain a rival.   That which
he gave, and they received, as love, was only a careless
distribution of superfluous time ; such love as man can
bestow upon that which he despises, such as has neither
hope nor fear, neither joy nor sorrow."

"You have reason, lady, to think yourself happy," said
Imlac, "that you have been thus easily dismissed.   How
could a mind, hungry for knowledge, be willing, in an
intellectual famine, to lose such a banquet as Pekuah's
conversation ? "

"I am inclined to believe," answered Pekuah, "that he

was for some tlme in suspense; for notwithstanding hic promise, whenever I proposed to despatch a messenger to Cairo he found some excuse for delay. While I was detained in his house he made many incursions into the neighbouring countries, and perhaps he would have refused to discharge me had his plunder been equal to his wishes. He returned always courteous, related his adventures, delighted to hear my observations, and endeavoured to advance my acquaintance with the stars. When I importuned him to send away my letters, he soothed me with professions of honour and sincerity; and when I could be no longer decently denied, put his troop again in motion, and left me to govern in his absence. I was much afflicted by this studied procrastination, and was sometimes afraid that I should be forgotten; that you would leave Cairo, and I must end my days in an island of the Nile.

"I grew at last hopeless and dejected, and cared so little to entertain him, that he for a while more frequently talked with my maids. That he should fall in love with them, or with me, might have been equally fatal; and I was not much pleased with the growing friendship. My anxiety was not long; for, as I recovered some degree of cheerfulness, he returned to me, and I could not forbear to despise my former uneasiness.

"He still delayed to send for my ransom, and would perhaps never have determined had not your agent found his way to him. The gold, which he would not fetch, he could not reject when it was offered. He hastened to prepare for our journey hither, like a man delivered from the pain of an intestine conflict. I took leave of my companions in the house, who dismissed me with cold indifference."

Nekayah having heard her favourite's relation, rose and embraced her; and Rasselas gave her a hundred ounces of gold, which she presented to the Arab for the fifty that were promised.

CHAPTER XL.

The History of a Man of Learning.

THEY returned to Cairo, and were so well pleased at finding themselves together, that none of them went much abroad. The Prince began to love learning, and one day declared to Imlac that he intended to devote himself to science, and pass the rest of his days in literary solitude.

" Before you make your final choice," answered Imlac, "you ought to examine its hazards, and converse with some of those who are grown old in the company of themselves. I have just left the observatory of one of the most learned astronomers in the world, who has spent forty years in unwearied attention to the motion and appearances of the celestial bodies, and has drawn out his soul in endless calculations. He admits a few friends once a month to hear his deductions and enjoy his discoveries. I was introduced as a man of knowledge worthy of his notice. Men of various ideas and fluent conversation are commonly welcome to those whose thoughts have been long fixed upon a single point, and who find the images of other things stealing away. I delighted him with my remarks. He smiled at the narrative of my travels, and was glad to forget the constellations, and descend fo ra moment into the lower world.

" On the next day of vacation I renewed my visit, and was so fortunate as to please him again. He relaxed from that time the severity of his rule and permitted me to enter at my own choice. I found him always busy, and always glad to be relieved. As each knew much which the other was desirous of learning, we exchanged our notions with great delight. I perceived that I had every day more of his confidence, and always found new cause of admiration in the profundity of his mind. His comprehension is vast, his memory capacious and retentive, his discourse is methodical, and his expression clear.

" His integrity and benevolence are equal to his learning. His deepest researches and most favourite studies are willingly interrupted for any opportunity of doing good by his counsel or his riches. To his closest retreat, at his most busy moments, all are admitted that want his assistance : ' For though I exclude idleness and pleasure, I will never,' says he, ' bar my doors against charity. To man is permitted the contemplation of the skies, but the practice of virtue is commanded.' " ·

" Surely," said the Princess, " this man is happy."

" I visited him," said Imlac, "with more and more frequency, and was every time more enamoured of his conversation : he was sublime without haughtiness, courteous without formality, and communicative without ostentation. I was at first, great Princess, of your opinion, thought him the happiest of mankind, and often congratulated him on the blessing that he enjoyed. He seemed to hear nothing with indifference but the praises of his condition, to which he always returned a general answer, and diverted the conversation to some other topic.

" Amidst this willingness to be pleased and labour to please, I had quickly reason to imagine that some painful sentiment pressed upon his mind. He often looked up earnestly towards the sun, and let his voice fall in the midst of his discourse. He would sometimes, when we were alone, gaze upon me in silence with the air of a man who longed to speak what he was yet resolved to suppress. He would often send for me with vehement injunction of haste, though when I came to him he had nothing extraordinary to say. And sometimes, when I was leaving him, would call me back, pause a few moments, and then dismiss me."

CHAPTER XLI.

The Astronomer discovers the Cause of his Uneasiness.

"At last the time came when the secret burst his reserve. We were sitting together last night in the turret of his house watching the immersion of a satellite of Jupiter. A sudden tempest clouded the sky and disappointed our observation. We sat awhile silent in the dark, and then he addressed himself to me in these words : 'Imlac, I have long considered thy friendship as the greatest blessing of my life. Integrity without knowledge is weak and useless, and knowledge without integrity is dangerous and dreadful. I have found in thee all the qualities requisite for trust : benevolence, experience, and fortitude. I have long discharged an office which I must soon quit at the call of nature, and shall rejoice in the hour of imbecility and pain to devolve it upon thee.'

"I thought myself honoured by this testimony, and protested that whatever could conduce to his happiness would add likewise to mine.

"'Hear, Imlac, what thou wilt not without difficulty credit. I have possessed for five years the regulation of the weather and the distribution of the seasons. The sun has listened to my dictates, and passed from tropic to tropic by my direction; the clouds at my call have poured their waters, and the Nile has overflowed at my command. I have restrained the rage of the dog-star, and mitigated the fervours of the crab. The winds alone, of all the elemental powers, have hitherto refused my authority, and multitudes have perished by equinoctial tempests which I found myself unable to prohibit or restrain. I have administered this great office with exact justice, and made to the different nations of the earth an impartial dividend of rain and sunshine. What must have been the misery of half the globe if I had limited the clouds to particular regions, or confined the sun to either side of the equator?' "

CHAPTER XLII.

The Opinion of the Astronomer is explained and justified.

"I suppose he discovered in me, through the obscurity of the room, some tokens of amazement and doubt ; for after a short pause he proceeded thus :—

" ' Not to be easily credited will neither surprise nor offend me, for I am probably the first of human beings to whom this trust has been imparted. Nor do I know whether to deem this distinction a reward or punishment. Since I have possessed it I have been far less happy than before, and nothing but the consciousness of good intention could have enabled me to support the weariness of unremitted vigilance.'

" ' How long, sir,' said I, ' has this great office been in your hands?'

" ' About ten years ago,' said he, ' my daily observations of the changes of the sky led me to consider whether, if I had the power of the seasons, I could confer greater plenty upon the inhabitants of the earth. This contemplation fastened on my mind, and I sat days and nights in imaginary dominion, pouring upon this country and that the showers of fertility, and seconding every fall of rain with a due pro-portion of sunshine. I had yet only the will to do good, and did not imagine that I should ever have the power.

" ' One day as I was looking on the fields withering with heat, I felt in my mind a sudden wish that I could send rain on the southern mountains, and raise the Nile to an inunda-tion. In the hurry of my imagination I commanded rain to fall ; and by comparing the time of my command with that of the inundation, I found that the clouds had listened to my lips.

" ' Might not some other cause,' said I, ' produce this

concurrence? The Nile does not always rise on the same day.'

"' Do not believe,' said he with impatience, ' that such objections could escape me : I reasoned long against my own conviction, and laboured against truth with the utmost obstinacy. I sometimes suspected myself of madness, and should not have dared to impart this secret but to a man like you, capable of distinguishing the wonderful from the impossible, and the incredible from the false."

"' Why, sir,' said I, ' do you call that incredible which you know, or think you know, to be true?'

"' Because,' said he, ' I cannot prove it by any external evidence : and I know too well the laws of demonstration to think that my conviction ought to influence another, who cannot, like me, be conscious of its force. I therefore shall not attempt to gain credit by disputation. It is sufficient that I feel this power that I have long possessed, and every day exerted it. But the life of man is short : the infirmities of age increase upon me, and the time will soon come when the regulator of the year must mingle with the dust. The care of appointing a successor has long disturbed me : the night and the day have been spent in comparisons of all the characters which have come to my knowledge, and I have yet found none so worthy as thyself.' "

CHAPTER XLIII.

The Astronomer leaves Imlac his Directions.

"' HEAR, therefore, what I shall impart with attention, such as the welfare of a world requires. If the task of a king be considered as difficult, who has the care only of a few millions, to whom he cannot do much good or harm, what must be the anxiety of him on whom depends the action of the elements and the great gifts of light and heat? Hear me, therefore, with attention.

"I have diligently considered the position of the earth and sun, and formed innumerable schemes, in which I changed their situation. I have sometimes turned aside the axis of the earth, and sometimes varied the ecliptic of the sun; but I have found it impossible to make a disposition by which the world may be advantaged : what one region gains, another loses by an imaginable alteration, even without considering the distant parts of the solar system with which we are acquainted. Do not, therefore, in thy administration of the year, indulge thy pride by innovation; do not please thyself with thinking that thou canst make thyself renowned to all future ages by disordering the seasons. The memory of mischief is no desirable fame. Much less will it become thee to let kindness or interest prevail. Never rob other countries of rain to pour it on thine own. For us the Nile is sufficient.'

"I promised that when I possessed the power, I would use it with inflexible integrity; and he dismissed me, pressing my hand. 'My heart,' said he, 'will be now at rest, and my benevolence will no more destroy my quiet: I have found a man of wisdom and virtue, to whom I can cheerfully bequeath the inheritance of the sun.'"

The Prince heard this narration with very serious regard ; but the Princess smiled, and Pekuah convulsed herself with laughter. "Ladies," said Imlac, "to mock the heaviest of human afflictions is neither charitable nor wise. Few can attain this man's knowledge, and few practise his virtues; but all may suffer his calamity. Of the uncertainties of our present state, the most dreadful and alarming is the uncertain continuance of reason."

The Princess was recollected, and the favourite was abashed. Rasselas, more deeply affected, inquired of Imlac whether he thought such maladies of the mind frequent, and how they were contracted.

CHAPTER XLIV.

The dangerous Prevalence of Imagination.

"DISORDERS of intellect," answered Imlac, "happen much more often than superficial observers will easily believe. Perhaps if we speak with rigorous exactness, no human mind is in its right state. There is no man whose imagination does not sometimes predominate over his reason, who can regulate his attention wholly by his will, and whose ideas will come and go at his command. No man will be found in whose mind airy notions do not sometimes tyrannize, and force him to hope or fear beyond the limits of sober probability. All power of fancy over reason is a degree of insanity; but while this power is such as we can control and repress, it is not visible to others, nor considered as any deprivation of the mental faculties: it is not pronounced madness but when it becomes ungovernable, and apparently influences speech or action.

"To indulge the power of fiction and send imagination out upon the wing is often the sport of those who delight too much in silent speculation. When we are alone we are not always busy; the labour of excogitation is too violent to last long; the ardour of inquiry will sometimes give way to idleness or satiety. He who has nothing external that can divert him must find pleasure in his own thoughts, and must conceive himself what he is not; for who is pleased with what he is? He then expatiates in boundless futurity, and culls from all imaginable conditions that which for the present moment he should most desire, amuses his desires with impossible enjoyments, and confers upon his pride unattainable dominion. The mind dances from scene to scene, unites all pleasures in all combinations, and riots in delights which nature and fortune, with all their bounty, cannot bestow.

"In time some particular train of ideas fixes the attention; all other intellectual gratifications are rejected; the mind, in weariness or leisure, recurs constantly to the favourite conception, and feasts on the luscious falsehood whenever she is offended with the bitterness of truth. By degrees the reign of fancy is confirmed; she grows first imperious and in time despotic. Then fictions begin to operate as realities, false opinions fasten upon the mind, and life passes in dreams of rapture or of anguish.

"This, sir, is one of the dangers of solitude, which the hermit has confessed not always to promote goodness, and the astronomer's misery has proved to be not always propitious to wisdom."

"I will no more," said the favourite, "imagine myself the Queen of Abyssinia. I have often spent the hours which the Princess gave to my own disposal in adjusting ceremonies and regulating the Court; I have repressed the pride of the powerful and granted the petitions of the poor; I have built new palaces in more happy situations, planted groves upon the tops of mountains, and have exulted in the beneficence of royalty, till, when the Princess entered, I had almost forgotten to bow down before her."

"And I," said the Princess, "will not allow myself any more to play the shepherdess in my waking dreams. I have often soothed my thoughts with the quiet and innocence of pastoral employments, till I have in my chamber heard the winds whistle and the sheep bleat; sometimes freed the lamb entangled in the thicket, and sometimes with my crook encountered the wolf. I have a dress like that of the village maids, which I put on to help my imagination, and a pipe on which I play softly, and suppose myself followed by my flocks."

"I will confess," said the Prince, "an indulgence of fantastic delight more dangerous than yours. I have frequently endeavoured to imagine the possibility of a perfect government, by which all wrong should be restrained, all vice reformed, and all the subjects preserved in tranquillity and innocence. This thought produced innumerable schemes of reformation, and dictated many useful regulations and salutary effects. This has been the sport and sometimes the labour of my solitude, and I start when I think with how little anguish I once supposed the death of my father and my brothers."

"Such," said Imlac, "are the effects of visionary schemes. When we first form them, we know them to be absurd, but familiarize them by degrees, and in time lose sight of their folly.".

CHAPTER XLV.

They discourse with an Old Man.

THE evening was now far past, and they rose to return home. As they walked along the banks of the Nile, delighted with the beams of the moon quivering on the water, they saw at a small distance an old man whom the Prince had often heard in the assembly of the sages. "Yonder," said he, "is one whose years have calmed his passions, but not clouded his reason. Let us close the disquisitions of the night by inquiring what are his sentiments of his own state, that we may know whether youth alone is to struggle with vexation, and whether any better hope remains for the latter part of life."

Here the sage approached and saluted them. They invited him to join their walk, and prattled awhile as acquaintance that had unexpectedly met one another. The old man was cheerful and talkative, and the way seemed short in his company. He was pleased to find himself not disregarded, accompanied them to their house, and, at the Prince's request, entered with them. They placed him in the seat of honour, and set wine and conserves before him.

"Sir," said the Princess, "an evening walk must give to a man of learning like you pleasures which ignorance and youth can hardly conceive. You know the qualities and the causes of all that you behold—the laws by which the river flows, the periods in which the planets perform their revolutions. Everything must supply you with contemplation, and renew the consciousness of your own dignity."

"Lady," answered he, "let the gay and the vigorous expect pleasure in their excursions : it is enough that age can attain ease. To me the world has lost its novelty. I look round, and see what I remember to have seen in happier days. I rest against a tree, and consider that in the same shade I once disputed upon the annual overflow of the Nile with a friend who is now silent in the grave. I cast my eyes upwards, fix them on the changing moon, and think with pain on the vicissitudes of life. I have ceased to take much delight in physical truth ; for what have I to do with those things which I am soon to leave ?"

"You may at least recreate yourself," said Imlac, "with the recollection of an honourable and useful life, and enjoy the praise which all agree to give you."

"Praise," said the sage with a sigh "is to an old man an empty sound. I have neither mother to be delighted with the reputation of her son, nor wife to partake the honours of her husband. I have outlived my friends and my rivals. Nothing is now of much importance ; for I cannot extend my interest beyond myself. Youth is delighted with applause, because it is considered as the earnest of some future good, and because the prospect of life is far extended; but to me, who am now declining to decrepitude, there is little to be feared from the malevolence of men, and yet less to be hoped from their affection or esteem. Something they may yet take away, but they can give me nothing. Riches would now be useless, and high employment would be pain. My retrospect of life recalls to my view many opportunities of good neglected, much time squandered upon trifles, and more lost in idleness and vacancy. I leave many great designs unattempted, and many great attempts unfinished. My mind is burdened with no heavy crime, and therefore I compose myself to tranquillity; endeavour to abstract my thoughts from hopes and cares which, though reason knows them to be vain, still try to keep their old possession of the heart; expect, with serene humility, that hour which nature cannot long delay, and hope to possess in a better state that happiness which here I could not find, and that virtue which here I have not attained."

He arose and went away, leaving his audience not much elated with the hope of long life. The Prince consoled himself with remarking that it was not reasonable to be disappointed by this account; for age had never been considered as the season of felicity, and if it was possible to be easy in decline and weakness, it was likely that the days of vigour and alacrity might be happy; that the noon of life might be bright, if the evening could be calm.

The Princess suspected that age was querulous and malignant, and delighted to repress the expectations of those who had newly entered the world. She had seen the possessors of estates look with envy on their heirs, and known many who enjoyed pleasures no longer than they could confine it to themselves.

Pekuah conjectured that the man was older than he appeared, and was willing to impute his complaints to delirious dejection; or else supposed that he had been unfortunate, and was therefore discontented. "For nothing," said she, "is more common than to call our own condition the condition of life."

Imlac, who had no desire to see them depressed, smiled at the comforts which they could so readily procure to themselves; and remembered that at the same age he was equally confident of unmingled prosperity, and equally fertile of consolatory expedients. He forbore to force upon them unwelcome knowledge, which time itself would too soon impress. The Princess and her lady retired; the madness of the astronomer hung upon their minds; and they desired Imlac to enter upon his office, and delay next morning the rising of the sun.

CHAPTER XLVI.

The Princess and Pekuah visit the Astronomer.

THE Princess and Pekuah, having talked in private of Imlac's astronomer, thought his character at once so amiable and so strange that they could not be satisfied without a nearer knowledge, and Imlac was requested to find the means of bringing them together.

This was somewhat difficult. The philosopher had never received any visits from women, though he lived in a city that had in it many Europeans, who followed the manners of their own countries, and many from other parts of the world, that lived there with European liberty. The ladies would not be refused, and several schemes were proposed for the accomplishment of their design. It was proposed to intro-duce them as strangers in distress, to whom the sage was always accessible; but after some deliberation it appeared that by this artifice no acquaintance could be formed, for their conversation would be short, and they could not decently importune him often. " This," said Rasselas, " is true; but I have yet a stronger objection against the mis-representation of your state. I have always considered it as treason against the great republic of human nature to make any man's virtues the means of deceiving him, whether on great or little occasions. All imposture weakens con-fidence and chills benevolence. When the sage finds that you are not what you seemed, he will feel the resentment natural to a man who, conscious of great abilities, discovers that he has been tricked by understandings meaner than his own, and perhaps the distrust which he can never after-wards wholly lay aside may stop the voice of counsel and close the hand of charity; and where will you find the power of restoring his benefactions to mankind, or his peace to himself?"

To this no reply was attempted, and Imlac began to hope that their curiosity would subside; but next day Pekuah told him she had now found an honest pretence for a visit to the astronomer, for she would solicit permission to continue under him the studies in which she had been initiated by the Arab, and the Princess might go with her, either as a fellow-student, or because a woman could not decently come alone. "I am afraid," said Imlac, "that he will soon be weary of your company. Men advanced far in knowledge do not love to repeat the elements of their art, and I am not certain that even of the elements, as he will deliver them, connected with inferences and mingled with reflections, you are a very capable auditress." "That," said Pekuah, "must be my care. I ask of you only to.take me thither. My knowledge is perhaps more than you imagine it, and by concurring always with his opinions I shall make him think it greater than it is."

The astronomer, in pursuance of this resolution, was told that a foreign lady, travelling in search of knowledge, had heard of his reputation, and was desirous to become his scholar. The uncommonness of the proposal raised at once his surprise and curiosity, and when after a short deliberation he consented to admit her, he could not stay without impatience till the next day.

The ladies dressed themselves magnificently, and were attended by Imlac to the astronomer, who was pleased to see himself approached with respect by persons of so splendid an appearance. In the exchange of the first civilities he was timorous and bashful; but when the talk became regular, he recollected his powers, and justified the character which Imlac had given. Inquiring of Pekuah what could have turned her inclination towards astronomy, he received from her a history of her adventure at the Pyramid, and of the time passed in the Arab's island. She told her tale with ease and elegance, and her conversation took possession of his heart. The discourse was then turned to astronomy. Pekuah displayed what she knew. He looked upon her as a prodigy of genius, and entreated her not to desist from a study which she had so happily begun.

They came again and again, and were every time more welcome than before. The sage endeavoured to amuse them, that they might prolong their visits, for he found his thoughts grow brighter in their company ; the clouds of solicitude vanished by degrees as he forced himself to entertain them, and he grieved when he was left, at their departure, to his old employment of regulating the seasons.

The Princess and her favourite had now watched his lips for several months, and could not catch a single word from which they could judge whether he continued or not in the opinion of his preternatural commission. They often contrived to bring him to an open declaration ; but he easily eluded all their attacks, and, on which side soever they pressed him, escaped from them to some other topic.

As their familiarity increased, they invited him often to the house of Imlac, where they distinguished him by extraordinary respect. He began gradually to delight in sublunary pleasures. He came early and departed late ; laboured to recommend himself by assiduity and compliance ; excited their curiosity after new arts, that they might still want his assistance ; and when they made any excursion of pleasure or inquiry, entreated to attend them.

By long experience of his integrity and wisdom, the Prince and his sister were convinced that he might be trusted without danger; and lest he should draw any false hopes from the civilities which he received, discovered to him their condition, with the motives of their journey, and required his opinion on the choice of life.

" Of the various conditions which the world spreads before you which you shall prefer," said the sage, " I am not able to instruct you. I can only tell that I have chosen

wrong.   I have passed my time in study without experience :
in the attainment of sciences which can for the most part
be but remotely useful to mankind.   I have purchased
knowledge at the expense of all the common comforts of
life : I have missed the endearing elegance of female friendship, and the happy commerce of domestic tenderness.   If I
have obtained any prerogatives above other students, they
have been accompanied with fear, disquiet, and scrupulosity ;
but even of these prerogatives, whatever they were, I have,
since my thoughts have been diversified by more intercourse
with the world, begun to question the reality.   When I have
been for a few days lost in pleasing dissipation, I am always
tempted to think that my inquiries have ended in error, and
that I have suffered much, and suffered it in vain."

Imlac was delighted to find that the sage's understanding
was breaking through its mists, and resolved to detain him
from the planets till he should forget his task of ruling
them, and reason should recover its original influence.

From this time the astronomer was received into familiar
friendship, and partook of all their projects and pleasures :
his respect kept him attentive, and the activity of Rasselas
did not leave much time unengaged.   Something was always
to be done : the day was spent in making observations,
which furnished talk for the evening, and the evening was
closed with a scheme for the morrow.

The sage confessed to Imlac that since he had mingled
in the gay tumults of life, and divided his hours by a succession of amusements, he found the conviction of his authority
over the skies fade gradually from his mind, and began to
trust less to an opinion which he never could prove to others,
and which he now found subject to variation, from causes in
which reason had no part.   "If I am accidentally left alone
for a few hours," said he, "my inveterate persuasion rushes
upon my soul, and my thoughts are chained down by some
irresistible violence ; but they are soon disentangled by the
Prince's conversation, and instantaneously released at the

entrance of Pekuah. I am like a man habitually afraid of spectres, who is set at ease by a lamp, and wonders at the dread which harassed him in the dark; yet, if his lamp be extinguished, feels again the terrors which he knows that when it is light he shall feel no more. But I am sometimes afraid, lest I indulge my quiet by criminal negligence, and voluntarily forget the great charge with which I am entrusted. If I favour myself in a known error, or am determined by my own ease in a doubtful question of this importance, how dreadful is my crime!"

"No disease of the imagination," answered Imlac, "is so difficult of cure as that which is complicated with the dread of guilt; fancy and conscience then act interchangeably upon us, and so often shift their places that the illusions of one are not distinguished from the dictates of the other. If fancy presents images not moral or religious, the mind drives them away when they give it pain; but when melancholy notions take the form of duty, they lay hold on the faculties without opposition, because we are afraid to exclude or banish them. For this reason the superstitious are often melancholy, and the melancholy almost always superstitious.

"But do not let the suggestions of timidity overpower your better reason : the danger of neglect can be but as the probability of the obligation, which, when you consider it with freedom, you find very little, and that little growing every day less. Open your heart to the influence of the light, which from time to time breaks in upon you : when scruples importune you, which you in your lucid moments know to be vain, do not stand to parley, but fly to business or to Pekuah ; and keep this thought always prevalent, that you are only one atom of the mass of humanity, and have neither such virtue nor vice as that you should be singled out for supernatural favours or afflictions."

CHAPTER XLVII.

The Prince enters, and brings a new Topic.

"ALL this," said the astronomer, "I have often thought;
but my reason has been so long subjugated by an uncon-
trollable and overwhelming idea, that it durst not confide in
its own decisions. I now see how fatally I betrayed my
quiet, by suffering chimeras to prey upon me in secret; but
melancholy shrinks from communication, and I never found
a man before to whom I could impart my troubles, though
I had been certain of relief. I rejoice to find my own sentiments confirmed by yours, who are not easily deceived, and
can have no motive or purpose to deceive. I hope that
time and variety will dissipate the gloom that has so long
surrounded me; and the latter part of my days will be spent
in peace."

"Your learning and virtue," said Imlac, "may justly give
you hopes."

Rasselas then entered, with the Princess and Pekuah, and
inquired whether they had contrived any new diversion for
the next day. "Such," said Nekayah, "is the state of
life, that none are happy but by the anticipation of change:
the change itself is nothing; when we have made it, the
next wish is to change again. The world is not yet
exhausted; let me see something to-morrow which I never
saw before."

"Variety," said Rasselas, "is so necessary to content, that
even the Happy Valley disgusted me by the recurrence of its
luxuries; yet I could not forbear to reproach myself with
impatience when I saw the monks of St. Anthony support,
without complaint, a life, not of uniform delight, but uniform
hardship."

"Those men," answered Imlac, "are less wretched in
their silent convent than the Abyssinian princes in their
prison of pleasure. Whatever is done by the monks is in-

cited by an adequate and reasonable motive. Their labour
supplies them with necessaries; it therefore cannot be
omitted, and is certainly rewarded. Their devotion prepares
them for another state, and reminds them of its approach,
while it fits them for it. Their time is regularly distributed;
one duty succeeds another; so that they are not left open
to the distraction of unguided choice, nor lost in the shades
of listless inactivity. There is a certain task to be performed at an appropriated hour; and their toils are cheerful,
because they consider them as acts of piety, by which they
are always advancing towards endless felicity."

"Do you think," said Nekayah, "that the monastic rule
is a more holy and less imperfect state than any other?
May not he equally hope for future happiness who converses
openly with mankind, who succours the distressed by his
charity, instructs the ignorant by his learning, and contri-
butes by his industry to the general system of life; even
though he should omit some of the mortifications which are
practised in the cloister, and allow himself such harmless
delights as his condition may place within his reach?"

"This," said Imlac, "is a question which has long
divided the wise and perplexed the good. I am afraid to
decide on either part. He that lives well in the world is
better than he that lives well in a monastery. But perhaps
every one is not able to stem the temptations of public
life; and if he cannot conquer, he may properly retreat.
Some have little power to do good, and have likewise little
strength to resist evil. Many are weary of the conflicts
with adversity, and are willing to eject those passions which
have long busied them in vain. And many are dismissed
by age and diseases from the more laborious duties of
society. In monasteries the weak and timorous may be
happily sheltered, the weary may repose, and the penitent
may meditate. Those retreats of prayer and contemplation
have something so congenial to the mind of man, that
perhaps there is scarcely one that does not purpose to

close his life in pious abstraction, with a few associates serious as himself."

" Such," said Pekuah, " has often been my wish ; and I have heard the Princess declare that she should not willingly die in a crowd."

" The liberty of using harmless pleasures," proceeded Imlac, " will not be disputed ; but it is still to be examined what pleasures are harmless. The evil of any pleasure that Nekayah can image is not in the act itself, but in its consequences. Pleasure in itself harmless may become mischievous by endearing to us a state which we know to be transient and probatory, and withdrawing our thoughts from that of which every hour brings us nearer to the beginning, and of which no length of time will bring us to the end. Mortification is not virtuous in itself, nor has any other use but that it disengages us from the allurements of sense. In the state of future perfection to which we all aspire there will be pleasure without danger, and security without restraint."

The Princess was silent, and Rasselas, turning to the astronomer, asked him whether he could not delay her retreat by showing her something which she had not seen before.

" Your curiosity," said the sage, " has been so general, and your pursuit of knowledge so vigorous, that novelties are not now very easily to be found ; but what you can no longer procure from the living may be given by the dead. Among the wonders of this country are the catacombs, or the ancient repositories in which the bodies of the earliest generations were lodged, and where, by the virtue of the gums which embalmed them, they yet remain without corruption."

" I know not," said Rasselas, " what pleasure the sight of the catacombs can afford; but, since nothing else is offered, I am resolved to view them, and shall place this with my other things which I have done, because I would do something."

They hired a guard of horsemen, and the next day visited the catacombs. When they were about to descend into the sepulchral caves, "Pekuah," said the Princess, "we are now again invading the habitations of the dead; I know that you will stay behind. Let me find you safe when I return." "No, I will not be left," answered Pekuah; "I will go down between you and the Prince."

They then all descended, and roved with wonder through the labyrinth of subterraneous passages, where the bodies were laid in rows on either side.

CHAPTER XLVIII.

Imlac discourses on the Nature of the Soul.

"WHAT reason," said the Prince, "can be given why the Egyptians should thus expensively preserve those carcases which some nations consume with fire, others lay to mingle with the earth, and all agree to remove from their sight as soon as decent rites can be performed."

"The original of ancient customs," said Imlac, "is commonly unknown, for the practice often continues when the cause has ceased; and concerning superstitious ceremonies it is vain to conjecture; for what reason did not dictate, reason cannot explain. I have long believed that the practice of embalming arose only from tenderness to the remains of relations or friends; and to this opinion I am more inclined because it seems impossible that this care should have been general; had all the dead been embalmed, their repositories must in time have been more spacious than the dwellings of the living. I suppose only the rich or honourable were secured from corruption, and the rest left to the course of nature.

"But it is commonly supposed that the Egyptians believed the soul to live as long as the body continued undissolved, and therefore tried this method of eluding death."

"Could the wise Egyptians," said Nekayah, "think so grossly of the soul? If the soul could once survive its separation, what could it afterwards receive or suffer from the body?"

"The Egyptians would doubtless think erroneously," said the astronomer, "in the darkness of heathenism and the first dawn of philosophy. The nature of the soul is still disputed amidst all our opportunities of clearer knowledge; some yet say that it may be material, who, nevertheless, believe it to be immortal."

"Some," answered Imlac, "have indeed said that the soul is material, but I can scarcely believe that any man has thought it who knew how to think; for all the conclusions of reason enforce the immaterality of mind, and all the notices of sense and investigations of science concur to prove the unconsciousness of matter.

"It was never supposed that cogitation is inherent in matter, or that every particle is a thinking being. Yet if any part of matter be devoid of thought, what part can we suppose to think? Matter can differ from matter only in form, density, bulk, motion, and direction of motion. To which of these, however varied or combined, can consciousness be annexed? To be round or square, to be solid or fluid, to be great or little, to be moved slowly or swiftly, one way or another, are modes of material existence all equally alien from the nature of cogitation. If matter be once without thought, it can only be made to think by some new modification; but all the modifications which it can admit are equally unconnected with cogitative powers."

"But the materialists," said the astronomer, "urge that matter may have qualities with which we are unacquainted."

"He who will determine," returned Imlac, "against that which he knows because there may be something which he knows not, he that can set hypothetical possibility against acknowledged certainty, is not to be admitted among reasonable beings. All that we know of matter is, that matter is inert, senseless, and lifeless ; and if this conviction cannot be opposed but by referring us to something that we know not, we have all the evidence that human intellect can admit. If that which is known may be overruled by that which is unknown, no being, not omniscient, can arrive at certainty."

"Yet let us not," said the astronomer, "too arrogantly limit the Creator's power."

"It is no limitation of Omnipotence," replied the poet, "to suppose that one thing is not consistent with another, that the same proposition cannot be at once true and false, that the same number cannot be even and odd, that cogitation cannot be conferred on that which is created incapable of cogitation."

"I know not," said Nekayah, "any great use of this question. Does that immateriality, which in my opinion you have sufficiently proved, necessarily include eternal duration."

"Of immateriality," said Imlac, "our ideas are negative, and therefore obscure. Immateriality seems to imply a natural power of perpetual duration as a consequence of exemption from all causes of decay: whatever perishes is destroyed by the solution of its contexture and separation of its parts; nor can we conceive how that which has no parts, and therefore admits no solution, can be naturally corrupted or impaired."

"I know not," said Rasselas, "how to conceive anything without extension: what is extended must have parts, and you allow that whatever has parts may be destroyed."

"Consider your own conceptions," replied Imlac, "and the difficulty will be less. You will find substance without extension. An ideal form is no less real than material bulk ; yet an ideal form has no extension. It is no less certain, when you think on a pyramid, that your mind possesses the idea of a pyramid, than that the pyramid itself is standing. What space does the idea of a pyramid occupy more than the idea of a grain of corn? or how can either idea suffer laceration? As is the effect, such is the cause; as thought, such is the power that thinks, a power impassive and indiscerptible."

" But the Being," said Nekayah, " whom I fear to name, the Being which made the soul, can destroy it."

"He surely can destroy it," answered Imlac, " since, how-ever imperishable, it receives from a superior nature its power of duration. That it will not perish by any inherent cause of decay or principle of corruption, may be shown by philosophy; but philosophy can tell no more. That it will not be annihilated by Him that made it, we must humbly learn from higher authority."

The whole assembly stood awhile silent and collected. " Let us return," said Rasselas, "from this scene of mor-tality. How gloomy would be these mansions of the dead to him who did not know that he should never die; that what now acts shall continue its agency, and what now thinks shall think on for ever. Those that lie here stretched before us, the wise and the powerful of ancient times, warn us to remember the shortness of our present state; they were perhaps snatched away while they were busy, like us, in the *choice of life.*"

" To me," said the Princess, " the choice of life is become less important; I hope hereafter to think only on the choice of eternity."

They then hastened out of the caverns, and under the protection of their guard returned to Cairo.

CHAPTER XLIX.

The Conclusion, in which Nothing is Concluded.

IT was now the time of the inundation of the Nile. A few days after their visit to the catacombs the river began to rise.

They were confined to their house. The whole region being under water, gave them no invitation to any excursions; and being well supplied with materials for talk, they diverted themselves with comparisons of the different forms of life which they had observed, and with various schemes of happiness which each of them had formed.

Pekuah was never so much charmed with any place as the Convent of St. Anthony, where the Arab restored her to the Princess, and wished only to fill it with pious maidens and to be made prioress of the order. She was weary of expectation and disgust, and would gladly be fixed in some unvariable state.

The Princess thought that, of all sublunary things, knowledge was the best. She desired first to learn all sciences, and then proposed to found a college of learned women, in which she would preside, that, by conversing with the old and educating the young, she might divide her time between the acquisition and communication of wisdom, and raise up for the next age models of prudence and patterns of piety.

The Prince desired a little kingdom in which he might administer justice in his own person and see all the parts of government with his own eyes; but he could never fix the limits of his dominion, and was always adding to the number of his subjects.

Imlac and the astronomer were contented to be driven along the stream of life without directing their course to any particular port.

Of those wishes that they had formed they well knew that none could be obtained. They deliberated awhile what was to be done, and resolved, when the inundation should cease, to return to Abyssinia.